If We Were Kin

If We Were Kin

*Race, Identification, and Intimate
Political Appeals*

LISA BEARD

OXFORD
UNIVERSITY PRESS

Oxford University Press is a department of the University of Oxford. It furthers
the University's objective of excellence in research, scholarship, and education
by publishing worldwide. Oxford is a registered trade mark of Oxford University
Press in the UK and certain other countries.

Published in the United States of America by Oxford University Press
198 Madison Avenue, New York, NY 10016, United States of America.

Library of Congress Cataloging-in-Publication Data
Names: Beard, Lisa, author.
Title: If we were kin : race, identification, and intimate political appeals / Lisa Beard.
Description: New York, NY : Oxford University Press, [2023] |
Includes bibliographical references and index.
Identifiers: LCCN 2022058426 (print) | LCCN 2022058427 (ebook) |
ISBN 9780197517338 (hardback) | ISBN 9780197517321 (paperback) |
ISBN 9780197517352 (epub) | ISBN 9780197517345 | ISBN 9780197517369
Subjects: LCSH: Political science—United States—Philosophy. |
Kinship—Political aspects—United States. | Identity politics—United States. |
Race relations—Political aspects—United States. |
Sexual minorities—Political aspects—United States. |
Political sociology—United States.
Classification: LCC JA71 .B4134 2023 (print) | LCC JA71 (ebook) |
DDC 320.01—dc23/eng/20221223
LC record available at https://lccn.loc.gov/2022058426
LC ebook record available at https://lccn.loc.gov/2022058427

DOI: 10.1093/oso/9780197517338.001.0001

Paperback printed by Marquis, Canada
Hardback printed by Bridgeport National Bindery, Inc., United States of America

Contents

Acknowledgments

My deepest thanks to the race and gender justice and queer and trans liberation activists whose world-making work and whose political visions and freedom dreams are at the heart of this book. I am grateful to Southerners On New Ground organizers for meeting with me on front porches, in coffee houses, at Gaycation, and in feminist bookstores. Special thanks to Caitlin Breedlove for accompanying me in the archives in Durham, Mary Hooks for her support in late stages of the project, and Pat Hussain and Serena Sebring for speaking with me about drafts of chapter 4.

My graduate mentors on my dissertation committee opened their office doors to countless hours of conversations, and they shepherded my project on its own terms, creating wide space for its shape to emerge rather than imposing conventional frameworks or tidy closures. Joe Lowndes and Dan HoSang have been incredible co-advisors. Joe traveled with me through so many of the richest theoretical and historical dimensions of this project, and in our conversations always draws out what's at the heart of my work. I'm constantly learning from the ways Dan stays close to what is at stake politically in a project, and I leave each of our meetings with the title of another amazing book in my hands. Ernesto Martínez' mentorship, warmth, and how he has slowed down with my writing and close readings has been an extraordinary gift. My work has been distinctly shaped by conversations with Alaí Reyes-Santos about kinship, solidarity, and political community. Priscilla Yamin has been a brilliant guide as I developed my historical analysis of late twentieth century race and gender politics.

Enormous gratitude to Tiffany Willoughby-Herard belongs across so many paragraphs of these acknowledgments, for her exceptional feedback on every chapter, her mentorship and friendship, and her visionary change-making work.

A Chancellor's Postdoctoral Fellowship at UC Riverside provided invaluable research support and intellectual community. I am deeply indebted to my fellowship mentor Bronwyn Leebaw for her amazing support, co-thinking, and generative feedback as I pivoted from dissertation to book. Special thanks also to Farah Godrej, Francisco Pedraza, the UCR Political Science and Ethnic Studies Departments, Kimberly Adkinson, Mark Lawson, and the intergenerational Presidential and Chancellor's Postdoctoral Fellowship community across the UCs. I am extremely grateful to Tiffany Willoughby-Herard, Shana Redmond, Chip Turner, Melvin Rogers, and Mark Golub for traveling to Riverside to participate in, and to Bronwyn Leebaw for convening, an incredible day-long manuscript workshop. It was one of the most memorable days in the journey of this book.

This project received generous research support from the Wayne Morse Center for Law and Politics Dissertation Fellowship; the Center on Diversity and Community; the Center for the Study of Women and Society; the Department of Indigenous, Race, and Ethnic Studies; and the Department of Political Science at the University of Oregon; as well as from the Future of Minority Studies Research Project; UC Riverside's Chancellor's Postdoctoral Fellowship Program; and Western Washington University's College of Humanities and Social Sciences and Office of Research and Sponsored Programs.

It was a gift to work with the exceptional archivists and librarians at the Schomburg Center for Research in Black Culture; the Manuscripts and Archives Division of the New York Public Library; the Sallie Bingham Center for Women's History and Culture at Duke University; the LGBT Community Center's National History Archives; the Lesbian Herstory Archives; the John F. Kennedy Presidential Library Archives; and the Oregon Shakespeare Festival Archives. Special thanks to Cheryl Beredo, Natiba Guy, Caitlin McCarthy, Tal Nadan, Alison Quammie, and Kelly Wooten.

It has been a joy to work with Angela Chnapko and Alexcee Bechthold at Oxford University Press. I thank Angela for her clear eyes on my project since our first meeting. I am indebted to Annie Menzel and an anonymous reviewer for their incredibly generative feedback on the manuscript. Special thanks to Alexandra Chiou for permission to print her exquisite art on the book cover. An earlier version of chapter 2 appeared *Contemporary Political Theory* 15, no. 4 (2016), and I thank Sam Chambers and the reviewers for their helpful comments.

For hosting presentations of parts of this project, warm thanks go to Vilna Bashi Treitler, Pei-te Lien, and Roberto Strongman and the Departments of Black Studies and Political Science at UC Santa Barbara; Catherine Ceniza Choy and the Department of Ethnic Studies at UC Berkeley; Susan McWilliams and the Department of Political Science at Pomona College; Bronwyn Leebaw and John Medearis at UC Riverside's

Department of Political Science; Joshua Dienstag and the UCLA Political Theory Workshop; and Miriam Abelson and the Department of Women, Gender, and Sexuality Studies at Portland State University. Thanks to Lynn Fujiwara, Tiya Miles, and the Department of Indigenous, Race, and Ethnic Studies at the University of Oregon for engaging an earlier version of chapter 2 at the Peggy Pascoe Memorial Lecture graduate paper workshop. I've received excellent feedback on this project and ongoing inspiration from colleagues in the National Conference of Black Political Scientists; the Western Political Science Association; the American Studies Association; the American Political Science Association; the Caribbean Philosophical Association; the National Women's Studies Association; the Critical Ethnic Studies Association; and the Politics of Race, Immigration, and Ethnicity Consortium.

My research and writing group of the past five years has read chapter drafts with precision and care—thank you to Tiffany Willoughby-Herard, Jeanne Scheper, Khanum Shaikh, LaShonda Carter, Deshonay Dozier, Salvador Zárate, Natalia Molebatsi, and everyone from earlier years, especially Jasmine Syedullah, April Jackson, Kat Cosby, and Gabriela Corona. Warm thanks also to Miriam Abelson, Lawrie Balfour, Natasha Behl, Eva Bertram, Anita Chari, Anand Commissiong, Heath Fogg Davis, Alfonso Gonzales, Cory Gooding, Zachary Hicks, Vicki Hsueh, Murad Idris, Mzilikazi Koné, James Martel, Lida Maxwell, Desireé Melonas, Zein Murib, Joshua Plencner, Heather Pool, Anna Sampaio, George Shulman, Dean Spade, Courtney Thorsson, Chithira Vijayakumar, Nancy Wadsworth, and Jasmine Noelle Yarish for their feedback on different parts of this project. Thank you also to Nic Francisco, Stefanía García, Anne Huffman, Aylie Baker, Jed Walsh, and Ariel Powell-Córdova. I am grateful to Laura Holliday and Berkeley Goodloe at Academic Writers Studio for their support, with special thanks to Laura for her outstanding editorial guidance.

Warm thanks to Ginetta Candelario, Greg White, Randy Bartlett, Heather Andrea Williams; and to Vicki Spelman and Albert Mosley and the Kahn Institute at Smith College. At the University of Oregon, special thanks go to the Departments of Political Science and Indigenous, Race, and Ethnic Studies, and especially to Erin Beck, Gerald Berk, Anita Chari, Charise Cheney, Donella Elizabeth-Alston Cleveland, Chris Finley, Lynn Fujiwara, Alison Gash, Michael-Hames García, Jason Schreiner, and my graduate student friends. At Western Washington University, I thank my colleagues in the Political Science Department for their welcome and support, as well as

Dharitri Bhattacharjee, Josh Cerretti, Stefania Heim, Litav Langley, Peter Pihos, and Theresa Warburton.

The questions and dreams at the heart of this project grew out of community organizing, and I am indebted to the organizers, community health workers, and artist-activists who have taught me, with special thanks to the Slim Buttes Agricultural Project, Black Mesa Water Coalition, Challenging White Supremacy Workshop, East Bay Saturday Dialogues, Catalyst Project, and the Center for Transformative Change. My thinking has also been shaped by living in community, and I thank my co-operative housemates over the years for their activism and world-making.

Special thanks go to Mez Baker-Médard, Laura Burfoot, Lynelle Gamage, Sarah Barnard, Naunau Baker-Médard, Amrit Gupta, Tigre Lusardi, Urooj Mughal, Steph Thurman-Moore, Lydia Van Dreel, Mia Villanueva, Amanda Blaine, Olivia Corson, and other dear friends and chosen family—many of them named earlier in these acknowledgments—who have sustained and inspired me across the years of this project. I thank my lucky stars I had the brilliant cowriting companionship of Desireé Melonas and Jasmine Syedullah while I completed revisions. Gratitude to my extended family, my brother, Jamie, and my dad, the late John Beard. Special thanks to my mom, Liz Beard, whose enthusiasm and support throughout the years of this project has been immeasurable. Finally, I cannot adequately thank my partner, Scott, for spending countless hours reading and talking through the pages of this book and for accompanying me in this process with so much love.

Introduction

Intimate Appeals

Over five decades of organizing and building a political community across lines of race, region, class, and educational background, Ella Baker was known to ask nearly everyone she met the question, "Who are your people?"[1] As Barbara Ransby explains, when Baker invoked this question she meant it not only in geographic terms—Where do you come from?—but also in political terms—"Who do you identify with? When you have to take sides, where do you stand and who will be there with you?" As recorded by Ransby, Baker's question "Who are your people?" works as a provocation, a methodology of identification. Her capacious question holds together one's origin story ("Where do you come from?") together with a less fixed conceptualization of our identifications that is about who we choose to stand with ("When you have to take sides, where do you stand and who will be there with you?").

This book is about how people politically come to understand who they are, what are their interests, and how they are connected to others. It is about the *we* of politics, and how that *we* is made. How it is fought over. How it is remade. And why these struggles and processes matter to politics. More than *matter*—how they are at the very core of questions about power and political change.

Reigning frameworks in the study of politics—including notions of coalition building, interest groups, alliances, or instrumental politics of rhetorical persuasion—leave forms of identification sedimented in the background as a priori identities or prop them up front as a part of a mechanistic and calculated game. In both cases we are left with constrained accounts of our political world. Political identification cannot be captured by these frameworks and is a far more significant and profound political process than they allow. Identification is not a backdrop or explanatory variable—it is a phenomenon that deeply shapes the political world and is, itself, a primary object of contestation. Political actors from presidential candidates to grassroots organizers invest tremendous effort in crafting and contesting forms of identification

If We Were Kin. Lisa Beard, Oxford University Press. © Oxford University Press 2023.
DOI: 10.1093/oso/9780197517338.003.0001

and summoning people into identifying in certain ways. What is at stake in their appeals is the possibility of changing or upholding relationships of power.

Although this book stakes a wider claim about the centrality of identification to politics, I am especially after its deeper registers, and the attempts by political actors like Baker to get people to shift or reshape their foundational identifications. Specifically, these are appeals animated by a concept I call *boundness*, reconceiving the lines of relationship between self and other in ways that challenge the atomized and hierarchical gendered and sexualized racial formations that constitute political life in the United States. Boundness posits that lived conditions of violence and possibilities of freedom are co-constituted across lines of power and difference.

Appeals to boundness constitute a distinct lineage within the wider field of identificatory appeals in U.S. political culture. In different articulations, the concept can be traced across Maria Stewart's antislavery speeches, through Frederick Douglass' writings and Ida B. Wells' antilynching activism, and against the rise of the "race relations" paradigm in the twentieth century on into the contemporary moment. Boundness is deployed through an identifiable set of rhetorical strategies, including kinship language or language of *my people*, visceral appeals, compressions of space and time, and certain articulations of American national identity. As an alternative political ethos, boundness has been invoked in antiracist politics for over two centuries as an invitation, an ethic, a description of conditions, a philosophical provocation, and a form of address. Such appeals aim to trouble forms of historical amnesia and to provoke shifts in identification. In their appeals, political thinkers do not collapse but center difference and conditions of violence— mining the texture of difference in the structures of violence in which we live for an account of how we are connected.

Through their invocations of boundness, the primary actors in this book are doing more than trying to get people to recognize that their freedoms are "linked": their appeals generate and call people into sharing an idea of what freedom even is. They challenge us to face disavowed relationships and re-imagine new forms of being together politically. It is an intimate politics that centers the historical relationships of violence and lays claim to a different future. When James Baldwin invokes boundness in the 1960s, for example, he does not simply tell white people that they cannot be free unless Black people are free—he tells them they must understand precisely *how* they are connected to Black people and how they are constituted by histories of anti-Black violence. He tells them that they cannot be free unless they both confront and forfeit their white identity because that identity is predicated on violence and willful unknowing. They must, Baldwin says, give up safety for life.[2]

The thinkers and actors centered in the four main chapters of this book stand within traditions of Black, Latinx, and queer and trans of color political thought and political action, and the context of their appeals is a late twentieth–early twenty-first-century contested America. Their interventions not only demand a rethinking of fundamental assumptions in the study of politics but also provide critical resources for understanding the way power works in struggles to constitute a *we*, how commitments toward or away from racial justice politics are cultivated through battles over identification, and the dangers and possibilities that inhere in identificatory appeals. And, most importantly, their appeals advance powerful visions of reoriented political relationships rooted in mutuality and shared freedom.

Political Identification

Tarso Luís Ramos, executive director of Political Research Associates (PRA), a social justice think tank that has monitored the right wing for four decades, addressed a group of rural organizers in a church hall in eastern Oregon in the summer of 2017. The people in the audience that day were involved in struggles for racial, environmental, and immigrant justice across the state, many of them traveling from locales impacted by a growing militia presence, white supremacist organizing, escalating ICE raids, and depressed resource-extractive economies. A long-term movement strategist and investigative researcher, Ramos was well acquainted with this particular region and a number of the organizers, having worked at the Western States Center for twelve years before starting at PRA.[3] In his remarks, Ramos charted out some of the political landscape between the Reagan years and the contemporary moment and explained that his organization's purpose of monitoring and studying organized right-wing groups is "not to vilify the people who organize into [those groups], but to understand them, *and to compete for those people*."[4] When Ramos describes the work of competing for those people, he is naming the struggle to *lay claim upon* people's identificatory attachments, to compete for, as he put it, their "hearts and minds"—and to win.[5]

Ramos is mapping out a project in political identification—an interpretive battle waged, in this case, against right-wing organizers over the question of *how* and *with whom* different people will identify, a political struggle to call people into a way of understanding who they are, how they are connected to others, and what politics they are beholden to. Ramos was not proposing that progressive organizers attempt to call militia leaders into identification, but that they try to win the identifications of people who are being summoned by those leaders. Many liberals, Ramos explains, would cast aside those being summoned by the Far Right as "stupid and ignorant"—a response Ramos argued is not only "absurd and disgusting" but also "an excuse to not do the work" of trying to call them into identification with a different kind of politics. I take Ramos' statements as a point of departure to introduce three key dimensions of political identification central to this study.

First, identification is a political process in motion across place and time. In contrast to political science research that begins studies with identification and then asks about behavior, forms of identification are better understood as a *product* of politics—as being forged *through* political conflict.[6] Forms of identification can be deep or transitory, long-lasting or fleeting. Their structures are not predetermined, but constructed, multiple, and overlapping. They can be won or lost, sustained or abandoned. Those that seem well established or seem to rest on "natural affinities" have in fact been forged slowly over time in discursive processes through which otherwise disparate elements are sutured together into "associative chains."[7] Similarly, new forms of identification are constructed by pulling together existing ones and suturing them together in new combinations of meaning and political commitments.[8] As Stuart Hall shows, an emergent Black identity in Great Britain in the 1970s and 1980s came to "provide the organizing category of a new politics of resistance, among groups and communities with, in fact, very different histories, traditions and ethnic identities."[9] "The black experience" became a unifying identificatory framework, but one that did not erase ethnic and cultural differences. Ruth Wilson Gilmore has called this a "bottom-up politics of recognition" and observed it at an environmental justice and anti-prison conference in California in 2001 that bridged rural and urban organizing. Instead of describing the cooperation at the conference as "multicultural organizing" (a familiar lens or lexicon), she interprets it as a "syncretic rescaling of identity"—it was not just discrete groups coming together, but people came to recognize themselves and each other in a new way.[10] These cases cannot sufficiently be interpreted through the lens of a coalition or alliance—instead, political actors are themselves changed as they enter new constellations of political community and take on new forms of identification.[11] In part, these new forms of identification are constituted by visions for the future and through the processes of creating those visions. Tarso Luís Ramos, for example, invoked forms of identification rooted not in shared experiences or shared policy goals but in aspirations and visions of what might be possible.

Second, forms of identification matter politically because they concern the ways people recognize each other and how they affiliate or align themselves in political community. This is the question of the *we* of politics. When Gilmore explains that "organizing is always constrained by recognition," she means that political organizing is constrained by whether people can recognize and identify with each other and with a political agenda in some way.[12] Organizing is, she says, "*constrained by people's practices of identification*, fluidly laden with differences and continuities of characteristics, interests, and purpose through which they contingently produce their individual and collective selves" (emphasis added). As such, activism "always begins with the politics of recognition."[13] As I will explain more in chapter 4, this is not state recognition but a different genealogy of recognition politics that is about recognition of self and other.

In this way, forms of identification are relational. Identifications are identifications *with*—for example, with groups, nations, institutions, ideas, political visions, family members, community members, public figures, and places.[14] Taken together, forms of identification can be understood as relational orientations insofar as they are structured by their answer to the questions "*Toward whom and what politics do I face and care for? From whom and from what politics do I turn away?*" As Juliet Hooker explains, it is because we identify others as members of a community to which we also belong that we feel that we have obligations toward them.[15] It thus matters greatly where and how lines of identification are drawn and on what terms. Indeed, the relationship between identification and care/responsibility has a pivotal place in the long history of race-making, racial violence, and racial justice struggles in the U.S. and elsewhere. Care and responsibility have been and continue to be distributed through terms of social life and social death, as in the making of blood kin into property in the context of slavery, the forging of white political community through imagined fraternity and constructions of white womanhood, or contemporary disavowals of the death-dealing structures of mass incarceration.[16] The actors and political thinkers centered in the main chapters of this book are engaged in political struggles over identification that seek to intervene in these structures of (gendered and sexualized) racialized violence and racist ideology. They labor to dismantle deadly allocations of care and concern and to establish reoriented relationships with others.

Third, and finally, identification is a political practice that works at both conscious and unconscious registers. On the one hand, to the extent that they are voluntary or conscious, forms of identification can be harnessed in political work through questions like Ella Baker's "Who are your people?"—where there is potential through forms of political education or self-reflective practice to intentionally discard certain inherited identifications and to cultivate others. In ways that resonate with Baker's question, feminist philosopher María Lugones calls for identifications to be practiced as a conscious and ongoing act, insisting that "we have to constantly consider and reconsider the question: Who are our own people?"[17] Issuing her charge in *Pilgrimages/Peregrinajes: Theorizing Coalition Against Multiple Oppressions*, a book grounded in decades of grassroots organizing and popular education work, Lugones presents identification as a reflexive and iterative political practice of asking, answering, and re-asking this question.[18] The endeavor is not to *find* one's own people as if they are a preexisting formation awaiting discovery but to forge community through ongoing political praxis.[19] On the other hand, one of the difficulties of harnessing identification in political projects is that identificatory processes are not entirely conscious or voluntary—they also work at unconscious registers and are not entirely up to our own choosing. Lugones' and Baker's questions attempt to make the process of identifying "our people" more active and conscious. Other appeals might *answer* rather than *ask* the question for their audience. These appeals (including a number of those centered in the chapters that follow) hide the contingency or uncertainty of their claims, *telling* people who they are rather than *proposing* to them how to identify.

Audre Lorde delineates a political practice that would arise from one's answers to the questions raised by Baker and Lugones. In her 1982 address "Learning from the 60s" presented to the Harvard-Radcliffe Black Student Union, Lorde uses her own identifications as a site from which to theorize the relationship between who we call *our people* and how the answer to this question compels us to live differently. Lorde models/offers her listeners a reflexive practice:

I ask myself as well as each one of you, exactly what alteration in the particular fabric of my everyday life does this connection call for? . . . In what way do I contribute to the subjugation of any part of those who I define as my people? Insight must illuminate the particulars of our lives: who labors to make the bread we waste, or the energy it takes to make nuclear poisons which will not biodegrade for one thousand years; or who goes blind assembling the microtransistors in our inexpensive calculators?[20]

Lorde asks her audience to consider the ways they are, as Grace Kyungwon Hong puts it, "implicated in abandoning others to expendability."[21] Furthermore, Lorde tells us that the answer to the question "Who are your people?" only becomes substantive and meaningful with action, with "alter[ing]," the "particular fabric" of our everyday lives. Lorde performs identification not as an endpoint of a political practice but as something that is only made real through different kinds of inquiry and action. It is one thing to *say* who our people are, but that is empty until we change the way we live according to those webs of mutual care and concern.[22]

It is worth pausing here to distinguish between identity and identification. In short, the former is constituted by the latter—that is, political identity is made up of an assemblage of identifications and also, as I will show, disidentifications.[23] These diverse elements are themselves shifting and, taken together, have contradictory implications that must be papered over for an identity to cohere. At the collective level, as Cristina Beltrán has explained, forms of political identity can be understood as "moment[s] when diverse and even disparate subjects claim identification with one another." When Beltrán states that "Latino is a Verb" rather than a noun, she moves us into the terrain of political identity as something people "do" rather than something people "are." *Identification*, over and above identity, lets us get to the more microlevel or constitutive processes of subjectification to discursive practices.[24]

Boundness and Intimate Political Appeals

Forms of political identification are forged and called into being through practices of political appeal. Political appeals are speech acts that work through the art and language of persuasion.[25] They are discursive, emotional, and relational. An appeal itself does political work to constitute the status of the claimant, the one to whom the appeal is addressed, and their relationship to each other.[26] *Identificatory appeals* are speech acts meant to call people into forms of identification. In making these appeals, actors have to use what is available—including extant identifications, cultural reference points, ideas, histories, and imagined communities. They innovate, rework, recombine, and recirculate. The issuing of an appeal, though, is only one aspect of what is a relational practice. Will those summoned hear the call to identification? Will they receive it? Will they invest in the identification? As Hall explains, "the notion that an effective suturing of the subject to a subject-position requires, not only that the subject is 'hailed,' but that the *subject invests in the position,* means that the suturing has to be thought of as an *articulation,*" or, as Cristina Beltrán puts it, "an emotive and participatory encounter between subjects" rather than a one-sided process.[27]

Ultimately, we do not privately assemble our identificatory attachments. We are claimed and summoned. We are pushed away and excluded. Political actors, as Ramos put it, "compete" for people's identifications, and they compete to set the shape and agendas of those identifications. They tell us who we are politically and, in doing so, call us into ways of being in the world. And it is not just activists who share political commitments with Ramos doing this—this is all part of a much broader political landscape in which different actors are staking competing claims and advancing alternative interpretations about what it means to identify in certain ways. This is, I contend, a primary site of politics: places where identifications are forged, called out, fought over, reshaped, received, invested in, rebuked, summoned to mobilize action, or used to secure inaction.

Identificatory attachments are crafted through discourse and felt through desire/aversion, pleasure/shame, and inclusion/exclusion. Identifications *move* people politically. Political actors understand their connections to each other not through (as dominant frameworks in political science scholarship would have it) abstract ideas of interest groups or purely tactical notions of coalition but through mobile and partly elastic ideas of connection and disconnection, often understood in terms of familial notions of belonging and exclusion lived through an array of relationships. People understand themselves as being in support of gay marriage, against gun control, or as belonging to "Middle America" through feelings and concepts of connection, revulsion, care, pain, or anger.

If We Were Kin examines how concepts and registers of address attributed to the intimate sphere animate racial politics and contestations over political

identification. As a register of political appeal, the intimate is a scale of address that makes claims on familiarity, belonging, and proximity—actual
or imagined (as in the imagined intimacies of national belonging),
sanctioned or transgressive. Intimate appeals are sensory and affective, and
they are meant to tug at, hail, and locate their listeners in a constellation of
relationships in the past, present, and future. Sometimes they are attempts
to call listeners into positions of containment, subservience (e.g., in the Jim
Crow formulation, analyzed and challenged by Alice Childress, that Black
domestic workers were "one of the family"), or forms of contingent inclusion.[28] As showcased in the chapters that follow, intimate appeals may contain descriptive accounts of intimate ties that have been disavowed, or they
may be calls into visions of a shared future. Their tonalities are personal, familial, erotic, nostalgic, and prophetic. It is a fantasy of the field of political
science and of liberal ideology that politics operate in a tidy remove from
these registers—fields of political discourse are constituted in no small part
by intimate registers of address, and processes of political identification are
deeply propelled by these calls.

The intimate is an embodied and ideological site of political contest and
a locus of governance. It encompasses but is not reducible to the familial. To
be clear, intimacy in this sense does not imply consent, justice, tenderness, or
love. Scholars across disciplines and generations of antiviolence activists in
race and gender justice movements issue this critical warning.[29] In U.S. (racial, gendered, colonial) history, the intimate has been a site of violence, dehumanization, terror, and the regulation of identification and affective ties.[30]
As Patricia Hill Collins has shown, as a political idea, the intimate or familial
has functioned to produce and naturalize social and economic hierarchies.[31]
As Lauren Berlant has explained, in the late twentieth and early twenty-first
centuries, the intimate has been made the hearth of privatized citizenship,
homophobic anxieties, the ashes of a dismantled welfare state, and conservative delineations of the proper (gendered and racialized) relationship between public (patriotic) and private (sentimental) spaces.[32] Part of what is
at stake here is that to comprehend race politics, as Ida B. Wells and James
Baldwin warn, we must reckon with the intimate scale of race-making and
racial violence. To understand struggles over forms of racial identification,
we must understand their intimate registers of address.

Intimate political appeals, including the appeals to boundness that I examine in this book, pull on cultural scripts and fields of meaning from their
particular political-historical contexts. There is much to learn in these

appeals about the texture of the relationships of power that they seek to fortify or to upend and replace. Theorizing political identification at these sites of encounter is the endeavor of this book. *If We Were Kin* explores how actors *rework* rather than discard problematic themes of intimacy (e.g., kinship language) and harness the power and attraction of intimate public speech acts to summon people into identification. Whether it is, as the book explores in subsequent chapters, Sylvia Rivera using intimacy and shame together with language of "brothers" and "sisters," James Baldwin invoking a kind of psychoanalytic intimacy rooted in a kinship narrative, or grassroots organizer Suzanne Pharr invoking a small-town account of the intimacy of belonging and a language of "my people"—intimacy is a provocative register for identificatory appeals, one whose power lies in the sentiments of immediacy, familiarity, and mutual recognition.[33] Intimate appeals are not the only means through which identifications are built, but they are one series of mechanisms by which we can come to know identification and can register it as a political act.[34]

Political Conflict as Text

Against dominant presumptions of group-based interests and transactional notions of coalition, *If We Were Kin* shows how activists contest the very shape and meaning of identification. The unstated presumption is that interests are pre-political—that you *start* with a set of interests and then politics flow from there.[35] In this framework, differences in interests fuel political conflict, but interests are not themselves a product of politics. Already imbued with interests (and through those interests connected to others in interest groups), political actors enter the political arena and duke things out. Today, this conception of interests continues to strongly influence work in race, gender, and sexuality politics.[36] Seen in these terms, different groups represent and negotiate competing sets of interests. LGBTQ+ people, immigrants, women, Black people, and disabled people are understood as civil rights–focused interest groups, each oriented toward the state to secure resources.[37]

The trouble is that the interest group model fails in many ways to describe how politics actually works. For one thing, groups are *not* coherent, bounded, or discrete. As Cristina Beltrán demonstrates, facile reliance on a naturalized conceptualization of interest group politics obscures hierarchy and conflict within groups, flattening their historical production.[38] Additionally, the interest group model presents deeply constrained ways of thinking about coalition.[39] In an interest group framework, coalitions can only be understood as limited term—in a coalition, discrete groups, each with their own enduring set of interests, would align for a specific campaign or political action. As such, coalitions are temporary, strategic, and transactional formations. The political actors in the chapters that follow create something distinct from what the social sciences recognize as a coalition or alliance. Instead of forming tactical coalitions of discrete interest groups, they generate shared forms of identification that would bind people together in political community. Ultimately, the dominant model of interest group politics misses the action, misrepresenting as a stable object what is actually ongoing and contingent political activity. Rather than existing prior to politics, interests are, like forms of identification, the *product of* politics.[40] The question becomes *how* certain interpretations of conditions and ideas of interests come to prevail over others. This alternative approach plumbs the relations of power at work within invocations of interests. It begins with the ways in which forms of political identification are forged through conflict and in language and sees interests as arising from those identifications.[41] Politics is generated in many places, and so an account of the production of forms of identification requires looking not only at recognizable sites within political science, like presidential politics or political speeches, but also sites like radio shows, national television, grassroots meetings, essays, and protests. *If We Were Kin* examines the endeavor to shape identifications as itself a political project, one which exceeds certain notions of political campaigns (e.g., winning an election, passing legislation, or increasing representation) and which is central to the making and remaking of the political world.

   Each chapter in this book slows down with detailed moments in political discourse and organizing to theorize how people on the ground conceptualize and pursue identification to reconfigure relationships of power. My focus is not on the *internal* world of a person's identificatory attachments (i.e., how someone might personally experience, be moved by, or change one's attachments) but on practices of identification as they occur within public discourse and political organizing spaces. Here is the drama and fire of public contestations over forms of identification—the emotional pulls, the making of an *us* by delineating a *them*, the kinship language, the values talk, the jeremiads and theologically charged references, and the invocations of dangers and threats that might bind a vulnerable *we*. The political action is in these details, and so this is where I linger. I use a close-reading practice informed by political and literary theory, interpretive political science, and cultural studies to explore sites of political appeal and political confrontations as text. Micro-speech practices are at center stage: I ask what claims actors make, how they make those claims, how they link elements together, and how they include their audience in their narratives. I mine transcripts of political appeals not only for their metaphors, registers of address, repetitions, and performative utterances but also for questions of embodiment (body language, gestures, tone, volume, pauses, and interaction) and for the ways in which actors pull upon and engage their historical context. My approach is a kind of midlevel theorizing that toggles between political history and theory and stays close to sites of encounter—those sites that Lori Marso describes as the "affective and agonistic struggle and potential transformation" that together constitute politics.[42]

The work of forging and reconfiguring forms of identification is uncertain, volatile, messy, and historically contingent. Some attempts succeed and some fail (and further, those that succeed are never fully secure, and those that fail are not total failures). Indeed, it is often through apparent failures in politics—e.g., lost elections—that new articulations of ideologies and identities are attempted, enunciated, and over time can come to take hold.[43] The study of the formation of political identification and struggles over them thus requires a somewhat different approach than one that depends on traditionally legible political wins such as electoral victories. My sites of study are not chosen because they have historically won in terms of becoming dominant interpretations but because the specifics of the cases illuminate actors' attempts to reconstitute forms of identification and reconstitute structures of care and responsibility within and across political communities.

In its choices of texts, historical moments, and thinkers, *If We Were Kin* joins other scholarship invested in rethinking the sources of political theory. The book centers political organizing, as Cheryl Harris has put it, "not just as an application [of knowledge and theory] but as a place where knowledge is produced."[44] It comes to political theory through critical race theory; Black political thought and Black feminist theory; queer of color theory; women of color feminist theory; and other scholarship on race, intersectionality, and political thought. As a field, political theory has been haunted by its disavowal of race in the same way that, as Toni Morrison has explained, American literature and literary theory is constituted by its continual invocation and disavowal of Blackness.[45] Most often, as Cristina Beltrán explains, political theorists approach Black or Latinx or Indigenous political thought as an "emancipatory supplement" to the western canon. These are, as Beltrán has put it, "theoretical drive-bys" and "fleeting references, in which race scholars become talisman rather than text." In this dynamic, the logic of the emancipatory supplement is to adorn rather than unsettle and replace.[46]

Taking Gilmore's assertion that political organizing is "constrained by recognition," *If We Were Kin* uses the concept of boundness to theorize forms of solidarity that are rooted in deeper registers of commitment and mutuality and that build from rather than elide difference. The book asks how political actors harness the contingency of identification and mobilize it as a political practice, attempting to shape formations of political community that ultimately exceed prevailing notions of coalition and solidarity. The chapters that follow also take up questions about the relationship of identification and solidarity raised in ethnic studies and critical race and gender studies, including warnings about the difference between transactional versus transformational forms of solidarity, the tepid political charge of allyship, the perils of crafting identifications, and the question of when and how solidarity works.[47]

Chapter Road Map

Trans liberation activist Sylvia Rivera's identificatory appeal at the 1973 Christopher Street Liberation Day Rally (a predecessor to today's Pride parades) in New York City is at the heart of chapter 1. In her speech, Rivera excoriated white middle-class LGB people for their racialized, classed, and gendered disidentifications with her and with LGBTQ people who were in prison or who were houseless. At a moment when the gay liberation movement was beset by ideological rifts between incremental civil rights approaches and more radical critiques, Rivera attempted to summon her audience away from assimilatory politics and toward deeper forms of solidarity across race and class lines. Rivera intervened against these lethal sortings, not to add trans representation to the coattails of white middle-class gay and lesbian incorporation, but to hold out for a vision in which no one is left behind. Chapter 1 reads Rivera's speech in relationship to a broader archive of her political organizing work in order to explore her account of how people are connected to each other through constellations of mutuality, debt, kinship, and shared freedom. It examines Rivera's multivalent appeals as countercalls—issued horizontally and vertically, claiming and defending genealogies of transformative multi-issue liberation struggles within a broader contest over what gay forms of identification would come to mean politically. The chapter examines the relationship between practices of identification and disidentification and the role of the prophetic in struggles over identification. Finally, following Rivera's testimony, the chapter asks how access to participating in identificatory struggles is policed and how the costs and dangers are differently distributed among participants in these struggles.

Chapter 2 focuses on James Baldwin's invocations of boundness and his complicated use of a kinship narrative in his identificatory appeals. In the 1960s, in contrast to Black nationalist and integrationist responses to racial domination, and as an intervention into white liberal forms of political identity, Baldwin repeatedly asserted that Black and white people are related by blood and are therefore morally bound together. The chapter examines Baldwin's invocations of boundness in four main texts—"White Man's Guilt," *The Fire Next Time*, a 1963 Public Broadcasting Service interview, and a 1968 speech in London—and shows how the concept animates his calls for shifts in identification. The chapter places Baldwin's invocations within a wider lineage of intimate political appeals that extends from Maria Stewart's antislavery speeches in the 1830s, through Ida B. Wells' journalism and antilynching activism at the turn of the century, and on into the late twentieth century.

Chapter 3 explores how a series of civil rights and Black Lives Matter activists have issued appeals to state officials in an attempt to forge deep identifications with struggles to end anti-Black violence. Specifically, it examines sites of appeal to state officials concerning the urgency of and questions of responsibility for ending racialized violence and theorizes the relationship between boundness and distance in these exchanges. The chapter reads three historical moments/texts—James Baldwin's May 1963 telegram to Attorney General Robert Kennedy, the May 1963 Baldwin-Kennedy Summit (with a focus on Lorraine Hansberry's remarks at the meeting), and an August 2015 meeting between Hillary Clinton and Black Lives Matter activists Daunasia Yancey and Julius Jones—first, to elucidate how appeals to boundness intervene in distancing practices of white identifications, and second, to theorize the point of entry presented in these exchanges for a politics of responsibility to and identification with the work of ending anti-Black violence. In these exchanges, Lorraine Hansberry, Jerome Smith, Lena Horne, James Baldwin, Daunasia Yancey, and Julius Jones refuse the narrow scope of interaction that the white liberal state officials offer and uphold. Through the structure and tenor of their appeals, they map out each official's responsibility to end racialized violence, drawing on the concept of boundness to map out their political project. Their encounters shed light on the relationships between hearing, feeling, knowledge production, and action in political identification.

The short interlude takes a turn from sites in race and gender justice politics to examine intimate registers of address in an identificatory appeal on the Far Right. Specifically, it explores Pat Buchanan's speech at the 1992 Republican National Convention in which he sutured together a spectacle of gendered and racialized *others* into a threat to an imagined *us* and performed a kind of political friendship that would draw white people into a form of mutual recognition. The speech illuminates the construction of ideas of white nationalist kinship through a web of demonological and intimate political appeals; the role of racialized and gendered nostalgia and myth-making in claims of a *we*; the layers of identificatory appeals in party politics; and the ways struggles over identification defy formal measures of political "victory" or "failure." The chapter also historicizes how discourses of identity politics have been mobilized by the right. Buchanan's work to forge identifications in 1992 is emblematic of the identificatory landscape faced by the organizers in chapter 4—his appeals working through racialized and gendered demonology marshaled in the early 1990s (into the contemporary era) in both distinct and overlapping ways by actors from the Far Right to the liberal Left.

Practices of identification can be read in their singular moments (e.g., in specific speeches), but they are at work within longer reaching discursive threads. Chapter 4 attends to this feature most closely by exploring the long-term identificatory appeals issued by Southerners On New Ground (SONG), a movement organization self-described as a "kinship organization" that has, for nearly thirty years, built "a beloved community" of southern LGBTQ+ people in a fight against rural abandonment, right-wing Christian infrastructure, racism, and economic oppression.[48] In the early 1990s, just as emergent national LGBTQ formations were being constructed through disavowals of connection to communities of color, working-class communities, and rural communities, SONG set out to craft forms of LGBTQ identification that understood queer liberation as bound to racial and economic justice. Drawing on oral histories, original interviews, SONG writings, and political education materials, this chapter examines how SONG has reworked ideas of kinship and boundness and has used political imagination, world-making practices, and invitations to "marry the movement" to construct a shared form of identification and build a social movement organization across lines of race, class, abilities, gender, age, immigration status, and sexuality. The final section of the chapter explores appeals to boundness issued in one of SONG's 2014 direct action campaigns for immigrant justice.

The conclusion explores the implications of appeals to identification as interpretive political acts. It turns to a series of solidarity statements issued within immigrant justice struggles in the 2010s, reading these statements as appeals into expansive forms of political identification that refuse logics of racialized carcerality, anti-Black racism, and assimilation. It closes with final reflections on what is at stake in appeals to boundness, on the fantasies that bracket certain patterns in the study of political identification, and on the freedom dreams called forth in intimate appeals.

1

"For *Your* Gay Brothers and *Your* Gay Sisters in Jail"

Sylvia Rivera's Countercall

> It came down to a brutal battle on the stage that year at Washington
> Square Park between me and people I considered my comrades and
> my friends.
>
> —Sylvia Rivera, "Queens in Exile: The Forgotten Ones"

On Sunday June 24, 1973, fifteen thousand people marched through New York City to celebrate the fourth annual Christopher Street Liberation Day (CSLD).[1] The commemorative march began at the site of the 1969 Stonewall rebellion and ended with a rally at Washington Square Park.[2] Partway through the rally, trans liberation activist Sylvia Rivera fought her way to the stage to speak. Rivera, a frontline activist in New York City gay liberation organizing, had been cut from the rally program, as had two drag queen performance artists.[3] Rivera, enraged by the racialized, classed, and gendered turn in the parade politics away from trans and street people, and thus from the roots of the Stonewall uprising, would not let such omissions go unchallenged.[4] Once on stage, Rivera faced a cacophony of booing, jeering, and applauding. In her four-minute speech, she excoriated the movement for its growing white middle-class politics of assimilation and reminded the crowd, in no uncertain terms, of the history of the gay liberation movement, of their obligations to their gay brothers and sisters in jail, and of their debts owed.

Rivera's 1973 speech works in her moment and ours as an identificatory appeal and is a part of a larger body of appeals that she issued across multiple decades of political organizing work. As Melvin Rogers explains, political appeals are speech acts that work through the art and language of persuasion. In their conveyance and reception, appeals are discursive, emotional, and

If We Were Kin. Lisa Beard, Oxford University Press. © Oxford University Press 2023.
DOI: 10.1093/oso/9780197517338.003.0002

relational. An appeal does political work to constitute the claimant, the one to whom the appeal is addressed, and their relationship to each other.[5] Appeals require an audience, and they rely on that audience's judgment—they work as a call and response in a "discursive field of answerability."[6] *Identificatory appeals* in particular are those speech acts meant to summon people into identification. In this chapter, I examine how Rivera's identificatory appeal was staged through an opening framework of intimate obligation and worked through a complex push and pull with her listeners. She called her listeners into belonging through a rubric of kinship and responsibility just as she distanced herself from them and mapped out sharp lines of difference between their positionality and hers.

The primary record of Rivera's speech is a black-and-white four-minute video clip.[7] It is critical to mark—and I will return to this at the end of the chapter—that the contemporary circulation of Rivera's speech and the political life it leads today in LGBTQ+ public discourse is indebted to archival activism by writer, activist, and filmmaker Tourmaline. Much of the archive of Rivera's organizing work, as well as that of Rivera's comrade Marsha P. Johnson, has been gathered, digitized, revitalized, and brought into public discourse through Tourmaline's efforts—often at physical and personal risk to her own body as she has navigated archival institutions and library security as a Black trans woman.[8] Tourmaline's digitized records and film portfolio together constitute a political intervention into the historical erasure and flattening of trans and gender nonconforming people of color who were revolutionaries and who forged life-giving practices of community care. Rivera's 1973 speech in particular has been further amplified by public intellectual and activist Janet Mock.

Rivera's speech sheds light on the interplay between practices of identification and disidentification and the ways political actors attempt to summon people into identification. Her battle to the stage illuminates how access to participating in conflicts over identification—over how people will understand who they are, what their interests are, how they are connected to others, and what politics they are beholden to—is policed, and signals the very differently distributed costs and dangers borne by participants in these struggles. In this chapter, I read Rivera's 1973 speech at the CSLD rally, her 2001 speech at the Latino Gay Men of New York's (LGMNY) Pride celebration, materials from the dispersed archive of Street Transvestite Action Revolutionaries (STAR), oral history accounts of Rivera's organizing work within STAR, and archived interview excerpts in order to examine her account of how people are connected to each other through constellations of obligation, mutuality, debt, and a concept of boundness.[9] Rivera's identificatory appeals were multivalent and worked both vertically and horizontally. To be clear, they weren't issued primarily or most importantly to white gay middle-class people. Her foundational political project was one that would bind trans and queer people of color to each other, especially people who were drag queens, sex workers, and houseless.

Rivera in Her Time

Sylvia Rivera was a self-described revolutionary who organized in New York City and New Jersey to confront police violence, criminalization, transphobia, economic injustice, gendered/racialized violence, and the conditions of houseless people. Rivera was born in the Bronx and identified as Venezuelan and Puerto Rican.[10] She lived on and off New York City streets beginning when she was ten-and-a-half-years old.[11] She was politicized by her involvement in the late 1960s in the peace movement, the civil rights movement, and the women's movement.[12] Rivera explains that although she participated in the Stonewall rebellion, she did not more fully join the gay liberation movement as a political person until 1970, when she began organizing with the New York City chapter of the Gay Liberation Front (GLF) and then, in 1971, with the newly formed Gay Activists Alliance (GAA), where she quickly became a frontline activist—participating in sit-ins, soliciting petition signatures, lying in front of traffic during demonstrations, and changing the terms of central political debates.[13] Rivera took the first arrest in the fight to pass the city's first gay rights bill.[14] Her activism exceeded GAA, and, ultimately, Rivera found the organization to be not radical enough for her political commitments.

Rivera's closest friend, Marsha P. Johnson, was a revolutionary Black and disabled trans woman who participated in the Stonewall rebellion and was an artist; a performer and a member of the group the Hot Peaches; a sex worker; and an activist who organized people in jails, prisons, hospitals, psychiatric wards, and at AIDS vigils.[15] Both Rivera and Johnson were well known in New York City gay activist communities in the early 1970s and at the time of the 1973 CSLD march. They inhabited and staked a claim as revolutionary and gender nonconforming people in spaces like GAA and GLF and pushed the politics of those spaces.[16]

In September 1970, Rivera and Johnson cofounded an organization called Street Transvestite Action Revolutionaries, or STAR.[17] In its founding, STAR articulated a trans and queer politics that centered drag queens, sex workers, houseless trans and queer people, and trans and queer people who were poor. One of STAR's first public appearances included participating in a 10,000-person march organized by the Young Lords from East Harlem to the United Nations to demand an end to police repression.[18] In the coming months, Rivera attended the second People's Revolutionary Convention in Washington, DC, where she met Huey Newton.[19] With GLF and GAA, STAR organized demonstrations against the prison system and helped form an organizing committee on the status of gay people in prisons (STAR was credited on the front page of the February 1971 *Gay Flames* journal for raising awareness in the lesbian, gay, and trans community of the conditions of lesbians, gay men, and trans people held in prisons, hospitals, and juvenile centers in New York City).[20] STAR members traveled to the March 1971 gay liberation mobilization at the Albany State House, organized a demonstration to "stop job discrimination against transvestites," helped run an early gay community center, testified in support of the New York City gay rights bill Intro 475, held fundraising dances and a bake sale, and wrote articles for the gay liberation press.[21]

Rivera's work within STAR illuminates the ways identificatory appeals are not only issued through speeches but also through the daily labor of organizing work. At the center of STAR's work was a youth house called STAR House on East Second Street in which Johnson, Rivera, and other STAR members, as Rivera explained, "fed people and clothed people. We kept the building going. We went out and hustled the streets. We paid the rent. We didn't want the kids out in the streets hustling."[22] They wanted to create a "place . . . for all the young runaway future drag queens or transvestites . . . because we knew what it was to be out in the streets at the age of eleven hustling."[23] Rivera herself was only nineteen when she cofounded STAR, and a number of her "kids," she reflected in an interview years later, were a similar age or even older than her.[24] But they were her juniors and they were Johnson's juniors in living on the street, and Rivera and Johnson nurtured them by making sure they did not have to hustle. In an interview later in her life, Rivera cited *this* kind of political care work—caring and sustaining each other against logics of disposability—as what it means to be in community, in contrast to the work of well-funded gay organizations that did not attend to the basic needs of unhoused and cash poor trans and queer people.[25]

Before opening STAR House, Rivera had secured the promises of professionals within GAA, GLF, and the wider gay community that they would help paint and clean up the building and offer educational programs to teach her "kids" and help them "get a high school diploma so they could get something better in life than what we were doing in selling our bodies out in the streets just to keep surviving."[26] However, no one from GAA or GLF came to help, and while STAR members fixed the building and sustained STAR House, it was ultimately lost in an eviction.[27] STAR had envisioned additional projects—including dance fundraisers, establishing a second STAR house, opening a telephone hotline, creating a recreation center, starting a bail fund for arrested queens, and securing a lawyer for queer and trans people in jail—but without more resources and community support, STAR was unable to implement them.[28] The scope of STAR's political visions forms a critical archive—and although it was short-lived as an organization, activists and scholars recognize the significance of its legacy.[29] A critical part of this legacy is a set of identificatory appeals that were material and that addressed an audience of young trans and queer people around the language of kinship as the context for their survival.[30]

"Ya'll Better Quiet Down"

STAR was at the front of the 1973 CSLD march, along with the popular 82 Club drag performance troupe and the drag queen–led political organization Queens Liberation Front (QLF) (Figures 1.1 and 1.2). This lineup with drag queens at the lead had been secured by CSLD Committee secretary (and QLF and STAR member) Bebe Scarpinato to honor the roots of Stonewall.

The context of the 1973 parade was the final years of the Vietnam War, Nixon's second inauguration earlier that year, and the cumulative effects of COINTELPRO on the Black Panther Party, the Young Lords, and other radical movement organizations.[31] The U.S. gay liberation movement was beset by ideological rifts between incremental civil rights approaches (anchored, for example, by the National Gay and Lesbian Task Force and other national groups); transphobic articulations of white lesbian feminist politics; white and middle-class–dominated gay direct action groups; and radical critiques

Figure 1.1 Sylvia Rivera and Bebe Scarpinato power salute, Christopher Street Liberation Day, 1973. Photograph by Richard C. Wandel. Courtesy of LGBT Community Center National History Archive.

that linked LGBT issues to anti-prison activism, race and gender justice, and class justice politics.[32]

The march ended at Washington Square Park for a two-hour rally, billed as a Gay Pride Gala that almost exclusively featured musical entertainment rather than speeches.[33] The day's events were already marked by a number of trans exclusions.[34] Schedules distributed by the CSLD Committee (CSLDC) warned that anyone besides cis women were unwelcome at Lesbian Pride Week events, which included a separate women's contingent at the march. The group Lesbian Feminist Liberation (LFL) circulated anti-trans flyers among parade participants.[35] As Rivera explained in a later interview, she had been invited by parade organizers in the months prior to give a speech at the rally but was not included in the final program; and Billy and Tiffany, two drag queen performance artists, were nearly cut from the program at the last minute.[36] Refusing to let the unfolding politics go unanswered, Rivera fought her way to the stage, and was "beaten up and punched around by people I thought were my comrades, to get to that microphone. I got to the microphone, and I said my piece."[37]

Figure 1.2 Marsha P. Johnson and Sylvia Rivera, Christopher Street Liberation Day, 1973. Photograph by Leonard Fink. Courtesy of LGBT Community Center National History Archive.

When perhaps it became clear they could not easily contain Rivera, Grand Marshal Jean DeVente and another parade marshal turned to the crowd, asking them whether to let Rivera speak—and once they heard a number of people shouting in the affirmative, the assistant marshal proclaimed, "that's the end of the conversation!" and went to fetch Rivera rather than asking to hear the *no* votes. Emcee Vito Russo, looking dejected as he held onto

Figure 1.3 Sylvia Rivera, Christopher Street Liberation Day, 1973. Bettye Lane Gay Rights Movement Photographs, Manuscripts and Archives Division, the New York Public Library. Courtesy of Gary O'Neil.

the microphone with drooping shoulders, pleaded for unity, and promised dissenters that Jean O'Leary of LFL would also get to speak.

When Rivera arrived on stage she met an onslaught of booing, jeering, and yelling as well as some applause, whistling, and cheering (Figure 1.3). She wore a full-length sparkly jumpsuit fastened in the front by a ring pull zipper down her midline, large bracelets on one wrist, and a necklace, and her hair was dyed a light color. She waved and greeted the crowd, "Hi, Baby!"[38] Her chest was heaving as she breathed. As the booing persisted, Rivera swiveled the microphone stand behind her and then took it in both hands as though to anchor herself while she paused. She surveyed the scene. DeVente reached to take the microphone stand away, but Rivera held onto the microphone. Rivera reprimanded those who were jeering at her, "YA'LL BETTER *QUIET DOWN*," then turned and walked a small lap around the stage as if to re-group. She returned to the front of the stage, leaning forward toward the crowd and amplifying her voice to berate them: "I've been trying to get up here *ALL DAY* for *YOUR* gay brothers and *YOUR* gay sisters *IN JAIL!*[39] *They write me every motherfucking week and ask for your help, and you all don't do a goddamn thing for them!*"

Rivera confronted the people in front of her, asking rhetorically if they had ever been beaten up or raped in jail, and reported that their brothers and sisters have been. "Now *think about it*," she instructed. The crowd be-came quiet. Rivera continued, telling them that she had been to jail, and she had been beaten and assaulted many times "by men, heterosexual men that do *not belong* in the homosexual shelter!" She blasted them for trying to shame her off the stage: "You all tell me 'go' and hide my tail between my legs. *I will not no longer put up with this shit!*"[40] In this way, Rivera set the terms of engagement with people who, moments before, had refused to hear her and had tried to silence her. She detailed the physical and mate-rial costs she had paid for the movement: "I have been beaten. I have had my nose broken. I have been thrown in jail. I have *lost my job*. I have *lost my apartment* for gay liberation—*and you all treat me this way?! What the fuck's wrong with you all!?! THINK ABOUT THAT!*" The crowd erupted in cheers and clapping, which all but eclipsed what had earlier been jeering and booing.

Rivera advised the crowd, "I do not believe in revolution, but you all do. I believe in the gay *power*. I believe in us getting our rights or else I would not be out there fighting for our rights." She warned them not to forget Bambi L'Amour, Andorra Martin, Kenny Messner, "and the other gay people that are in jail," and, sharing the address of STAR House, invited them to come visit the people at STAR: "The people that are trying to do something for *all* of us and *not men and women that belong to a WHITE MIDDLE CLASS WHITE CLUB! AND THAT'S WHAT YOU ALL BELONG TO!!*" Rivera closed her speech with a call and response and received loud participation, yelling "*REVOLUTION NOW!!!*," and spelling, letter by letter, "GAY POWER!" By the end, she crouched down with her shoulders curved inward, as from over-exertion. Her voice became more hoarse and faint in her final words, just as the crowd became louder. She faced downward into her hands, almost as if kneeling in prayer.

Identification and Distance

In her brief speech, Rivera confronts and contests white, middle-class LGB forms of political identification that would not see gay liberation as bound to race, class, and trans justice. Rivera first "disrupts" the gathering to make her appeal.[41] She begins by cataloging how the crowd has failed in their obligations to their trans and gender nonconforming kin in jail. She positions herself, the people before her, and the people in prison as belonging to each other and re-narrates their purpose. She challenges the predominantly white, middle-class, cisgender LGB people standing in the sun in Washington Square Park to understand themselves as connected to people who are socially positioned quite differently—i.e., to gender nonconforming people who are in jail and without political redress or the ability to march in the streets while confined by the state. Rivera stands as an intermediary—triangulating between the park and the prison, the inside and the outside—as someone who that day walks in the "free world" like the other rally participants, but who walks with the embodied knowledge and shared experience of imprisonment, assault, and economic marginalization of her sisters and brothers in jail.[42] By the end of her speech, through a powerful rhetorical and performative act, Rivera has many of those who would have silenced her instead chanting "GAY POWER!" with her in a call and response. She and many of the rally attendees are in opposition to start with: the people jeering do not see that they are connected to Rivera. However, by the end of her speech, she has drawn them through a narrative that calls them out and calls them in, at least in that moment, into reoriented relationships and shared identification.

In part, the political fight in Washington Square Park that day was a fight over what gay forms of identification would mean *politically*—that is, what are the political imperatives and interests of "gay politics"? Gay identity does not describe a simple and stable set of interests, desires, or identities that cohere over the course of the rally or even that decade. Rather, there are multiple emerging, competing, and contested meanings of *gay* at play. Rivera's speech lifts these tensions to the surface, denaturalizing the pull by dominant LGB groups toward white assimilatory politics. Instead, she holds ground for a different possibility for gay identity: one that would prioritize prison abolition, antiracism, class justice, and trans liberation. She calls the movement into STAR's politics.

When Rivera proclaims at the 1973 rally that she does not "believe in revolution like you all do"—she is not rejecting *revolution* (she identified as a revolutionary, and STAR identified as a revolutionary organization) but is rejecting the watered-down terms of white middle-class gay revolution. When Rivera declares that she instead believes in "gay power" she invokes a phrase that, as Roderick Ferguson explains, "could only exist because of the nearness of the black revolution" (a fact that Rivera and Johnson understood) and that enunciates STAR's firmly anticarceral politics.[43] STAR's original name was Street Transvestites for Gay Power and one of their first signed statements, issued in the wake of the 1970 Weinstein Hall occupation at New York University, confronted sit-in participants and the wider gay community with the question: "GAY POWER—WHEN DO WE WANT IT? OR DO WE?"—riffing on a popular protest chant and calling a bluff.[44] In their statement, STAR asks people to take stock—were people looking for just "a few laughs and a little excitement" and did they otherwise intend to keep running? Did people understand that they were going to have to fight? Did they understand that the fight requires a total commitment? STAR explains that they will have to fight until they win or the police will get stronger. This is *gay power* for STAR—it is defined against police power; it sees localized fights for rights as bound to broader struggles across the country; and it sees that abandoning ship in one site endangers the whole.

In ways that resonate with contemporary debates about homonormativity and assimilation, at the rally Rivera raises the critical question of what gay identity means in terms of *with whom* one identifies, with whom one disidentifies, and whose interests are served by those identifications and disidentifications. The stakes of her intervention only intensified in the next decade with the establishment of a well-funded LGBTQ nonprofit industrial complex and a focus on what Yasmin Nair has called the "holy trinity" of mainstream gay and lesbian politics: gay marriage, gays in the military, and hate crime legislation.[45] Rivera contests the ways mainstream forms of gay identity were being built not only through identifications with whiteness and middle-class values but also powerfully through forms of disidentification with poor LGBTQ people, LGBTQ people of color, and LGBTQ people in prison.

Disidentification and Rivera's Countercall

Rivera refuses these practices of disidentification. Here I mean disidentification as a disavowal—a process in which people turn away from and refuse identification with others (others with whom they could find points of connection or for whom they could be mistaken) through practices that uphold relationships of power. At the rally, Rivera attempts to summon her listeners into identification with a political vision and with other sexual and gender outsiders. The booing that greets her is constituted by the people in the park's middle- and upper-class aspirations, their assimilatory identifications with whiteness, and their disidentification with Rivera and who and what politics she represents.

As Eve Sedgwick explains, identification is not only a positive act—that is, accepting and even appropriating someone else's ways—it is also negative in the sense that, as Natasha Lushetich has puts it, "it clearly marks that which the subject does not want to be in order to arrive at what the subject wants to be."[46] In other words, there is no identification without some kind of disidentification—the grounds of who we are is defined in part by who we are not. The booing in Washington Square Park is a performance of demarcation of space and political identity.[47] The crowd refuses, until the end of the speech, to be summoned by Rivera.

Rivera's appeal is a countercall. If interpellation is the process through which subjects are summoned by dominant ideologies through different forms of address, and if *misinterpellation* is, as James Martel explains, the process through which those not intended for a call show up for it, then *counterinterpellation* names the process of issuing alternative calls that go against the grain of dominant calls.[48] These are rival calls. They work to defy, invert, or subvert the roles and lines of relationship mapped by dominant calls. They claim alternative possibilities. Countercalls are always already in circulation, but dominant calls often drown them out or simply interfere with their transmission and uptake. Countercallers may use the very same technology or airwaves as dominant calls, repurposing these tools for a different project—as in Fanon's account of Algerian revolutionaries' appropriation of the radio, or as in Rivera seizing the microphone and the stage from an antipolitical gala.[49] Rivera calls upon the crowd as people who are socially and politically indebted to her and who are related to her as political kin. Rivera's interventions thus lay out a particular form of counterinterpellation in which actors make appeals or bids that would cast as *horizontal* the relationships of power that those being bid upon have inhabited as vertical. Mainstream gays shun her, but she claims them against their retreat. Here, Rivera is not simply positioning horizontal kinship against vertical assimilation but rather positioning one form of kinship (a queer kinship that is anti-assimilationist) against another that is in process (in which homonormativity is privileged over other forms of kinship). This second kind of kinship appeal—one that appeals to the heteronormative family—has grounded the very kind of gay white assimilationist politics that Rivera is challenging.[50]

The tension between Rivera's appeal and the people's booing lies in the fact that many of the rally attendees were busy identifying with an assimilationist white gay politics that must, to exist, expel Rivera. The booing can be read as an attempt not only to shame her off the stage but also to flood the aural field and render her message incomprehensible. Rivera herself represents an obstacle to their aspiring identification with white middle-class political community—thus the hissing and booing. Their performed separation from her, as well as from the political meaning signified by her presence, is not very secure—otherwise, the rally may have worked through a *different* kind of violence that would tokenize and incorporate Rivera rather than try to expel and eject her. The emcee's and many of the audience's disidentifications with Rivera form a trail, archived on video, of their anxieties about their connection and boundness to Rivera and the larger frame of who and what politics she signifies. These disidentificatory acts and refusals would not be necessary if white liberal gay people's own identificatory longings and aspirations were not threatened by the figure of Rivera and her disruptive rescripting of gay politics and history.

In this way, the dominant LGB movement actually needed Rivera as an *other* in order to consolidate itself. The crowd was in the midst of a disidentification/identification entanglement, and this was what manifested at Washington Square Park. Some of Rivera's first words were an attempt to quiet the crowd, and she waited and walked around the stage when they would not stop. When she returned to the front of the stage, she amplified her voice to speak above the booing. In her speech, Rivera confronts the crowd's repudiations along multiple and mutually constituted axes of transphobia, class hostility, the criminalization and incarceration of poor people of color, and white supremacy. Rivera tutors her listeners—teaching them that their kin are not white straight people, but queer and trans people of color like her who spent time in jail to get everyone free.[51]

Rivera already had a substantial record of claiming the place of trans people within the gay liberation movement, especially through her activism within GAA and GLF. In her 1973 speech, Rivera also claims trans women's place in—and as being in fact the vanguard of—the women's movement, explaining that the sisters who are in jail fighting to get bail and fighting "for their sex changes or to become women *are* the women's liberation." She explained that the gay brothers and sisters in jail don't write to women's or men's groups; "they write to STAR, because *we're* trying to do something for them."[52] Here, as Susan Stryker and Talia Bettcher trace, Rivera was in conversation with and pulled on tenets of the women's movement, chastising her listeners for their antagonism toward and neglect of trans people who have experienced forms of gender and sexual violence that feminists typically decried.[53] She calls out white middle-class cisgender feminists and homonormative elites on their empty claims of kinship and community and instead testifies to a kinship with those who are criminalized and those who are compelled to disrupt.

At the rally, disidentifications with trans women and other gender nonconforming people were led most vociferously and earnestly by a group of white lesbian feminists and their gay male supporters like Russo. Their efforts to expel Rivera and performers Tiffany and Billy should be understood as connected to events at the West Coast Lesbian Feminist Conference held in Los Angeles two months prior, where keynote speaker Robin Morgan and other participants verbally attacked lesbian and trans songwriter and activist Beth Elliott. Morgan's accusation that Elliott was invading women's space constituted, as activist Jeanne Córdova attests, a deeply formative incident for transphobic lesbian feminist politics that would endure in the months and decades ahead.[54] LFL president Jean O'Leary had attended the West Coast conference, and the night before the CSLD parade, she and

other members of LFL drew upon Morgan's remarks to fashion their statement against trans women.[55] At the CSLD parade, Rivera and other queens
were told by LFL members that they were a "threat" and "an embarrassment
to women."[56] In an interview two decades later, Rivera reflected wryly that
this was a time when drag queens weren't needed anymore by the movement and a time when the LFL was militant in demanding the expulsion of
trans women from the movement.[57] In her speech at the 1973 rally, O'Leary
misgendered Rivera, defended the LFL's "rational" approach of "negotiat[ing]
for a week and a half" to try to get a spot on the program against Rivera's
"interruption," then read a statement that attacked transfeminine people for
"impersonat[ing] women for reasons of entertainment or profit."[58] Here,
O'Leary marshals an Enlightenment narrative in which LFL stands in as a
white and masculinized subject, who is virtuous and reasonable in political
approach, against Rivera—who is figured as an excessively emotional and
impatient racialized and feminized *other* who is unable to follow codes of
procedure and therefore unfit for group-level citizenship and even dangerous
to the movement itself. O'Leary reads Rivera's and other queens' gender performance through a framework of cisgender authenticity (in which gender is
imagined not to be a performance) defined in contrast to what LFL described
as a kind of extractive gender nonconformity (in which gender is performed
for "entertainment and profit"), and ultimately poses cis women, particularly
cis lesbians, as victims of theft and parody.

In addition to confronting disidentifications with trans people, Rivera
also condemns disidentifications with people who are incarcerated and
confronts gay elites for pursuing a vision of freedom complicit with the
prison state. In doing so, Rivera enunciates an anticarceral politics that
was already being articulated across racial justice, feminist, and gay liberation activism. The early 1970s was in fact a peak time in anticarceral
organizing—from international defense campaigns to prison rebellions. It
was a time when police and carceral violence became sharpened as a central
issue for the Left, and the walls separating radical social movements from
the country's prisons became more permeable.[59] As Regina Kunzel explains,
in the 1970s, gay activists joined others on the radical Left in theorizing
connections between the inside and the outside of prisons. They initiated a
wide range of projects on behalf of imprisoned people they called "brothers"
and "sisters"—publishing newsletters, investigating and publicizing
prison conditions, offering legal counsel, assisting people on parole, and
sponsoring pen-pal projects. Out of these powerfully imagined connections

emerged a rhetoric and politics of unity based on an assumed kinship between gay people in prison and gay activists on the outside. The language
of brotherhood and sisterhood "infused the rhetoric and ideology of gay
prison advocacy," inspiring strong commitments to a range of activist efforts
on behalf of people in prison.[60]

It is worth repeating that the political roots of the CSLD rally itself lay in
the Stonewall rebellion, and that the Stonewall rebellion was an interracial
uprising primarily by drag queens, gender-nonconforming people, lesbians,
and gay men against the police—a fact eclipsed in the 1980s and 1990s with
the rise of assimilationist gay politics and which recent activism and scholarship has worked to restore. The first commemorative march, held one
year after the 1969 rebellion, maintained a strong critique of the carceral
state and included on its route a visit to the New York Women's House of
Detention.[61] Historically, the Women's House of Detention had imprisoned
many renowned activists, including Dorothy Day, Elizabeth Gurley Flynn,
Ethel Rosenburg, and Angela Davis, and at the time of the 1970 march, it was
holding Joan Bird and Afeni Shakur, two of the defendants in the Panther
21 conspiracy case. In the early 1970s, numerous radical grassroots organizations were involved in organizing protests in front of the "House of
D" to amplify the conditions and demands of prisoners.[62] When the 1970
march arrived at the jail, the protest chants changed from "Whose streets?
Our streets!" to "Free our sisters! Free ourselves!,"[63] with Johnson, Rivera,
and thousands of others forging "a politics of solidarity that argued trans
and queer liberation were coterminous with the struggle against the prison
industrial complex."[64] The demonstration should also be understood as a
trans-feminist articulation of anticarceral politics, linked to work by groups
like the Third World Women's Alliance who organized around Shakur's and
Bird's cases.

By 1973, Rivera sensed a moment of danger as an antiviolence analysis
dropped out of gay and gender activist politics. (Indeed, the first keynote
speaker at the gala—activist Barbara Gittings—led the crowd in cheers at
the prospect of gay professional associations, including cheers for gay police
officers). When Rivera warns people in Washington Square Park not to forget
Bambi L'Amour, Andorra Martin, Kenny Messner, and the other gay people
in jail, and invites them to visit STAR House to learn more "about the people
that are in jail," she labors against the mounting mechanisms of disappear-
ance, disposability, and forgetting that surround and enable the carceral state.
Furthermore, in her interventions, Rivera anticipates contemporary analyses

that map the expansion of liberation struggles on the U.S. Left within a context of state violence and nation-building—as in the case of the backdrop of the Vietnam War harboring the civil rights movement, or U.S. militarism in the Middle East harboring the expansion of sexual freedom in the U.S., increasing the capacity for inclusion of queer subjects within the context of U.S. nationalism and militarism.[65]

Rivera attacks whiteness and middle-class investments in the same breath, describing them as bound together in the figure of a "club." She attacks the crowd's racialized class aspirations—their reaching not for the end of criminalization and police violence broadly but instead for state protection of their own personal safety—safety that encases a specific racialized class of gay people from the criminal justice system and from being criminalized while condemning others to social death by that same system.

There is a way in which the speech can be misread as an individualized moral dispute between Rivera and those who taunted her, bypassing the scope of Rivera's political intervention and overlooking the material context of white gay people's incorporation. Rivera's call is a bid into STAR's expansive and formidable political vision—ranging from the community control of hospitals to the transformation of mental health services to universal access to healthcare to the end of job discrimination. It is a vision that centers mutual care and refuses a politics of disposability. An oversimplified reading of the moment can also overlook the structural recruitment of white middle-class gays and lesbians toward a politics of incorporation, in ways that obscure how we understand our own political moment. Rivera bears witness to liberalism's fixation on differentiating between "good" and "bad" subjects, and its incorporation of those perceived to be more valuable. Rivera intervenes against these lethal sortings, not to *add* trans representation to the coattails of white middle-class gay and lesbian incorporation but to hold out for a vision in which no one is left behind. Hers is a vision incompatible with liberalism. At the CSLD gala, Rivera confronts those who are being sorted differently than her and drawn toward the pursuit of equality through a single-axis framework rooted in the claim that "but for my sexual orientation, I, too, could be a full member." Rivera sounds an alarm, warning white and middle-class LGB people that their celebration is in fact a profound narrowing of a political vision, one that forfeits genealogies of multi-issue queer and trans liberation struggles.

Prophecy, Sacrifice, and Debt

Rivera's identificatory appeal works through the literary and political genre of prophecy. She bears witness, poses fateful collective choices, and speaks to the power of those choices. She announces truths that her audience is invested in denying, names the dangers of incorporation, and to tries to fore-stall those dangers. She dramatizes loss and hopes of redemption.[66] Prophecy is important in studying practices of identification because prophets invoke a *we* as a given and charge that *we* with ethical, moral, and affectively charged responsibilities. This is a realm that works through discourses of truth-telling rather than making proposals, through direct warnings rather than tenta-tive bids.

As George Shulman has explained, prophecy is a powerful register through which actors fighting to end racism and white supremacy can an-nounce disavowed realities that must be acknowledged.[67] But as Jasmine Syedullah observes, prophecy works differently in the hands of different people and in different kinds of projects.[68] Unlike the prophetic appeals of Martin Luther King Jr., Frederick Douglass, or James Baldwin, Sylvia Rivera's prophecy does not rely upon or seek to rebuild the nation-state. Hers is an anti-police politics that refuses the state; it refuses the bond of identification between the individual and the nation. Without the nation as a form of binding or as a dream for redemption, Rivera must find something else to work with.

Rivera constructs a web of responsibility, partly through a kinship trope and, relatedly, through her account of sacrifice and debt. She stages her accusations within an opening framework of intimate obligation. She leads with intimate appeals ("Hi, Baby") and maps out a constellation of relationships and political obligation through queering and trans-ing fa-milial language (a language that charts horizontal webs of responsibility rather than orienting toward the state and invoking individual rights as "gay citizens"). She thus begins with intimacy, then moves into reciting a litany of the crowd's failures: their active drifting away toward incorpora-tion, their disidentification not only with Rivera but also with other street queens, trans people, sex workers, people in jail, and people who live on the streets.

Although Rivera starts with intimacy, her speech is ultimately charged by a push-pull—pulling her audience together by invoking forms of binding *and* pushing them away by demarcating the lines dividing the group. She both invokes familial ties and confronts her listeners as a distinctively *non-familial* other. Not only are the people at the rally "brothers and sisters" with gay people in jail, but they are also strangers, even enemies. She rebuffs the crowd as "you people," in an ironic reversal that turns racist language against the racist. Her embodied gestures amplify her criticism—she points at the crowd to emphasize (or, as Ruth Osorio puts it, to "punctuate") the *you* and *your* of each accusation.[69] She holds on to the people in the park rather than discarding them (disidentifying with them in the Muñozian sense), and she holds onto rather than discards the movement that they together constitute. She interrogates and confronts the crowd's and the movement's transphobia, classism, and racism. This kind of disidentification, as José Esteban Muñoz has put it, "enables politics"—Rivera exposes the movement's encoded political messages and their "universalizing and exclusionary machinations" and she "recircuits their workings" to account for trans and queer people of color, poor people, and sex workers, and to make possible a more capacious politics.[70]

The basis of Rivera's appeals to identification are the relationships that have been betrayed and which must be made right. The audience has failed in their obligations to their brothers and sisters who are in jail. Rivera charges her listeners with abandonment and neglect. And they have failed in their obligations to Rivera and to other trans activists. They owe their liberation to her (and to her sisters). They are bound to her through what she has given them—and yet they have failed to abide by the terms of this relationship. What binds the *we* for Rivera is *what people's liberation and dignity is made of*—upon whose labor has their freedom been built? For Rivera, the basis of shared identification is not a gay nationalism. Rather, her interlocutors are bound to her because of her sacrifice for their freedom. She chronicles the material sacrifices she has made for gay liberation—being beaten up, having her nose broken, losing her job, and losing her apartment—and she tutors her listeners on her proximity to violence in a way that works as a particular kind of authentication. She refuses white GAA members' claims upon the movement, figured through accounts of their own sacrifice of putting in time into meetings and coordination.[71] These are not the sacrifices Rivera is talking about. Instead, her ledger of debt and dues is about her and other street queens being frontliners who have physically met and absorbed state violence.[72] What freedom and dignity white middle-class gay people have tasted is constituted by her labor and her sisters' labor and their confrontations with the police. These dues cannot be repaid in a way that would neatly balance accounts and absolve, nullify, or unbind the connection—and this is because the sacrifices of the past constitute the present. The interest on the debt can only be paid by coming into STAR's politics.

Rivera uses shame to move her listeners politically. But as Juliet Hooker and Christopher Lebron clarify, shame is only salient within some kind of web of responsibility.[73] People will not feel shame about an unmet responsibility if they do not feel that responsibility in the first place. When Rivera shames the people in the park, she shames them *as kin*, as bound to her and to their brothers and sisters in jail. In leading with queer intimate forms of address, like "Baby," she establishes the rubric within which the listeners' failures mean anything politically.

Rivera patently flips people's attempt to silence her, expel her from the stage, and shame her out of her rightful place in the movement. She refuses the script. When she confronts the people in the park for telling her to "go and hide my tail between my legs" and announces that she will "no longer put up with this shit," she returns their shaming back to them and admonishes them for failing to remember their obligations and debts. She shames the crowd for their attempts to silence her and for their hostile conduct: "I have *lost my job*. I have *lost my apartment* for gay liberation—*and you all treat me this way?!*" Then she orders them to reflect upon these incredible failures by flipping back their condemnation: "*What the fuck's wrong with you all!?! THINK ABOUT THAT!*"

As James Baldwin tells us, every accusation contains a plea.[74] Rivera's plea is a call into identification and reoriented ethical political action. Rivera does not try to persuade her listeners into a kind of coalitional politics, but instead summons them into a thick identification rooted in an ethic of community care. Rivera's listeners would redeem themselves through a renewed commitment to their relationship with her and with their kin in prison and through their changed conduct going forward.

"I *gave them their pride* but they have not given me mine."

Three decades later, the tension between belonging/demarcation and sacrifice/debt structured Rivera's intervention in her 2001 keynote address for Latino Gay Men of New York's (LGMNY) monthly meeting at the Lesbian and Gay Community Services Center in New York City.[75] Partway through telling the story of the Stonewall rebellion, Rivera recounted that:

We were determined that evening that we were going to be a liberated, free community, which we did acquire that. Actually, I'll change the "we": *You* have acquired your liberation, your freedom, from that night. Myself, I've got shit, just like I had back then. But I still struggle, I still continue the struggle. I will struggle til the day I die and my main struggle right now is that my community will see the rights that are justly ours.[76]

Here, Rivera enunciates and then *rescinds* a *we*, splintering it into a sharply demarcated *you* and *I*, a *you* who has freedom, while "I've got shit, just like I had back then." Next, she pivots to claim her audience right in the midst of critiquing their elite gay politics: "I am tired of seeing my children—I call everybody, including yous in this room, you are all my children—I am tired of seeing homeless transgender children, young, gay, youth children. I am tired of seeing the lack of interest that this rich community has." Here, in a trans and queer kinship practice, Rivera locates her hearers in a lineage of ancestors and youth; she furnishes them with new terms for LGBTQ adulthood and a mandate for future conduct. Rivera went on to critique the resources going into remodeling the Center, confronting her audience for being able to "rerenovate a building for millions and millions of dollars and buy another building across the street and still not worry about your homeless children from your community, and I know this for a fact, because the reason that I have to get clearance every time to come into this building is because I saw many of the kids before the building was being renovated up the street, many of the children are sleeping on the steps of that church." Rivera recounts her own attempt to intervene, explaining that "I went in there with an attitude. I raised hell. Yes, maybe I did try to destroy the front desk, but I did not attack anybody."[77]

At this point in her life, Rivera was a movement elder, and she figures her relationship to her audience in maternal/parental terms. She charts an intergenerational constellation of kinship relationships layered upon the sibling relationships of her 1973 speech. Rivera confronts her audience about what happened when she raised hell at the Center: "My thanks for everything I have done for this freakin' community? Had me arrested and put in Bellevue!" She reprimands them for not showing up a month earlier to support Intro 475 at New York City Council—a proposal to add a definition of gender to New York City's Human Rights Law. "Where," she demands, "were my sisters and brothers? Where were my children that I liberated?"[78] They did not go to the City Council for this long-awaited day to support a bill made necessary by back-room dealings in 1973. Her children have not, as James Baldwin puts it, been "paying their dues."[79] There is a debt that has not been paid, and she insists that everyone know about it. In Rivera's appeal, the basis of their identification is rooted in what she gave them.[80] Her more privileged children are bound to her even as they turn away. Their self-absorption and assimilation are failures in their responsibilities to her. Even as her listeners are her "children," Rivera also hails them as the parents of homeless youth, criticizing their choice to pour resources into renovations and "still not worry about *your homeless children from your community*" (italics added), youth sleeping on the streets nearby the Center.[81]

Weeks later, in an interview by Kristianna Tho'mas, Rivera names the betrayal and unfulfilled reciprocity surrounding Pride itself and what mainstream gays and lesbians owe, explaining, "This is no longer my Pride. I *gave them their pride* but they have not given me mine."[82] Pride carries multiple meanings here: as the annual gathering/event, as material safety from being jailed or detained in a mental institution, as material change and organized revolt, and as a sense of self in political community.

Her demarcation that "this is *their* pride," or that "*you* have acquired your liberation" while "I've got shit" has resonances with the juxtapositions in Frederick Douglass' 1852 jeremiad, "What to the Slave Is the Fourth of July?" In his speech, Douglass creates rhetorical and political distance from his audience—he tells his audience that this is "*your* National Independence," "*your* political freedom," that what has brought "light and healing to you has brought stripes and death to me. This Fourth July is *yours*, not *mine. You* may rejoice, *I* must mourn" (italics added).[83] Douglass performs both identifications and disidentifications in his speech, and he sharply underscores the uneven life of such a national holiday as the Fourth of July or, in modern queer national parlance, Pride. Douglass and Rivera claim mutual connection and distance from their listeners in order to build identification within a freedom politics that would keep matters of racialized (for Douglass and Rivera) and also gendered (for Rivera) violence and difference at the fore.

Rivera understands her siblings' and her children's failures to honor their relationship with her as nothing less than a betrayal. People have failed in their commitments and bonds—and she registers this failure as heartbreaking. In reflecting on the continued marginalization of trans people within LGBTQ politics, Rivera explains that

I'm hurt and get depressed a lot about it. But I will not give up because I won't give the mainstream gay organizations the satisfaction of keeping us down. If we give up, they win. And we can't allow them to win. . . . We allowed them to speak for us for so many damn years, and we bought everything they said to us: "Oh, let us pass our bill, then we'll come for you." Yeah, come for me. Thirty-two years later and they're still coming for me.[84]

Rivera references the fight in the 1970s and 1980s to pass a New York City gay rights bill and the removal of trans people from its protections in December 1973.[85] Upon joining GAA in 1970, Rivera was a frontline activist in the effort to pass the bill. Rivera took one of the very first arrests for the campaign while collecting petitions and later, at a meeting of Village Independent Democrats, whacked city councilwoman Carol Greitzer over the head with a clipboard of petitions when Greitzer would not accept them (Greitzer went on to become the first sponsor of the bill).[86] She also infamously kicked off her heels and scaled the walls of City Hall in bell bottoms and a crop top in an attempt to gain access to the closed-door votes on the original bill.[87] Despite the blood and sweat that Rivera and her sisters poured into the bill, a closed circle of representatives from gay organizations (including GAA and the National Gay Task Force) conceded to an amendment that would remove antidiscrimination protections for trans and gender nonconforming people.[88] As Bebe Scarpinato and Rusty Moore note, Rivera's "first major deception at the hands of the gay movement occurred when drag rights were specifically excluded from the bill to make it more palatable to 'straight' people, and reflect the assimilationist attitude of the Gay Rights movement at the time." Scarpinato and Moore explain that "this betrayal was a lesson [Rivera] carried with her in all her future activism"—it anticipated and came to haunt a larger pattern of the treatment of trans inclusions within gay rights legislation, as in the (contested) 2007 decision of Democratic leaders in the House of Representatives to amend the proposed Employment Non-Discrimination Act by stripping protections for transgender people.[89] The New York Gay Rights Bill, passed in 1986, did not include trans people in its protections. Here and elsewhere, the liberal gay rights movement failed in its political obligations to trans people, incarcerated LGBTQ people, and houseless LGBTQ people, and Rivera testifies as a witness to these betrayals. In her 2001 keynote, she explains that every time the bill came up for a vote, she hoped it wouldn't pass "because of what they did to me. As badly as I knew this community needed that bill, I didn't feel it was justified for them to have it on my sweat and tears, or from my back."[90]

Although at the 1973 rally Rivera drew her listeners into identification in the course of four minutes, her appeal came at great personal cost, and she did not see those identifications take hold in the years that followed. Her reflections years later indicate that she did not think the movement came into a substantive, politically meaningful identification with STAR's politics that year or in the long run. Most of the people at the park may not have cared for very long after her speech about what they owed or how they may be bound to a wider vision of freedom. Rivera thus presents us with the long-term failures of the movement to hear or heed her calls. She testifies to the great expense, the danger, and the difficulty of political struggles to bid upon and shape forms of identification. She testifies that identificatory claims, especially those issued by more subaltern voices, may not take hold.

Violence and Access

The struggle at the rally between accessing and policing access to the stage illuminates the differently borne hazards and risks of participation in the struggle over identification and the questions of *who* gets to make appeals, through what venues, with what reach, and with what costs. As Ruth Osorio, drawing on Lindal Buchanan, explains, rhetorical "delivery does not begin with the speech itself but with the act of getting onto the podium—a more difficult—even perilous—task for marginalized rhetors speaking to a resistant audience."[91] Indeed, Rivera's delivery was marked by violence and confrontation before she even arrived on the stage.[92] She explained that people she had called her "comrades in the movement literally beat the shit out of me" and that "that's where it all began, to really silence us."[93] Even though people forcibly tried to stop her from taking the stage, Rivera got past the barricade—she recounts, "They beat me, I kicked their asses. I did get to speak. I got my points across."[94] She claimed them as belonging to her even as she condemned their actions: "I don't let too many people keep me down. Especially my own, especially my own. My own cannot keep me down."[95]

The political significance of the attempt to remove Rivera was unambiguously clear to her. She explains that for four years drag queens had "been at the vanguard of the gay movement and all of a sudden it was being taken away. We were being pushed out of something that we helped create."[96]

Queens Liberation Front (QLF) founder Lee Brewster also intervened at the gala, stepping onto the stage in a long gown as O'Leary finished her tirade. Brewster proclaimed, "I cannot sit and let my people be insulted," and, above the din of applause and the yells of "fuck you!," reminded the audience that what they were celebrating "was a result of what the drag queens did at the Stonewall," that "*we gave you your pride!*" Brewster spurned the audience ("Gay liberation: *SCREW YOU!*") and threw his tiara into the crowd, vowed to continue to bring people out of the closet through his magazine readership, then bid the movement farewell ("Goodbye. Good luck, my *sometimes friends!*") with a final throw of his coat into the crowd.[97] Rivera understood the attempt to block her and understood the attempted removal of drag queen performers from the program as practices in excising the figures who were at the center of the very event that the parade sought to commemorate.[98] These erasures reverberate with broader processes through which trans women of color's activism has been and continues to be erased from racial justice, feminist, and gay liberation politics. Tourmaline has described this as a process of "exile and isolation of trans folks from movements that trans folks had actually helped start."[99]

In the speech itself, Rivera testifies to the physical costs that she sustained for gay liberation—including violence upon her body and heightened economic and housing precarity. But her reflections years later also shed light on the physical and emotional costs of making the intervention at the CSLD rally. The experience had serious long-term emotional and political repercussions. She marks that STAR died that year, and she went into a deep depression. Rivera attempted suicide and was found by Johnson who sent her to the hospital where she received sixty stitches in her arm. She reflects that she was deeply "hurt and I felt that the movement had completely betrayed the drag queens and the street people and I felt that . . . the years that I had already given them had been wasted."[100] Although some people stood in solidarity with Rivera's intervention, including Lee Brewster's declaration as well as his withdrawing funding from the CSLDC, many people continued to blame her in later years for "ruining" the rally.[101] She explained in a 1994 interview that "still to this day, I have people come up to me from the old days and say, 'Well, you trashed us on the 4th anniversary.' I said, 'No, I just stood up for me.'"[102]

Rivera largely left the movement for twenty years, moving to Tarrytown, New York, where she worked as a food services manager, organized drag shows, participated in AIDS walkathons and the annual Pride march, and maintained limited contact with the New York City gay political move-ment.[103] In 1995 she lived with other houseless people at the Christopher Street Piers, and in 1997 she moved into the Transy House Collective in Brooklyn.[104] Upon more publicly reentering movement work in the late 1990s, Rivera organized numerous demonstrations, including a political fu-neral for Amanda Milan, and helped plan the first Brooklyn Pride March. She took arrest at an Amadou Diallo demonstration, at a political funeral for Matthew Shepard, and on behalf of multiple activist organizations.[105] In 1999, she was invited by the Italian Transgender Organization to address the World Pride rally in Rome. She worked in and then became a manager of a kitchen providing food for houseless people, now named the Sylvia Rivera Food Pantry. In January 2001, she revived STAR as Street Transgender Action Revolutionaries.[106] In 2002, she summoned leaders from the Empire State Pride Agenda Committee to her deathbed, where she delivered a series of demands, negotiated to include a transgender person on their board, and urged them to ensure transgender protections in the Sexual Orientation Non-Discrimination Act (SONDA).[107]

Speaking Forward and Contemporary Containment

Today, Rivera's 1973 speech has a political life that evidences both the con-tinued reach of identificatory appeals from the past and the mechanisms of their ongoing containment. On the one hand, the footage of the speech is a critical record in its circulation and revival by Tourmaline, and today inhabits an important place in public discourses within trans and queer of color abolitionist politics. In an intergenerational prophecy, Rivera's speech moves through public presentations, essays and books, Twitter, YouTube, performance art, and classrooms.[108] It is called upon as a political mandate from a movement elder, as a resource for navigating a paradoxical moment of increasing trans visibility and heightened violence against trans women of color.[109] It is called upon as a resource for resisting trans assimilation into mainstream LGBTQ politics, respectability politics, and liberal state-sanctioned representation.

On the other hand, even as Rivera's speech circulates widely, public ac-cess to the footage carries its own story of containment. The primary copy of Rivera's speech was filmed by the lesbian feminist L.O.V.E. Collective (Lesbians Organizing for Video Experience), a group that in the 1970s and 1980s documented lesbian life and politics in New York, including demonstrations by LFL.[110] Members of the L.O.V.E. Collective were at the 1973 CSLD events in order to film lesbian performers, but when Rivera took the stage, the collective kept their camera rolling.[111] In this way, it is miraculous that the footage exists because the camera was not there for Rivera or STAR's freedom dreams. It was there to bear witness to the parade events in service of political projects that so often excluded Rivera. The footage is an example of radical trans histories being "accidentally archived," as Tourmaline has put it—including within, as Jeannine Tang explains, the records of people who were in fact antagonistic to trans people and their politics.[112]

Ultimately, the Lesbian Herstory Archives in Brooklyn acquired the footage. Tourmaline uploaded a recording of the film to Vimeo in 2012, clarifying that she "stole it and uploaded it . . . as a form of direct action against assimilation and historical erasure of trans life."[113] The post is part of her practice of restitching political relationships and imaginaries across generational lines, against the disjunctures produced through legacies of HIV/AIDS, poverty, criminalization, trans pushout from the LGB movement, and premature death.[114] In these ways, Tourmaline's posting—and the broader scope of her archival activism—can itself be understood as an identificatory appeal, one that calls trans and queer people into identification with STAR's politics and into right relationship with radical elders. Five years later, Tourmaline's posting was removed under the auspices of copyright protection, and the footage reappeared elsewhere on YouTube, titled as the "original authorized" copy and bearing the watermark "LoveTapesCollective." Alternative postings and re-postings of the footage flourish, but as Tourmaline and others have noted, the fact that the recording continues to be legally claimed by a collective that was historically more aligned with O'Leary's LFL rather than with Rivera raises critical questions about who "owns" trans of color history.[115]

Multivalence, Presence, and Absence

Rivera's appeals are multivalent and multi-sited. She summons both her antagonists in the gay movement and her sister queens, through different but sometimes overlapping tonalities and registers. None of STAR's identificatory projects were automatic or seamless. With Johnson, Rivera called to other street queens and homeless gay youth in conversations on sidewalks and in city parks, at the piers, in hotel rooms (where Johnson and Rivera provided shelter), and at STAR house. They issued appeals through practices of mutual aid, teaching their children that they didn't have to hustle, but if they did, "you have to put back into helping *all* of us."[116] Johnson and Rivera issued these appeals at material registers (e.g., housing, food, physical safety) as well as relational ones (e.g., through practices of mothering and accompaniment).[117] Temporally, these appeals concretely faced the conditions of the present and practiced political imagination for the future against forms of violence and disposability. The appeals summoned their sisters as "STAR people." Many of the traces of these appeals are ephemeral but live on in the stories and lives of their children and sisters.[118]

Rivera and Johnson also organized people in GAA and GLF, many of whom were antagonistic to STAR people and STAR's politics. Rivera's and Johnson's political appeals to white middle-class gay people constituted a different kind of reach, toward those who would disavow them. Rivera structured her CSLD appeal around shared history, which is not a fabrication: when Rivera took the stage it was not as an outsider; she had already inhabited a place in meeting spaces and in frontline activism. She also structured her appeal around having shared siblings, around her conviction about the necessity to unite against straight society itself, and around visions for a shared future. She and Johnson had issued these horizontal appeals vertically not only at CSLD events but also at protests, in meeting rooms, and at sit-ins. The context of the dominant gay movement in 1973 included demonological accounts of gay people, and, for some gay people, siren calls to homonormative whiteness as a way out of criminalization and state-sanctioned death. Seizing the microphone, Rivera broke into that din with her countercall. She knew that this brief encounter would not be sufficient for her identificatory project, and so she calls people at the gala to visit STAR House to learn more about their brothers and sisters. She calls them into identification as a process.

Rivera invoked the first-person plural at only one point in her speech: when she said she believes in "us getting our rights or else I would not be out there fighting for our rights." Rivera did not—and, given the hostile political conditions she faced at the rally, perhaps could not—rely on a preexisting *we* to invoke shared identification. Her accusations, however, indirectly invoked a *we*: she tried to draw the people in the park into identification with people in prison, and *back* into identification with her and with a wider vision for gay liberation. Ultimately, however, her substantive political and ethical challenge to the *we* may be so great that it breaks rather than bends the connection.[119]

Rivera's identificatory appeal works through a push-pull of belonging and distance, of friend and enemy, mapped within and across the same crowd in ways that tie that crowd to those who Rivera makes present in their absence: trans and queer people in prison. While for Rivera, identification is made up of ethical and political responsibilities to those who have less political power, she confronts and attempts to summon a crowd for whom those responsibilities are increasingly hollowed out. Rivera's call at the park does not just seek to interpellate her listeners *as they are* into horizontal relationships, but to show that this counterinterpellation must be *transformative* in order to be redemptive—transformative in the sense that they reorient themselves toward STAR's politics and toward their kin in jail and who live in the streets. They can only be redeemed if they are "Baby" instead of "you people.[120]

2

"Flesh of Their Flesh, Bone of Their Bone"

James Baldwin's Kinship Politics

> What the Americans do not realize is that a war between brothers, in
> the same cities, on the same soil, is not a *racial* war but a *civil* war. But
> the American delusion is not only that their brothers all are white
> but that the whites are all their brothers.
>
> —James Baldwin, "An Open Letter to My Sister Angela Y. Davis"

On Saturday February 3, 1968, over a hundred students filled the main hall at
the West Indian Students' Centre in London to hear James Baldwin and Dick
Gregory speak.[1] With standing room only, extra seats were tucked in on both
sides of the speaker's table, and people stood leaning against the curtained
walls. A row of miniature flags decorated the fireplace mantle at the head
of the room. The audience was interracial but mostly Black, and mixed
gender but mostly men. The political climate of the moment was marked by
the recent Tet offensive in Vietnam, the previous summer's riots in Detroit,
the growing profile of the Black Panther Party for Self-Defense, hardening
restrictions on immigration in Britain, the failures of Britain's weak 1965
Race Relations Act, and heated debates over the place of interracial solidarity and coalition within racial justice movements. Baldwin stood as he
spoke, leaning forward to rest his hands on the low table. Across his remarks,
Baldwin invoked his lineage—explaining that his "entry into America is a bill
of sale" and describing being formed in a "certain crucible"—and offered an
account of race at once deeply internationalist and rooted in the U.S. context.[2]
He summoned layers of belonging between the Caribbean and Harlem, while
also meditating on the ruptures of the slave trade and the histories that bind
him specifically to the United States. He located America's "racial problem"—
a term he refuses and upends—as rooted in a foundational history of violence
and disavowal. In contrast to Black nationalist and integrationist accounts of

If We Were Kin. Lisa Beard, Oxford University Press. © Oxford University Press 2023.
DOI: 10.1093/oso/9780197517338.003.0003

racial domination, Baldwin demanded a reckoning with the enfleshed and intimate history of the production of race.

Using this speech as an entry point, this chapter locates the concept I call *boundness* in James Baldwin's work and asks how Baldwin's articulation offers an alternative and embodied way to theorize racial identity, racialized violence, and interracial solidarity. Across the 1960s, Baldwin's interventions in U.S. racial politics challenged and exceeded dominant frameworks of race.[3] Unlike the framework of race as a social construction, Baldwin rejected biological notions of race by focusing attention *toward*, rather than away from, the body. He attended not only to discourse, institutions, and structures but also to blood, bone, and breastmilk and to embodied relationships within systems of domination and oppression. Baldwin brings us forward to the body in his antiracist project, contributing to political theory, critical race theory, and Black feminist phenomenology by centering an embodied account in theorizing race as a social construction.[4]

The concept I call boundness is, I argue, at the core of Baldwin's identificatory appeals in the 1960s and is crucial to understanding Baldwin's contributions to theorizing race and antiracist politics today. While Baldwin invokes different forms of boundness across his work, this chapter examines in particular his account that white and Black people in the U.S.—even though they have been subjected to centuries of racist laws, policies, ideologies, and other forms of violence—are related by blood and are therefore morally bound together. Baldwin posits a peculiar kinship narrative that foregrounds racialized/sexual violence, addressing the histories of southern plantations and Jim Crow spaces where lines of racial difference were drawn between people related by blood with, as Christina Sharpe has put it, "blood *becom[ing]* property . . . in one direction and kin in the another."[5] Following this narrative, white racial identity and white supremacist ideology function quite well in integrated spaces because both are foundationally *structured* by a history of race-making at an intimate scale—by the disavowal of "flesh and bone" kin and the transformation of kin into property. This form of boundness appears across Baldwin's work— in his fiction and nonfiction, in his writing and public commentary, and in his early and late work. Extending work by Maria Stewart in 1831, Ida B. Wells in 1892, and Beah Richards in 1951,[6] and anticipating work by contemporary social theorists on the production of racial difference in exceedingly intimate spaces,[7] Baldwin re-reads white-on-Black violence as a kind of intrafamilial violence that itself *produces* race. On this basis, he makes the claim that white and Black people's lives are co-constituted and their freedom is bound together.

To be clear, Baldwin's invocation of boundness through the kinship narrative does not translate usefully across many relational formations of race in the U.S., and Baldwin's account is vexed when it reproduces the settler imaginaries of American nationalism or when it privileges race over all other forms of difference.[8] Part of what makes Baldwin's enunciations of boundness so provocative and more broadly significant, however, is the space he opens to examine the relationship between intimacy and identification, the racial politics of kinship and nation,[9] and the political possibilities of bringing attention to the body into our understandings of race.[10]

While my argument is anchored across Baldwin's wider corpus, to explicate how boundness functions in his work, I do a close reading of passages from four texts—"White Man's Guilt," *The Fire Next Time*, a 1963 Public Broadcasting Service interview, and his 1968 speech in London.[11] In these texts, Baldwin invokes boundness with a number of rhetorical tools including familial language, destabilized racial categories, and racially ambiguous pronouns.[12] He selectively removes racial signifiers (for example, "white") from particular nouns (for example, "woman" or "brother") to foreground the intimate spaces in which racial violence has occurred and occurs. These particular texts are chosen not because they are his most famous (though this can be said of *Fire*), but because they allow me to focus on the rhetorical provocations that can be found throughout his oeuvre and theorize their implications.

Baldwin as Theorist

With Stephen Marshall, I read Baldwin as a theorist who provides critical insights into and challenges to the American political imaginary.[13] Lawrie Balfour and others have located in Baldwin's work not only a profoundly useful account of the relationship between racial history and U.S. democracy but also language through which to publicly engage race and racism today.[14] In Stephen Marshall's and George Shulman's readings, Baldwin's (queer) prophetic critique offers a political practice of "love as provocation"—the political actor is "the lover" who struggles with and on behalf of a beloved society.[15] I show that Baldwin's proposed political actor is also familial, moved to action through the relational political orientation of kinship. Baldwin's invocations of the past are often both interracial and familial, meant to, as Eddie Glaude, Jr. has put it, "orient us appropriately" toward self-examination and new forms of identification.[16] At different points, each of these scholars observes that Baldwin conceptualizes Black and white people as linked to each other; here, I want to talk about Baldwin's kinship narrative as a specific political theoretical intervention, a critical concept that reconfigures how to think about race and political community.

In Baldwin's work, boundness functions as a standpoint of critique and a political strategy to provoke shifts in identification.[17] Its power lies in the disruptive capacity of centering intimacy and impurity in theorizing race. In what Christina Sharpe calls the "monstrous intimacies" of slavery and its afterlife, ideas of racial categories are produced and maintained through violence and terror at an intimate scale. Baldwin foregrounds what Hortense Spillers has called an "incestuous, interracial genealogy" in which people related by blood were divided into categories of "kin" and "property," with the latter inheritable by the former.[18] As he invokes this history, Baldwin uses intimacy as a rhetorical technique—to demand change from white people, to critique dominant conceptions of legal and cultural integration, and to intervene in conversations in and about Black separatist politics.

In Baldwin's account, claims about purity are essential to white supremacy: purity is an illusion and a mechanism of control.[19] Ideas of racial purity are central to the notion of hypodescent: whiteness as a mythical political subjectivity and racial identity is defined by the imagined absence of any African ancestry.[20] Purity is defined against—defined by not-being—the "other," who is marked as impure or tainted and therefore "unfit" and worthless.[21] As María Lugones explains, the "lover of purity" "parades himself as pure" and aims to control the other. He is disembodied, a "fiction of his own imagination" and is "radically self-deceiving" in that he denies his own multiplicity and disowns his urges and deeds.[22] Against this disavowal, Baldwin bears witness to what the "lover of purity" has done. He argues that an underlying set of mechanisms, including self-deception, violence, and the construction of kin as *the other*, lie at the core of white racial identity.

Baldwin in His Time

Baldwin was not only a writer but also a significant public figure and an active participant in Black freedom struggles in the 1960s. He toured widely to speak for the Congress of Racial Equality and the Student Nonviolent Coordinating Committee, participated in voter registration drives and civil rights marches, spoke on television shows and radio programs, and was associated with movement leaders including Martin Luther King Jr., Malcolm X, Angela Davis, Medgar Evers, and Huey Newton.[23]

Baldwin theorized from within the shifting political and ideological frameworks of the 1950s and 1960s—a landscape defined by Cold War politics and anticommunist discourse; anticolonial struggles and the transatlantic exchange of Black political thought; the civil rights movement and the ascent of the liberal race paradigm; and the rise of Black nationalism in northern urban centers.[24] Although Baldwin defined himself as a faithful witness and *not* as a spokesperson, he was nonetheless described by some as "the voice of the revolution."[25] Henry Louis Gates, Jr. has argued that "by the early '60s [Baldwin's] authority seemed nearly unchallengeable. What did the Negro want? Ask James Baldwin."[26]

But Baldwin had complicated answers. Lawrie Balfour argues that Baldwin's political "fall out of fashion" later in the 1960s was fundamentally because of his appreciation of and insistence on the complexity of American racial politics.[27] Baldwin refused the choice between integration and separation as a false choice, and I argue that his conceptualization of boundness is at the heart of this refusal.

Flesh and Bone

At the West Indian Students' Centre in 1968, Baldwin invoked the concept I call *boundness* along multiple lines. Partly he does so through his compression of space—insisting to the largely Caribbean diasporic audience, for example, that he is part of the history of the Caribbean and that they "are part of the history which occurred in Harlem" (this spatial dimension of boundness will be examined at length in chapter 3). He also invokes boundness through compressing time and through a kinship narrative; the latter is my focus here. In the second half of his London address, Baldwin insists that to understand U.S. racial politics,

what you have to look at is what is happening in this country. And what is really happening is that brother has murdered brother, knowing it was his brother. White men have lynched Negroes knowing them to be their sons. White women have had Negroes burned knowing them to be their lovers. . . . That "great western house" I come from is one house, and I am one of the children of that house, simply I am the most despised child of that house. And it is because the American people are *unable* to face the fact that in fact I am *flesh of their flesh, bone of their bone, created by them. My blood, my father's blood is in that soil. They can't face that.*[28]

Describing the U.S. wryly as "that great western house," Baldwin repeats eight times in different ways his claim to belonging—as in his reference to the "house I come from" or his being "flesh of their flesh." He also names the white Americans' rejection of him, but that rejection is undermined each time by Baldwin's insistence on his very certain belonging. Baldwin argues that at the heart of American racial politics is white people's denial of their *flesh and bone* relationship with Black people—they make themselves into "blood strangers" and commit horrifying violence against their kin on land that is drenched in blood.[29]

In this passage, Baldwin does not read white-on-Black violence as raceless violence, but neither does he read it as violence done by one "distinct race" of people upon another "distinct race" of people. When he first introduces the kinship narrative, Baldwin strategically refuses the language of "distinct races" to enact a conceptual shift in our understanding of this violence. His refusal emphasizes that the murderers have killed their kin. Baldwin's audience can infer the racial identities of the "brother who has killed his brother," but in the initial absence of signifiers, the relationship between the brothers is conspicuously defined by kinship. Race is still present in this passage and even in some of the later signifiers, but by removing some of the racial signifiers, Baldwin demands that his audience face the intimacy of the violence. The violence cannot be explained *by race* as if race is essential and precedes the kin relationship.

In his 1965 essay "White Man's Guilt," published in *Ebony* magazine, Baldwin juxtaposes white-on-Black violence with white and Black relatedness.[30] Baldwin gives an account of white southern law enforcement officers barring courthouse doors against an unarmed group of Black people. Baldwin then immediately destabilizes the category of Black, specifying that, "more precisely, [the guards] were faced by a group of unarmed people arbitrarily called black whose color really ranged from the Russian steppes to the Golden Horn to Zanzibar."[31] Baldwin continues, drawing close in to a single sheriff and recounting how the sheriff begins to club the people down. Just at the cusp of physical violence, Baldwin foregrounds the flesh and bone relationship between the sheriff and the people who stand before him. In doing so, Baldwin is not denying the reality of the social category of Blackness, but he disrupts the logic by which white supremacy requires an undifferentiated category as a precursor to this kind of violence:

> Some of these people might have been related to him by blood. They are assuredly related to the black mammy of his memory and the black playmates of his childhood. And for a moment, therefore, he seemed nearly to be pleading with the people facing him not to force him to commit yet another crime and not to make yet deeper that ocean of blood in which his conscience was drenched, in which his manhood was perishing. The people did not go away, of course; once a people arise, they never go away. . . . So the club rose, the blood came down, and his bitterness and his anguish and his guilt were compounded.[32]

Baldwin lays out a narrative in which the sheriff pauses *because* of his relatedness to the people in the crowd. The sheriff can barely bear the tension between, on the one hand, the knowledge of his intimate connection with the people before him and, on the other hand, the scope and obligations of his white racial identity and his position as a law enforcement officer at that place and time. The only "nonviolent option" conceivable to the sheriff requires that the people return to submission—he hopes they submit so that he will not "have to" attack them. Baldwin describes the sheriff's conscience as already "drenched" with an "ocean of blood"—which becomes compounded by the choice to attack once again. This is the crux of the mechanics of white moral damage—with every additional action of committing violence toward known kin and insisting upon *unknowing*, white people become more wretched.

Baldwin finds that white people, with an unparalleled shrillness, deny their embodied relationship with Black people. His invocation of a flesh and bone connection is juxtaposed with a persistent white denial of that connection. His own family members "can't face" his membership in the "great western house." In the scene above, the sheriff's denial is incomplete—he cannot fully repress his connection to the crowd or his awareness of his own moral damage. His knowledge of his relatedness is a key part of the tension in the scene, but he chooses to reinvest in denial when he attacks. Baldwin thus illuminates the *willful* unknowing or nonrecognition that constitutes "white innocence" and is so central to white racial identity. Paradoxically, what is at stake in his intervention is less about recognizing *the other* per se but recognizing the self as related to the other.[33]

Baldwin's invocation of a narrative of Black–white kinship lies within a lineage of Black political discourse in the U.S. that stretches from the early nineteenth century into the late twentieth century. In this lineage, intimate appeals are used to confront racial violence and racial domination. In an 1831 speech to a mixed-race audience in Boston, abolitionist Maria Stewart declared that when God someday intervenes and stops white people from enacting violence against Black people, Black people

> will not come out against you with swords and staves, as against a thief [Matthew 26:55]; but we will tell you that our souls are fired with the same love of liberty and independence with which your souls are fired. We will tell you that too much of your blood flows in our veins, too much of your color in our skins, for us not to possess your spirits. We will tell you that ... it is the blood of our fathers, and the tears of our brethren that have enriched your soils. AND WE CLAIM OUR RIGHTS.[34]

Stewart frames her appeal within a raced narrative of national values and traces bloodlines *against* white myths of purity. Foretelling the end of slavery as divinely ordained, she foreshadows a distinctly fraternal confrontation in its wake. She demands accounting for the labor of and violence against Black people—both of which have made and shaped the country—and, on these terms, she announces a collective claim to political rights.

Stewart's provocation and claim reverberates, in different ways, throughout the political speeches, literature, visual art, and journalism of a number of Black public intellectuals over the next two centuries. Frederick Douglass' *Narrative* evokes the image of the master's "white" son whipping his "Black" half-brother while the master-father stands idly by.[35] In the 1890s, journalist and vindicationist Ida B. Wells mapped, at the risk of her own life, the connections between lynching; economic/political power; the myth of the Black male rapist and the surrounding moral panic; and white disavowal of interracial intimacy. Ralph Ellison's novels and essays in the mid-twentieth century evoke images of Black wet nurses and other Black caretakers—male and female—who give life to white citizens who forget the source of their life. In her poem, "A Black Woman Speaks," delivered to an audience of mostly white women at the 1951 Chicago Peace Congress, Beah Richards marked how white women have passed their children onto Black women:

> And so you passed them, your children, on to me.
> Flesh that was your flesh and blood that was your blood
> drank the sustenance of life from me.
> And as I gave suckle I knew I nursed my own child's enemy. [. . .]
> I kept your sons and daughters alive.
>
> But when they grew strong in blood and bone
> that was of my milk
> you
> taught them to hate me.
> Put your decay in their hearts and upon their lips
> so that the strength that was of myself
> turned and spat upon me,
> despoiled my daughters, and killed my sons.[36]

Collapsing time, Richards demands a reckoning with a history of weaponizing Black women's life force against them and their children—a history of white women training their children to commit violence against the Black women who nursed those children as infants and gave them life. While Baldwin accounts for the white sheriff's disavowal of the Black woman who raised him, Richards theorizes this connection as in fact a disavowed flesh and bone relationship—that "blood and bone / that was of my milk," "strength that was of myself" turned against her.

Kinship tropes are profoundly complicated and fraught. They are deployed in a range of nationalist articulations, where they often work to naturalize hierarchical and violent relationships and attempt to conjure unity in ways that sediment heteropatriarchal gender narratives.[37] In taking up these tropes, then, Baldwin faces multiple kinds of danger. First, in figuring the nation as kin, Baldwin risks reproducing a romanticized, familial, and exceptionalist American nationalism—a nationalism that binds a *we* in ways that rely on the production of remainders, strangers, and outsiders. A second danger in Baldwin's invocation of a kinship narrative concerns its treatment of the racialized-gendered sexual violence and terror at the foundation of the plantation and Jim Crow system. This danger lies in the ways in which shorthand retellings of the "monstrous intimacies" of slavery can transmogrify captivity, torture, and violation into "scenes of innocence" and "romance" that assuage the national imagination's grotesque nostalgia.[38] Third, in certain ways, Baldwin's narrative of Black–white kinship risks displacing and obscuring the profound ruptures of and ongoing violations of African and African American kinship in the context of chattel slavery.[39] As Hortense Spillers explains, enslavement was defined by classification as property *and by forced kinlessness*,[40] the latter instated not only through the denied genetic link between master/father and enslaved offspring as "the chief strategy of an undenied ownership"[41] but also foundationally through the violations of African and African American kinship. These breaches, Spillers explains, throw family meanings entirely into crisis; and kinship itself loses meaning since it "can be invaded at any given and arbitrary moment by the property relations."[42]

When Stewart, Wells, Richards, Ellison, and Baldwin invoke a kinship narrative, they demand confrontation with the exceedingly intimate scale of racial violence and foundational racial formations in the United States as well as with the legacies of those formations. Race has been made through intimate physical violence, through policing affective bonds, and through practices of disidentifying with some people and identifying with others. Historically, in the production of colonial and racial subjectivities, where/how/with whom one belonged was—as Ann Laura Stoler has put it—"reckoned, in part, by cultivation of the self—by one's desires and by that for which *one ceased to long*," a process she has called "the education of desire" or "sentimental education."[43] In these mappings, Stoler explains, the threshold between "inside and out cuts through families and across them, traces through selective genealogies and adoption agencies, 'degrees of blood' and dense webs of fictive kin"—a social geometry that is central to Baldwin's account.[44]

Like Maria Stewart and Beah Richards, Baldwin reworks themes of intimacy and kinship in his narratives about U.S. racial history and in his political appeals. As Lawrie Balfour, drawing on Patricia Williams, has put it, this multivocal lineage of appeals issues a "reminder that getting the facts straight about this past requires of many Americans a willingness to become involved, personally, in a wrenching paradox."[45] Baldwin mines this paradox and uses it to intervene in multiple directions—to disrupt white supremacist obsessions with purity, to challenge Black nationalist "preoccupations with purity of lineage and politics," and to call people into new forms of identification.[46]

Interventions into Separatism

Even as Baldwin was connected to both integrationist and separatist movement spaces and leaders, Baldwin stood ideologically and politically in a
third space outside of the two frameworks.[47] What set Baldwin apart was
his conceptualizations of boundness and race, his premise of political action, and his theorization of the relationship between history and political
identification.

In *The Fire Next Time* Baldwin rhetorically invokes boundness to critique separatism and ideas of racial distinctness in a way that positioned
him outside of dominant Black nationalist politics. *Fire* had a wide
reach—it was at the top of nonfiction bestseller lists across the country
and garnered international recognition.[48] In *Fire*, Baldwin articulates
his disagreement with the idea that Black and white people are inherently separate and that white people are unredeemable.[49] In the second
half of the book, Baldwin describes visiting the home of the Honorable
Elijah Muhammad in Chicago. His narrative pace and his description of
his arrival give the reader a sense of the peacefulness of the space. When
he meets Muhammad, Muhammad says something that makes Baldwin
laugh and makes Baldwin "think of my father and me as we might have
been if we had been friends."[50] As he describes Muhammad's smile, he
conveys his longing for a loving rather than antagonistic relationship
with his own father. However, as much as he is accepted by the community, Baldwin knows that he cannot fit in when, at the dinner table, people
speak about white people as "white devils." Baldwin tells the reader that he
does not think of white people as "devils" though it is a reasonable conclusion given the brutality of anti-Black violence.[51] He explains that in "the
beginning . . . a Negro just cannot *believe* that white people are treating
him as they do. . . . And when he realizes that the treatment accorded him
has nothing to do with anything he has done, that the attempt of white
people to destroy him—for that is what it is—is utterly gratuitous, it is not
hard for him to think of white people as devils."[52]

In *Fire* and in public remarks, Baldwin theorizes that part of the power of
the Nation of Islam's political appeals to Black people lies in a certain intimacy of description, in starkly naming the conditions of Black life and Black
death, of "articulat[ing] [Black people's] suffering" and "corroborat[ing] their
reality."[53] On this ground, Nation leaders make prophetic claims upon a *we*—
a *we* that shares a past and, compellingly, a future, in the vision that all Black

people will be saved in the impending total destruction of white people. Baldwin anticipates and even dreads that at this meal he would be summoned to identify. He describes the "stifling feeling that *they* knew I belonged to them but knew that I did not know it yet" and the sense that Muhammad and his followers were waiting patiently, confident that Baldwin would discover this belonging for himself.[54] Muhammad invokes a *we* that is a priori—that includes Black people in its bounds whether or not they individually identify with the Nation or subscribe to its prophecy. Baldwin rejects the prophecy; he feels drawn into identification on interpersonal and relational levels but cannot abide by the "invented past" or the political mandates of the identification.[55] What stands out across Baldwin's description of the meeting is the juxtaposition of intimacy and nonbelonging—from Baldwin's pull toward Muhammad's "peculiar authority" and his feeling as though he was a young person interacting with a father figure or preacher,[56] to Baldwin's conclusion as he departed that they "would always be strangers and possibly one day enemies."[57]

In Baldwin's telling in *Fire*, Muhammad's denunciation of white people as devils is sharply contrasted with Baldwin's claim of friendship with some white people. Baldwin tells the reader, "I knew two or three people, white, whom I would trust with my life, and I knew a few others, white, who were struggling as hard as they knew how, and with great effort and sweat and risk, to make the world more human."[58] In Baldwin's reference to "people, white" and "a few others, white" we see his subtle pattern of disrupting the order of racial signifier and human noun. The people with whom Baldwin would trust his life are introduced first as people, then as white. In his reversal, the link between "people" and "white" is denaturalized, it is made shaky, rendering whiteness more of a condition than an essential characteristic. The comma further signals that the whiteness is not essential. Both the comma in "people, white" and the disruptive reordering of "white" and "people" invite a pause. They create a space we might fill, as though we could hear the longer phrase "people who think they are white" or "people who have decided they are white."[59]

It is not that Baldwin disagrees with Muhammad on the magnitude of white people's violence and failure at humanity. The difference is that Baldwin thinks that white people are not a "different people" from Black people and that they are redeemable (though not *as* "white people"). Baldwin also diverges from Muhammad's position because Baldwin insists that African Americans are bound to America.[60]

Muhammad's critique is important to Baldwin, and he represents it with respect even as he indicates his fundamental concerns. He warns that *"whoever debases others is debasing himself*. That is not a mystical statement but a most realistic one, which is proved by the eyes of any Alabama sheriff— and I would not like to see Negroes ever arrive at so wretched a condition."[61] We are reminded of the sheriff in "White Man's Guilt" who, by violently investing in a continued denial of his relatedness to the people in the crowd, compounds his spiritual and moral destruction.

Although Baldwin critically objects to certain separatist politics of Black nationalist projects, to understand this objection carefully we must make a distinction between separatism as an ontological logic and separatism as a practice. On the one hand, an ontological logic of separatism conceives of Black and white Americans as originally, ultimately, and rightly separate. Within this logic, redemption and liberation are imagined in separate histories, separate present moments, and separate futures. Separatism as a practice, on the other hand—that is, when Black people remove themselves from the presence of white people—is *not* inherently linked to either an ontology of separatism or an ontology of boundness. Boundness does not require or even recommend that Black people maintain engagement with white people. One can understand oneself to be bound to white people and use a practice of separatism from them as a political-interpersonal tactic when necessary. In this way, a practice of separation is not a refusal of boundness but an acknowledgment that Black people do not need to risk living with and orienting their lives toward white people. Baldwin himself spent a considerable portion of his life outside of America as a survival strategy, as "an exile because I can't live in America under the terms on which Americans offer me my life."[62] He sees his boundness as undisturbed by his practice of separation. In a 1961 Pacifica Radio discussion with Malcolm X and Leverne McCummins, Baldwin insists that even if he were to "leave this country tomorrow and never come back," he would "not cease to be an American Negro."[63]

Baldwin understands projects of separation based in an ontology of separatism—whether those projects be led by white or Black people—as not just futile but also morally dangerous. Even though Muhammad's ideology is justified, Baldwin argues that it is dangerous because Black people will damage themselves if they dehumanize and deny their relatedness with white people. He knows this intimately from studying and understanding the injury white people bring upon themselves through committing violence against and denying their boundness to their kin. Out of a fierce love, out of not wanting to see Black people "ever arrive at so wretched a condition" as white people have made for themselves, Baldwin rejects accounts that represent white people as inhuman by nature and he warns against narratives that map separated histories and futures.[64]

Interventions into Integration

Because Baldwin argued that Black and white people are bound together, critics often misread him as an integrationist.[65] However, although he was involved in and more aligned with the civil rights movement, he did not fit neatly into that movement because he theorized integration differently. As Marshall and Shulman explain, where members of Martin Luther King Jr.'s beloved community are tied together by an agape love, Baldwin's political actor is figured as "the lover."[66] If for King, rebirth implies transcending our embodied history, for Baldwin, redemption is found in accepting, not transcending, that history. It is found in facing our desire, mortality, and suffering, and it requires taking responsibility for our actions and our ancestors' actions.[67] With a writer's attention to language, Baldwin addresses at least three meanings of integration in his work—not only integration as a political movement seeking formal equality or the cultural incorporation of Black people into white society, but also integration as already achieved (Black and white people are related), and integration as a political project to force white people to face themselves.

First, Baldwin intervenes in dominant conceptualizations of formal integration, his ambivalence structured by a psychoanalytic attention to kinship and disavowal. In his 1968 speech in London, Baldwin precedes the passage about "brother killing brother" by naming the limitations of formal legal change. He says that Black people's

> plea is a very simple one. It's saying: Look at it. Forget all the mountains of nonsense that have been written and everything that's been said. Forget "the Negro problem." Don't write any Voting Acts, we had that—it's called the Fifteenth Amendment. We don't need the Civil Rights Bill of 1964. What you have to look at is what is happening in this country. And what is really happening is that brother has murdered brother, knowing it was his brother.[68]

In arguing that the Voting Rights Act is a repetition of the Fifteenth Amendment,[69] Baldwin is also claiming that to layer new policy upon existing policy to secure formal legal rights misses the point—it misses the foundational intimate violence and denial of kinship that has defined the categories of and the relationship between white and Black people in America in ways that permit such a clear evasion of the letter of the Constitution. Baldwin critiques the strategies of groups like the NAACP, whose leaders argued that securing liberal individual rights under the law should be the primary focus of antiracist work.

Baldwin is concerned about any integration project that attempts to more systematically incorporate Black people into existing white supremacist structures, invoking one of Lorraine Hansberry's provocations in asking, "Do I really *want* to be integrated into a burning house?"[70] Baldwin criticizes the directionality of dominant conceptions of both legal and cultural integration; integration is not an acceptable solution to him when it requires Black assimilation into white norms or structures, or when it is represented as an "improvement" for Black people.[71] In such a framework, Baldwin explains, "it is the Negro, of course, who is presumed to have become equal"—to have risen and improved to join white people—"an achievement that not only proves the comforting fact that perseverance has no color but also overwhelmingly corroborates the white man's sense of his own value."[72] As Baldwin explains in "On Being White . . . and Other Lies," integration into whiteness has always meant integration into a system based on violence and denial of history. White people and their institutions are not sane or safe for Black people or other people of color. Black integration into a white supremacist system provides legitimation for a colorblind story that anyone can succeed if they work hard enough.

Baldwin's second meaning of integration can be found in a provocative rhetorical move in his 1961 radio debate with Malcolm X and Leverne McCummins, where Baldwin recasts integration as a fait accompli in light of U.S. racial history. In Baldwin's account, Black and white people are already integrated in ways that belie their social and political segregation. Baldwin insists to Malcolm X that "whether I like it or not, whether you like it or not, this issue about integration is a false issue because we have been integrated here ever since we got here."[73] In this sense of the word, integration has already happened. Baldwin disrupts the imagined temporality of integration wherein separation is the starting point and forward progress means increased proximity. Baldwin posits that integration itself has been the site of violence and the site of the production of racial difference—as arrangements of domination and categories of "master" and "property" were codified through lines of race that would cut across blood relations. "Integration," he quipped at the West Indian Students' Centre, "precisely is our problem."[74] While some contemporary debates in political theory presume that interracial interaction increases identification and a sense of mutual obligation across lines of race, Baldwin upends this presumption.[75]

In "My Dungeon Shook," his 1962 open letter to his nephew, Baldwin gives us a third meaning of integration. Baldwin wants an integration project, but one that integrates new political subjects. Notably, these new political subjects are oriented to each other as kin. He describes white people as "your brothers—your lost, younger brothers" and writes that "if the word *integration* means anything, this is what it means: that we, with love, shall force our brothers to see themselves as they are, to cease fleeing from reality and begin to change it."[76] Here, Baldwin posits Black people as integrating their white family members into freedom—into new subjectivities—by forcing them to face and take responsibility for themselves and their lives.[77]

Baldwin warns his nephew to be clear about the terms of national discourse ("the storm which rages about your youthful head") about *acceptance* and *integration*. He tells his nephew that there is "no basis whatever for [white people's] impertinent assumption that *they* must accept *you*"—and explains that their freedom is dependent on "you . . . accept[ing] them . . . with love."[78] Rather than integration being signified by the movement of Black bodies across space (e.g., entering segregated institutions), in Baldwin's formulation, integration requires white people to stop movement—to stop flight from reality, to come into self-knowledge, and to reorient toward appropriate political action. If, as I explain in the next section, white racial identity is built through not only physical and psychic violence but also disavowal and fractured ways of seeing self and other, then integration here has an epistemological and political meaning—it is integration of disavowed knowledge that would necessarily undo the basis of white innocence and produce transformed political subjects. This is Baldwin's integration project—the project for which Baldwin enlists his nephew and which is not reconciled with Muhammad's or Malcolm X's politics. Baldwin writes to his nephew that Black people's freedom is tied to this kind of integration project, for "we cannot be free until they are free."[79]

Speaking with People Who Think They Are White

In addition to being in conversation with Black freedom struggles and so-cial movements, Baldwin speaks quite directly to white liberals in ways that are important in his time and in ours. I do not mean to posit white people as outside of integrationist politics—certainly Baldwin's critique of integra-tionist politics contains messages for white people. But Baldwin was also in a particular conversation with white liberals about their white racial iden-tity and about deeper forms of solidarity. As Juliet Hooker theorizes, soli-darity is an emotional and ethical orientation that moves us to action.[80] Its bedrock—what creates its conditions of possibility—is political identifica-tion. Not all forms of solidarity are the same, and this partly has to do with the form and depth (including intimacy) of the political identifications that undergird it. Critically for this study, solidarity is foreclosed by racism and white supremacy—racism profoundly delimits white people's empathy, iden-tification, and sense of responsibility across lines of race, making Baldwin's interventions profoundly relevant today.[81]

Baldwin is relentless and skillful in illuminating white denial, and he claims an intimacy with white people that transgresses a white sense of pri-vacy and separation. He says that part of his intimate project as an artist in society is to, like a lover, "reveal the beloved to himself and, with that reve-lation, to make freedom real."[82] What I want to underscore here is Baldwin's performance of intimacy in his interventions into white racial identity. In a short excerpt from a 1963 PBS special, *Take This Hammer*, Baldwin does some of this work. While much of the program follows his conversations with Black youth on sidewalks and street corners in San Francisco, or shows him traveling by car around the city, in this excerpt at the end of the film, Baldwin slowly smokes a cigarette while seated in an armchair.[83] The viewer's whiteness is not explicitly named but is implied. In his remarks, Baldwin addresses white people as a single person—first as "you" and later as "Baby"—rescaling an impersonalized public sphere dialogue about race into an intimate conversation. He tells the viewer that "what you say about somebody else . . . reveals you. What I think of you as being is dictated by my own necessities, my own psychology, my own fears and desires."[84] Baldwin explains that in this country, "we've got something called a 'n——' " (my re-daction[85]). In his explanation, the n-word is, from the beginning, detached and unpaired from Black people's bodies—instead it floats disembodied as an idea and invention, a problem that "we" have together. Baldwin says that

"I have always known that I am not a 'n———.' But if I am not the 'n———,' and if it's true that your invention reveals you, then who is the 'n———'?" He challenges continued white investment in the n-word and refuses to hold white people's problem for them: "You still think, I gather, that the 'n———' is necessary. Well, he's unnecessary to *me*, so he must be necessary to *you*. So I give you your problem *back*. You're the 'n———,' Baby, it isn't me."[86]

Baldwin's final remark has certain resonances with Sylvia Rivera's opening greeting, "Hi, Baby" at the hostile stage in Washington Square Park a decade later. Rivera invokes a queer intimate form of address, issuing that address at a public scale across the din of jeering and cheering and against the movement's disavowals. It is from here that she stages her interventions. Inversely, Baldwin begins his account at the wide scale of the national and ends speaking directly to the camera, to a "you" who is finally revealed as "Baby." His naming the viewer "Baby" works to unveil the terrain of his earlier narrative, cinching his epistemological and political intervention with intimate address.

In *Fire*, Baldwin explains that "the price of the ticket of the liberation of white people" is the "total liberation" of Black people—"in the cities, in the towns, before the law, and in the mind."[87] He also says that to get free, white people must take their projections back. They must "consent, in effect, to become black [themselves]" by relinquishing their masks and mirrors and taking responsibility for their "private fears and longings."[88] In the passage in *Take This Hammer*, Baldwin returns the n-word and all its meanings to white people. He "gives [them] their problem back"; for his sake and for theirs, he will not participate in the fictional subjectivity that they have invented.

Baldwin returns the n-word, and he insists that white people must let go of their white racial identities. Where identities are, as Ernesto Martínez has explained, "ways of knowing" that "reference and illuminate" aspects of the social world with varying degrees of accuracy, what is required to achieve whiteness in particular is a cognitive model that precludes self-transparency and impedes a genuine understanding of social realities—an epistemology of ignorance, to draw on Charles Mills.[89] To enter the "Racial Contract," white people enter into an agreement to misinterpret the world.[90] For Baldwin, as Martínez has theorized, to take responsibility for one's self and one's identity requires letting go of some forms of identification. This risk of the self may be destabilizing and chaotic, but it is necessary to be able to understand oppressive circumstances and sustain alternative social orders.[91] Baldwin insists that "as long as you think you are white, there is no hope for you," and that a white racial identity must be dismantled or left behind in order to know.[92]

Baldwin also demands that white racial identity must be dismantled because it is *defined by* and *generated through* violence. In "On Being White . . . and Other Lies," Baldwin writes that "white men—from Norway, for example, where they were 'Norwegians'—became white by slaughtering the cattle, poisoning the wells, torching the houses, massacring Native Americans, raping black women."[93] Rather than racial difference *producing* violence, racial boundaries and notions of racial difference are forged through violence. Baldwin emphasizes the agency that white people have in selecting and inhabiting a white identity. Baldwin calls whiteness a choice "absolutely, a moral choice (for there are no white people)."[94] In Baldwin's account, it is in no way possible to salvage or redeem this particular identity—it cannot and should not be saved.

To Baldwin, white people's "unutterably exhausting" innocence is widely dangerous—it is dangerous to their own souls, to Black people, to America as a country, and to the entire world.[95] He is furious about the magnitude of white people's failures and delays, even as he holds a vision for what he calls the "New Jerusalem"—he says he truly believes that "we can all become better than we are."[96] Baldwin's prophetic appeals are full of hope, rage, and sometimes despair, especially after leaders in the civil rights and Black Power movements, whom he reminds us were his friends, were killed.[97] Baldwin meets the moment with urgency and the message, as he writes in his 1972 open letter to Angela Davis, that "Black people must do what we can and fortify and save each other."[98] He still invokes boundness and the kinship narrative, but warns white Americans with a more condemnatory tone—as in his 1973 interview with Frank Shatz—that "only you can undo it. . . . You've got to save yourselves."[99]

Embodiment and the Complexity of Intimacy as a Political Strategy

In November 1985, John Callaway interviewed James Baldwin on *Chicago Tonight* to discuss Baldwin's newly published book, *The Evidence of Things Not Seen*. Callaway had interviewed Baldwin two decades prior, and their rapport was warm and familiar. Baldwin reflected on the "terrifying" state of "what we call 'race relations' " in the country, describing the gulf between national myths and the historical realities of Black and white ancestry. He told Callaway about his own grandmother, whom he had known but who died when he was five years old. She had been born into slavery. When Baldwin was an adult, he had learned that she had had fourteen children,

> and some of them came out white, and some of them came out black. And those who came out white, like my father's brother, Robert . . . and he looks just like my father. There is a [daguerreotype] of him up on the wall—my father's eyes, my father's cheekbones, my father's lips, my father's fore-head, and his hair straight like an Indian.[100] So he was white. My father was black—he ended up in Harlem and finally died in a madhouse. The point is the same woman produced both children. Now, this is the truth about the country.

> CALLAWAY (*softly*): We are one.

> BALDWIN: This is the truth about the country. Do you see what I'm saying?

> CALLAWAY: Yes sir.

> BALDWIN: And nobody wants to face it. That's what frightens me.[101]

Across Baldwin's work, boundness operates on multiple registers—for him, it has both literal and metaphoric meaning. Here, he invokes boundness in his own family network of blood and relation. Baldwin argues that America is defined by the *flesh and bone* relationships of so-called Black and white people and the disavowal of those ties.

In Baldwin's London speech, when he emphasizes that he is "flesh of their flesh, bone of their bone, *created by them*," he holds up the backs of his hands toward the audience as if he is offering evidence in the flesh.[102] This is a crucial performance of his embodied understanding of race and identity. Baldwin insists that our history is in us—psychically, psychologically, and physically. He interrogates race at a corporeal level, unraveling the discrete edges of racial categories that are drawn around and upon bodies. He calls us to look behind a veil—where we might see how our bodies have been shaped by the history of white supremacy without relying on familiar and discrete racial categories to do that seeing.

Whereas white racial identity relies on essentialized notions of racial difference, fabricates spatial separation, and invests in an epistemology of ignorance that belies embodied knowledge, Baldwin claims embodied knowledge and embodied interracial intimacy for his antiracist project. In doing so, he joins Stewart, Wells, and Richards to challenge the ways race and racial justice are understood and conceptualized. The embodied story Baldwin tells testifies to an intimate sexual and familial history in which lines of racial difference have been drawn across flesh and bone ties. Baldwin shows us that it is violence at this intimate level and disavowal of this kind of kinship that is foundational to the history of race-making in the United States. His choice to center the intimate and sexual politics of race is extremely complex. Invocations of intimacy in the history of U.S. slavery risk reinscribing histories of violence and forced submission as histories of consent and affection.[103] In master narratives, domination is reformulated as love—erasing terror, captivity, and sexual violence.[104] When Baldwin works at the juncture of kinship and disavowal in histories of slavery and Jim Crow, he comes into dangerous proximity to such reformulations. As Ann Laura Stoler warns, studies of the intimacies of domination must never err on the side of the "tender"—it is mandatory to face the violence and outrage.[105] With careful attention to intimate violence and disavowal, Baldwin foregrounds the silence of white women watching Black men "burned knowing them to be their lovers" and the decision of the white sheriff to attack people who were related to the memory of the woman who gave him, as Richards defines, the very "sustenance of life."[106]

Baldwin's enfleshed account has important resonances with Hortense Spillers' turn to the flesh as a "primary narrative." In Spillers' account in her groundbreaking essay "Mama's Baby, Papa's Maybe: An American Grammar Book," the flesh as narrative exceeds the captor's (mis)namings and registers the wounding, entrapment, and "ripped-apartness" of the captive body.[107] The flesh is written over by the captor's language—it is, as Sharon Holland puts it, "discursively besieged," but it precedes and exceeds the captor's (mis)namings and violations.[108] The flesh is, as Ashon Crawley puts it, "anoriginal," existing before language.[109] Together, Spillers and Baldwin name the unseeings enacted in the political memory of American racial grammars and they demand attention to a "flesh and blood" or "flesh and bone" archive. In Spillers' work, the flesh of the African woman is primary text and liberating force. Spillers goes back to "retriev[e]" African female bodies from under the "mighty debris of the itemized account, between the lines of the massive logs of commercial enterprise."[110] Baldwin's primary text is the embodied ties between Black and white people in the context of U.S. slavery and its afterlife. It is in this text that Baldwin locates the histories of disavowed violence that shaped the country and which must be faced. Baldwin also locates and reclaims in the flesh the sensual register of *life* and critical ways of knowing. Baldwin reclaims the body against what he names as the white Christian personality's "nearly pathological" worry about the flesh and the senses, against the perverse rubric in which, as he puts it in his 1968 London address, "I, precisely, am the flesh which the Christians must mortify. Now, according to me," Baldwin explains, "and what I hope for in the future, the flesh is all you have. . . . *Everything you find out, you find out through your senses.*" Moving his hands down in front of his face and torso, he locates life in "this frame, this tenement, this mortal envelope, which should be—instead of beating it with chains and hammering nails through it and hanging it on crosses—it should be *the* celebration!"[111] In reclaiming the body in these ways, Baldwin intervenes in the co-constituted histories of white Christian disembodiment and the physical and psychic intimate violence through which the people who think they are white have constructed racial difference as a system of domination.

To be clear, Baldwin is not proposing a kind of colorblind critique or postracial vision when he turns to the body's intimate story. Contemporary postracial or multicultural politics might use an account of Black–white kinship for an apolitical narrative about family, relatedness, and racial redemption. We can see this at work, for example, in Barack Obama's invocation in his 2008 campaign speech in Philadelphia that sutured his "marriage to a Black American who carries within her the blood of slaves and slaveowners"; together with his maternal grandparent's whiteness, racism, and background in wartime production; together with his Kenyan and immigrant heritage in a postracial appeal to American exceptionalism.[112] In contrast, Baldwin's account of Black and white kinship is centrally concerned with violence, power, and the long reach of the monstrous intimacies of slavery and Jim Crow *into the present*, where they in fact constitute the crises of the present.[113] Baldwin invokes the kinship narrative to apprehend contemporary racial politics and to bring its disavowals into sharper relief. His project does not try to disappear Blackness through amalgamation with whiteness. Instead, he aims to undo the imagined purity of whiteness by holding up a mirror and sending back its projections, by insisting that white people reintegrate what they have psychologically disowned. He highlights the blood level kinship and psychic shared life of Blackness and whiteness not as an invitation for a postracial intimacy but as a political strategy to intervene in central movement discourses, to hold white people accountable for their identities, and to provoke shifts in identification.

In these ways, Baldwin's interventions in the 1960s anticipate and speak forward to colorblind racial discourse in the late twentieth and early twenty-first centuries—a discourse that persists amidst (and in certain formations coarticulates and is harnessed within)[114] the reflowering of white nationalist appeals since the 2016 election. In the context of postracial ideology, a dominant racial logic of colorblindness has skimmed the thinned language of human unity from the surface of racial justice work and has repurposed that language to roll back and foreclose race-conscious policy and race-conscious dialogue for justice.[115]

Baldwin's attention to the body offers critical resources for antiracist work today. Centering the body in antiracist work may seem risky because the body is so wrapped up in the mythology and fetishization of race as biological. It is important to examine, however, because even though racial categories are not biological, racial histories are in many ways embodied.[116] The framework of race as a social construction is a critical antiracist response to discourses of race as biological, but it may accidentally forfeit or abandon the body by focusing so primarily on social structures, representation, and discourse. Baldwin turns to the racialized body—not just in its lived body experiences in the moment but also as containing a history of lived body experiences that come to bear on the present. For Baldwin, the body holds the history of the invention of race. His flesh and bone account holds on to the materiality of the body against the furthest deconstructions of poststructuralism and white queer theory, and against political and sociological studies of race that evacuate its intimate and enfleshed history. Baldwin explores how a robust examination of race and antiracist politics can take embodiment into account. He has us ask, *What intimate story does the body tell that is hidden by racism's disavowals? What political possibilities rest in the body's knowledge?*

In Baldwin's enunciations, boundness is an embodied concept of race that simultaneously destabilizes the presumed discreteness of racial categories and demands attention to the psychological and physical violence of race and racism. Baldwin offers an extended meditation on the role of denial in

American racism, one that serves as a rebuttal to postracial ideology.[117] He highlights the psychic and political terrain of race that is so unaddressed in American political culture and underscores the costs of this neglect. Baldwin disrupts the liberal idea that interracial proximity or intimacy necessarily produces racial justice. He disproves the premise that white people are "innocent" because they "just don't know better," revealing their complicity and the willfulness of their unknowing.

3

"You Have to Hear What's Being Said to You"

Hansberry and Horne's Interruption

On the afternoon of May 24, 1963, just weeks after the Children's Crusade in Birmingham, Alabama was met with fire hoses and police attack dogs, and as civil rights organizers continued to build national and international pressure on the U.S. federal government to take action against racial violence, James Baldwin convened a private meeting between prominent civil rights activists and advocates and Attorney General Robert Kennedy. Baldwin had telegrammed Robert Kennedy two weeks earlier, excoriating the Kennedy administration for its culpability in the violence in Birmingham. Kennedy invited Baldwin to meet, then asked him to assemble a "quiet, off-the-record" gathering the next day.[1]

The meeting was convened at the Kennedy family apartment in New York City and included playwright and activist Lorraine Hansberry; sociologist Dr. Kenneth Clark; performers Harry Belafonte, Lena Horne, and Rip Torn; Congress of Racial Equality (CORE) organizer Jerome Smith; civil rights leaders Edwin Berry, Clarence Jones, and June Shagaloff; James Baldwin's brother David Baldwin; Assistant Attorney General Burke Marshall, and five others.[2] By all accounts, the nearly three-hour meeting was marked, as Clark put it, by an "excruciating sense of impasse"—Kennedy not comprehending their insistence that he "*had* to understand the sense of urgency of the Negro people" and evidently compelled to "protect the image of liberal concern"[3] just as he was being asked—demanded—to face reality so that he may be propelled to change it.

Fifty years after the summit, in the midst of her 2015 campaign for the Democratic nomination, Hillary Clinton was publicly remonstrated about her role in mass incarceration after a community forum in New Hampshire. In a short clip viewed by seventy-six million people, Black Lives Matter activists Daunasia Yancey and Julius Jones confronted Clinton about her

If We Were Kin. Lisa Beard, Oxford University Press. © Oxford University Press 2023.
DOI: 10.1093/oso/9780197517338.003.0004

historic support for the war on drugs and called her into a political practice of acknowledgment.

Although a half century apart, I suggest that the activists in both moments are doing a linked type of political work, work that condemns and undercuts the distancing practices that constitute white identifications. I mean distance here in two ways: distance as the space between things (between people, between people and places, or between people and events), and distance as a *practice*—a spatial, temporal, and emotional practice. This kind of distance has to be continuously reasserted for the maintenance of white supremacy; it is not actual but performative.[4] The activists disallow white performances of distance from racial violence, and they condemn white evasions of responsibility for that violence.

This chapter turns to three interventions—Baldwin's May 1963 telegram to Robert Kennedy; the May 1963 summit (especially Hansberry's remarks at the meeting); and the August 2015 encounter between Clinton and activists Yancey and Jones—first, to elucidate the relationship between the political concept of boundness and the distancing practices of white identifications, and second, to theorize a point of entry for a politics of responsibility to and identification with the work of ending anti-Black violence.[5] In these political confrontations, Hansberry, Horne, Smith, Baldwin, Yancey, and Jones disobey the narrow scope of interaction that the white liberal state officials offer and uphold. Their encounters shed light on the relationships between knowledge, affect, and political action in U.S. racial politics.

At the 1963 summit, Lorraine Hansberry, in tandem with Lena Horne, presses Kennedy to *hear*, especially to hear the provocations of Freedom Rider and CORE organizer Jerome Smith. Hansberry challenges Kennedy to feel and respond to the urgency of addressing racial politics in decisive and meaningful ways. For Kennedy to hear Smith as Hansberry intends would mean for him to face all the contradictions that such a hearing would bring to a point of crisis in his own sense of the world and would in turn move him to critical action. Daunasia Yancey and Julius Jones similarly pressed Hillary Clinton to face her historical connection to anti-Black violence meted out through U.S. social policy across the previous two decades. The pathway into appropriate action, as presented by Yancey and Jones, is through an affective and historical grappling with the ways in which Clinton is bound to and partly responsible for that historical violence. Baldwin, Hansberry, and Horne press Kennedy as Yancey and Jones press Clinton to face and feel the reality of the violence and their responsibility to ending it, not as an end point of politics but as a *practice in knowledge production* and a *precondition of right action*. They insist that what is required to end conditions of racialized violence and death cannot be achieved through a discourse of statistics and policy proposals. They identify *hearing* and *feeling* as knowledge-production practices that are generative prerequisites of critical political action.

In this chapter, the sites of identificatory politics and appeals to boundness are located within presidential- and cabinet-level politics. In particular, these are moments in which Black artists, activists, and public intellectuals confront "dynastic liberals"[6] who in many ways, as high-ranking white state officials, stand in for the state and whose popular iconicity consolidates and is the drapery for white power. The interventions of Hansberry, Baldwin, Horne, Smith, Yancey, and Jones; their accounts of what counts as *political*; and their demands for practices of listening, witnessing, and knowing shed light on the state's racialized regimes of power and the ways they are constituted by macro- and micro-level practices of evasion and unknowing.

"Birmingham Is in Los Angeles"

In the previous chapter, I demonstrated how Baldwin invoked a concept of *boundness* as a political intervention into white innocence, into white performances of distance from racialized violence and responsibility, and into white people's frantic refusals to be with reality and, as Baldwin puts it, "to enter into black suffering."[7] He invoked the concept in different moments in different ways, through geographic, temporal, kinship, and national narratives. Here, I turn to Baldwin's 1963 telegram to Robert Kennedy to derive boundness in its spatial form and demonstrate how boundness intervenes in ontologies and practices of distance.

On May 12, 1963, Baldwin sent a telegram to Robert Kennedy from Los Angeles, where Baldwin had been on a three-week speaking tour for CORE, grabbing newspapers along the way to keep abreast of events in the South.[8] This was eight years since the brutal murder of Emmett Till in Mississippi and the launching of the Montgomery bus boycott after years of Black women's organizing against sexual assault of Black women by white men.[9] This was two years since the first Freedom Riders sponsored by CORE and the Student Nonviolent Coordinating Committee (SNCC) were beaten and firebombed by mobs as they attempted to desegregate interstate travel. And this was just ten days since the start of the Children's Crusade in Birmingham, Alabama.

Over these years, as civil rights organizers escalated their direct action campaigns across the U.S. South, activists were maimed, sexually assaulted, jailed, threatened, and murdered by law enforcement agents, civilians, and vigilante groups. Television and newspaper images of burning buses, white mobs, and attack dogs circulated across national and international audiences, and John F. Kennedy was facing mounting political pressure to address civil rights issues. Baldwin wrote to Robert Kennedy:

> THOSE WHO BEAR THE GREATEST RESPONSIBILITY FOR THE CHAOS IN BIRMINGHAM ARE NOT IN BIRMINGHAM. AMONG THOSE RESPONSIBLE ARE J. EDGAR HOOVER, SENATOR EASTLAND, THE POWER STRUCTURE WHICH HAS GIVEN BULL CONNOR SUCH LICENSE, AND PRESIDENT KENNEDY, WHO HAS NOT USED THE GREAT PRESTIGE OF HIS OFFICE AS THE MORAL FORUM WHICH IT CAN BE. THE CRISIS IS NEITHER REGIONAL NOR RACIAL. IT IS A MATTER OF THE NATIONAL LIFE OR DEATH. NO TRUTH CAN BE BINDING UNTIL THE AMERICAN PEOPLE AND OUR REPRESENTATIVES ARE ABLE TO ACCEPT THE SIMPLE FACT THAT THE NEGRO IS A MAN.[10]

The "chaos in Birmingham" refers to the police dogs, high-pressure fire hoses, and police beatings that met the Children's Crusade marches led by the Southern Christian Leadership Conference from May 2 to May 10.[11] Especially during those first two weeks of May, images of Birmingham had saturated domestic media and reached international news, and questions of how to understand those images—especially questions about who was responsible for the violence, and how onlookers were connected to the events even from afar—animated the often quite frenetic interpretations underway in national discourse. In the white-dominated media and national imagination, Birmingham was a receptacle or repository of projections that racial violence is *distant*. Whether northern white media or political elites explained the "causes" of the Birmingham events as being rooted in southern racism or as rooted in the protestors not being "patient" enough (e.g., "these things take time")—in both cases Birmingham was imagined by viewers outside the South as definitively far away.[12]

When Baldwin insists that the Birmingham crisis is "not regional," he invokes boundness in its spatial form to intervene in white practices of distancing. His message to Robert Kennedy that the violence in Birmingham and the conditions it exposed were *not* confined to the South was a message that threaded through his work that spring. Like Ella Baker and Ida B. Wells before him, Baldwin was a consummate writer, vindicationist, and organizer. His social commentary emerged from a long genealogy of Black intellectuals whose social thought, political commentary, and oratory offered the most insightful and meaningful synthesis of their contemporary culture.[13] Traveling through California in May 1963, Baldwin bore witness to Birmingham from afar, from the "golden state" itself—a place ensconced in a self-image of paradise and racial liberal enlightenment constituted by the disavowal of its own foundational and contemporary racialized settler violence.[14] Across his talks and in his writing that month, he confronted white liberals with the message that most threatened West Coast innocence—a prophetic insistence that "Birmingham is in Los Angeles."[15] In the essay he penned around that time, "The White Problem," Baldwin explained that

> [w]hite people are astounded by Birmingham. Black people aren't. White people are endlessly demanding to be reassured that Birmingham is really on Mars. They don't want to believe, still less to act on the belief, that what is happening in Birmingham . . . is happening all over the country, and has been for countless generations; they don't want to realize that there is not one step, one inch, no distance, morally or actually, between Birmingham and Los Angeles.[16]

Baldwin describes how in the wake of their "astonishment" about Birmingham, white people reach for reassurance and comfort, whether from other white people in a reestablishment of mutually created reality[17] or from Black people in a form of what Tiffany Willoughby-Herard has called "mammy work"—the physical, emotional, and epistemological caretaking work by Black people, especially by Black women, of white people and their life worlds.[18] To seek reassurance that Birmingham is "on Mars" is an attempt to place Birmingham back where it was before the news, outside of consciousness; to site it outside of a sphere of political responsibility; to resettle it against a possibility that what is happening there actually reflects and helps illuminate conditions of violence in West Coast or northern cities.

Baldwin theorized space in his role as a witness with roots in Harlem and a life in France—a person who traveled widely, who had a distinctly different role than other movement actors, and who needed to move across wide geographies to "write the story, and to get it out."[19] In his work, Baldwin bends space. He becomes a wandering and diasporic figure, moving across space nationally and transnationally, subverting what Willoughby-Herard has called "the cage of the nation,"[20] refusing the terms on which white Americans, as he put it, "offer me my life,"[21] and refusing the promise of the nation just as he understood his identity to be bound to other Americans.

While Baldwin bears witness to Birmingham as an ethical-political practice, a practice *within and in service of* the project of ending the violence, white people's reeling back and desire to observe Birmingham from afar is a move that constructs the self as spectator. It is a move that constructs white people as discrete from rather than bound to Birmingham and positions the violence that month as an "event" rather than an ontology or the ongoing nature of things. White enactments of distance work along temporal, geographic/spatial, moral, and emotional lines. Enactments of distance are evidence of disavowed knowledge of responsibility, disavowed histories of harm, and disavowals of the mutually constituted reality of social value and social death. Baldwin endeavors to close the distance just as white people seek its comfort. He insists that the violence is close and that the violence is a white problem. He shrinks the space between Birmingham and Los Angeles in exponential increments—from the space between planets, to that of a human stride, to an inch, to no distance. In this iterative way, Baldwin pulls Birmingham closer and closer materially, morally, and politically. As Katherine McKittrick explains, "Geography is not . . . secure and unwavering; we produce space, we produce its meanings, and we work very hard to make geography what it is."[22] Baldwin collapses the distance from Birmingham, reconfiguring it spatially, politically, and morally to tell a different and incisive story about responsibility and boundness. He upends the *spatiality of white disavowal* and does so along two lines: by insisting that white lives in one place are bound to racial violence in another place, and by awakening people to the racial violence that is endemic to how space is organized in the United States.[23] White liberal identity is constituted through distancing practices, and this is what Baldwin attacks with such ferocity.

In the telegram, Baldwin also attacks Robert Kennedy's liberal distancing practices in his inventory of state actors who are politically responsible for the violence in Birmingham. Baldwin's deck of culpability places President Kennedy squarely among some of the very figures the Kennedys would like to define their virtue against. Robert Kennedy would not like to see his own brother—and by extension, himself—identified with Senator Eastland (the Mississippi senator who had vociferously led opposition to *Brown v. Board* and who was chairman of the Senate Judiciary Committee at that time), or J. Edgar Hoover, or as being a part of the structure that enabled Bull Connor's actions. And yet, Robert Kennedy had not provided leadership around advancing civil rights despite appeals to his office.[24] In such an accounting, Baldwin challenges Kennedy's comfortable distance from the violence in Birmingham, just as King did in his critique of the white clergy in his "Letter from Birmingham Jail" just a few weeks prior.[25] Robert Kennedy's fate, Baldwin suggests, depends on taking responsibility for Birmingham because John F. Kennedy, and by extension his brother, represent the body of the nation, and so the prophecy of the fire next time would threaten to split them.[26]

Baldwin makes two additional political claims about responsibility and consequence in his appeal. First, in his insistence to Kennedy that the crisis is not racial, Baldwin pushes back against the dominant framework of "race relations"—the reigning paradigm in the academy and national discourse that expertly flattens, depoliticizes, and glosses racial terror and hierarchy. This was the paradigm through which Gunnar Myrdal's *American Dilemma* was written and the framework through which leading social scientists made their paltry gestures at engaging race when they did so at all.[27] Baldwin disrupts the notion that race, as a coherent set of formations and set of people, and racial difference *produced* the crisis in Birmingham; he rejects any notion that race precedes and explains politics rather than race being a product of politics. Rather than being regional or racial, Baldwin tells Kennedy, the crisis in Birmingham is a "matter of the national life and death." His prophetic caution joins those of Frederick Douglass and Martin Luther King Jr.—who also tie the urgency of ending racial terror to the fate of the nation—and foreshadows the warnings that would be issued to Robert Kennedy in person two weeks later.[28] To be clear, national claims are always racial claims, so Baldwin's statement on one level conceals some of the political operation of the nation and trades in nation-building. We should understand Baldwin's rhetorical strategy as reflecting the severe constraints of making moral appeals within a regime of racial terror and as reflecting his politics of boundness.[29] As Charles Mills explains, the Racial Contract is not only political and epistemological but also moral. Racialized violence constitutes the moral landscape of whiteness and the nation. In the moral codes of the Racial Contract, anti-Black violence actually "makes" white people "good" and "right": the racialized violence that constitutes white identity is not amoral within but *constitutive to* that identity.[30] To say that the violence must stop because it is morally wrong to harm people thus does not give Baldwin enough leverage in national discourse. Baldwin uses the nation to register his warning that people must change their conduct. White people cannot survive the end of the nation to which they, as Baldwin puts it, "ow[e] [their] entire identity."[31] In Baldwin's account, it is not a question of whether the nation *should* be the horizon of political imagination, the basis of theorizing white-on-Black violence, or an object of redemption—instead, Baldwin claims, white and Black Americans are constituted by the nation; they may physically depart (as Baldwin himself often did) but they are bound to it.

In the short lines of the telegram, Baldwin blasts and summons Kennedy. He refuses the terms of white liberal responses to Birmingham, from the cloaked claims of spatial innocence to claims of virtue defined on little more than disidentification with explicit segregationists. Baldwin invokes an intimate political geography against white evasions. He demands that Kennedy reckon with his own responsibility for and to Birmingham and that he step into right political action. His appeal is a mandate for Kennedy's political office and conduct going forward.

"That Is the Voice of Twenty-Two Million People"

Ten days after sending the telegram, Baldwin received an invitation from Robert Kennedy for breakfast at his home in Virginia. At their meeting, Kennedy asked Baldwin to assemble a group of Black leaders for a meeting at the Kennedy family apartment in New York City the next day.[32] Baldwin accepted Kennedy's invitation and organized a meeting within twenty-four hours, inviting people he trusted, "black or white," who "had paid some dues and who knew it" and who would not feel compelled to represent an organizational point of view.[33] Baldwin reached out to Harry Belafonte, Lena Horne, Martin Luther King Jr. (who could not attend), Edwin Berry, and June Shagaloff, then reached Kenneth Clark in his office at 1 a.m. David Baldwin invited Lorraine Hansberry and Jerome Smith.[34] Baldwin's friends, he explains, were "fairly rowdy, independent, tough-minded men and women," and he counted on them to convey to Kennedy the "seriousness of the problem."[35] A number of the delegates were politically active artists at a time when, as Richard Iton explains, a line between the roles of artist and political activist was being drawn.[36] Along with other prominent artists—including Ossie Davis, Ruby Dee, and Nina Simone—Hansberry, Baldwin, Belafonte, and Horne had collaborated or would collaborate in various constellations to coordinate fundraising events and political/artistic actions in solidarity with the southern freedom struggle, including demonstrations, public appeals, fundraisers, and boycotts.[37] Baldwin had met Smith during his second trip to the South.[38] Hansberry and Smith had met in New York, and she would collaborate with Smith on a fundraising rally scheduled for June.[39]

For the story that follows, Hansberry in particular should have a special introduction. As an artist, writer, and political activist, Hansberry's political identifications were transnational and critically attuned to questions of race, gender, and power; and they were self-consciously resistant to Black middle-class or Black elite disidentifications with working-class Black people. As a young person, Hansberry's parents—both migrants from the South—were actively involved in fights against racial segregation and discrimination in Chicago, and her father, a successful entrepreneur, poured much of his wealth into a legal battle against residential segregation that went to the Supreme Court.[40] Although her family was middle class, U.S. residential segregation laws meant, as Hansberry explained, "intimacy with all classes and all kinds of experiences" in the South Side of Chicago.[41] Part of her refusal of middle-class values included a refusal to *dis*identify with the Black working class.[42] She fiercely identified with working-class Black people who were her childhood playmates and schoolmates. In ways that began in her youth, Hansberry understood Black working-class people to be politically the most important to collective Black liberation and Black futurity.[43] In a 1959 interview about *A Raisin in the Sun*, Hansberry explained that "whatever we ultimately achieve, however we ultimately transform our lives, the changes will come from the kind of people that I chose to portray" in *Raisin*, which centered a Black working-class family. "They are," Hansberry insisted, "more pertinent, more relevant, more significant—and most important, more *decisive*—in our political history and our political future."[44] Hansberry's political identifications and conceptualizations of boundness were also deeply transnational. Her journalistic, editorial, essay, and dramatic writing conveyed her belief that she and other African Americans were tied internationally to Black liberation struggles, and she understood that white supremacist ideologies would try to compel her away from these understandings and connections. In her 1959 speech "A Negro Writer and His Roots: Toward a New Romanticism," Hansberry vowed not to "allow the devious purposes of white supremacy to lead me to any conclusion other than what may be the most robust and important one of our time: that the ultimate destiny and aspirations of the African people and twenty million American Negroes are inextricably and magnificently bound up together forever."[45] Across her writing, Hansberry mined the profundity of everyday people as they were situated within raced, classed, gendered, and colonial contexts, and she embedded in her plays political possibilities for the future. Hansberry had been a devoted writer since 1950, when she began at Paul Robeson's journal, *Freedom,* in Harlem. She began playwrighting full time in 1956, and soon thereafter, under a pen name or signed with her initials, she published letters to the editor and short stories in the lesbian journal *The Ladder* and the homophile periodical, *ONE.*[46] As a playwright and in her short stories, Hansberry was self-consciously a realist. In contrast to naturalism, which "takes the world as it is," in realism, Hansberry explains, "the artist who is creating the realistic work imposes on it not only what *is* but what is *possible.*"[47] Hansberry's writings and public speeches on race, gender, sexuality, class, political change, whiteness, colonialism, and revolution constitute a powerful well for the study of politics, and she leaves a critical body of theoretical work on political identification, boundness, Black radicalism, Black feminist internationalism, and Black futurity.[48]

On the day of the summit, Hansberry, Horne, Belafonte, Clark, Smith, Jones, Berry, James and David Baldwin, and the other invitees gathered at 24 Central Park South to meet with Robert Kennedy and Burke Marshall. The moment was especially ripe for commanding the attorney general's ear. In May 1963, mounting pressure from direct action campaigns and international outcry at the images of racial violence in Birmingham had created a window of opportunity. There was a crisis in image and pressure to act. The meeting was private and, in a way, intimate—unrecorded, lengthy, unstructured, unpublicized, and at the Kennedy family apartment—quite unlike most formal political meetings with state officials.

The event is best reconstructed through first-person accounts, especially Hansberry's comments three weeks later at a fundraising rally in Croton, New York; Baldwin's 1979 essay, "Lorraine Hansberry at the Summit";[49] Dr. Clark's WBGH-TV interview of Baldwin recorded immediately after the summit meeting; interviews of Dr. Clark and Baldwin by Jean Stein in 1970; Lena Horne's, Harry Belafonte's, and Clarence Jones' autobiographies; and a television interview filmed eighteen years later with four of the original delegates.[50] Although the story was immediately picked up by many news outlets, the coverage had varying levels of accuracy, some including embellishment, misquotations, and fabrication—issues that have been subtly reproduced in some of the secondary literature on the summit and that create historical and interpretive challenges for its reconstruction.[51]

The summit was convened from 2 p.m. until 5:40 p.m. on Friday, May 24, 1963. Clark and Berry had brought charts and statistics on issues of education, housing, and employment, and the meeting began quietly until Jerome Smith started weeping, rocking in grief and pain, as if he'd just had a traumatic flashback.[52] Twenty-five-year-old Smith was a very experienced activist and Freedom Rider who had co-founded New Orleans CORE and was a task force organizer and field secretary. He had been severely beaten during the 1961 Freedom Ride to McComb, Mississippi, the Mother's Day Freedom Rides, and other actions, and was in New York City at the time for medical treatment. This was not Smith's first encounter with representatives of the Kennedy administration. He had spoken with Burke Marshall on the phone after being nearly killed in McComb and had not received support.[53] His experiences in the southern freedom struggle gave him ample reason to be skeptical about the U.S. government.[54] Clark recalled that Smith presented a kind of evidence in the flesh at the summit, "literally showing the consequences of being beaten."[55]

When Smith started weeping, Robert Kennedy had been explaining how he and his brother had done more for civil rights than any other administration, "implying," Clark remembered dryly, "that we should be grateful," and giving the impression that he hoped the delegates would endorse the administration's efforts.[56] Smith told Kennedy that he was "nauseated by the necessity of being in [the] room" and that the Justice Department is "full of shit"—that he'd seen them "stand around and do nothing more than take notes while we're being beaten."[57] Smith insisted that the Kennedys should not be worried about communists or America's foreign enemies because the real dangers in America were *inside* its borders. He described to Kennedy some of what he had been through in the South and made it clear he could not be sure how much longer he could remain nonviolent. Kennedy turned away from Smith, with his body, as though to say (in Baldwin's translation for us), "I'll talk to all of *you*, who are civilized. But who is *he*?"[58]

Hansberry stopped Kennedy. Baldwin wrote that although he knew Hansberry was sitting, she was standing in his memory because she towered as she warned Kennedy that " 'You have a great many very accomplished people in this room, Mr. Attorney General, but the only man you should be listening to is that man over there. That is the voice,' she added, after a moment during which Bobby sat absolutely still staring at her, 'of twenty-two million people.' "[59]

Kennedy was visibly shaken. It was clear to Jones that Kennedy had "never had any group of people, let alone Negroes, talk to him like that."[60] Because Kennedy did not appear to understand Hansberry, Lena Horne "eventually—and as the afternoon wore on, perpetually—attempted to clarify" Hansberry's point, insisting to Kennedy: "You have to hear what's being said to you."[61]

Baldwin, suspecting that the answer would make things more plain to Kennedy, asked Smith if he would take up arms to defend America. In an interview years later, Baldwin said he would never forget Smith's face at that moment as he answered Baldwin's query, replying, "Never! Never! Never!"[62] Kennedy was utterly shocked by Smith's answer, unable to comprehend how an American citizen could feel this way.

Kennedy insisted that, given his Irish-American family's ability to rise despite a recent history of immigration and experiences of anti-Irish discrimination, a Black person would surely be president within forty years. Kennedy seemed to feel, Horne remembers in her autobiography, "that this would establish some sort of identification, some sort of rapport, between us. It did not. In fact, it had the opposite effect."[63] Repeating the message he'd delivered to West Coast liberals earlier that spring that "I've been here 350 years, but you've never seen me,"[64] Baldwin explained that Kennedy's remark was utterly absurd—that Kennedy's ancestors immigrated long after Black people were here—that now a Kennedy could already be president, while Black people, "as the present meeting illustrated, [were] 'still required to supplicate and beg you for justice.' "[65]

After Kennedy's response to Smith's comments, Horne recalled in her memoir, the Black delegates "took a very hard line," asking, in different ways, why the federal government continued to promote rather than place economic sanctions on southern industry, and why pressure could not be brought to bear on northern-controlled industry whose southern branches, such as northern-owned steel mills in Birmingham, colluded with "a Southern style of discrimination."[66]

The delegates also confronted Kennedy about school desegregation. Horne and others affirmed the strong stand the Kennedy administration had taken around James Meredith's matriculation at the University of Mississippi that year, but they pressed Kennedy to understand "how much more . . . had to be done, and quickly."[67]

Robert Kennedy complained that he had come to the group for "ideas," and it was proposed that the president personally escort two Black students as they integrated the University of Alabama the next month, confronting George Wallace's state troopers charged with blocking their way and thus making it clear that "whoever spits on that child will be spitting on the nation."[68] Jones recalls that Kennedy laughed aloud when he heard the suggestion, and Baldwin explains that Kennedy rejected the proposal as a "meaningless moral gesture." Hansberry confronted Kennedy, telling him that "we would like . . . from you a moral commitment."[69] The attorney general scoffed when Jones suggested that John F. Kennedy revive Franklin D. Roosevelt's fireside chats and prepare a series of short speeches against segregation and discrimination.[70]

Hansberry told Kennedy that he and his brother were representative of the "best that a white America has to offer," and so, she said, "if *you* can't understand what this young man [Smith] is saying," and "if *you* are insensitive to this," "then we are without any hope at all," and "there's no alternative except our going in the streets."[71] Refusing any assumption that delegates might publicly defend the administration, Horne told Kennedy that if *he* was so confident about the administration's civil rights record, *he* could go tell that to people in Harlem, but he would have to go alone, she announced, "because *we* don't want to get shot."[72]

The meeting ended with a politics of impasse and refusal—with, in Baldwin's retelling, Hansberry standing up, issuing Kennedy a prophetic warning, and leaving.[73] In her warning, Hansberry flipped what had been Smith's most recent remark—regarding his concern about the "perpetual demolition" faced by Black men.[74] She told Kennedy that while she understood Smith's comment about the difficulties facing Black men, she was not worried about them—that she thought Black men had done "really beautifully, as far as she was concerned, all things considered." "But," Hansberry warned, "I am very worried about the state of the civilization which produced that photograph of the white cop standing on that Negro woman's neck in Birmingham."[75] She then smiled in such a way that, as Baldwin recalled, he was "glad that she was not smiling at me."[76] She extended her hand, bid Kennedy goodbye, and left the meeting, followed by the other delegates.

Outside the apartment building, Hansberry walked alone toward Fifth Avenue. As Baldwin recalled, she had her hands clasped over her abdomen as she walked in an "absolutely private place," with her eyes darker than he had ever seen them before. Baldwin explained that "we were all, in our various ways, devastated."[77] Clark described it as "the most intense, traumatic meeting in which I've ever taken a part . . . the most unrestrained interchange among adults, head-to-head, no holds barred . . . *the* most dramatic experience I have ever had."[78]

Hearing as Political Practice

The summit could be plumbed for the mechanics of its failures and "bitter misunderstanding."[79] It could offer a cartography of the distancing enacted by white people, in this case by Robert Kennedy.[80] There is much to attend to on this matter—Kennedy's stiff silences, his attempt to steer the conversation toward statistics and legislation, his invocation of his family's story of immigration and encountering anti-Irish discrimination, his crossed arms, his projections of "emotionality" onto his interlocutors contra the "rationality" he reserved for his own self-image, or his reflections later to an aide that the group seemed "possessed," hyper-emotional, and impossible to speak with.[81] But beyond a kind of phenomenology or repertoire of Kennedy's failures and beyond a catalog of white disidentification, there are critical resources to be located in the summit concerning the point of entry for a kind of reckoning, a bid to action, and the possibilities of reconfigured identifications mapped out especially by Hansberry and Horne.

What Hansberry and Horne *demanded* of Kennedy at the meeting is named by Baldwin as *hearing*. Baldwin writes that although he thought he was watching everything, he knows he was watching Hansberry's face during the meeting: "She wanted him to *hear*." He describes how her face "changed and changed, the way Sojourner Truth's face must have changed and changed or, to tell the truth, the way I have watched my mother's face change when speaking to someone who could not hear—who yet, and you know it, will be compelled to hear one day."[82] Here, Baldwin places Hansberry within an intergenerational trinity of prophets, who are Black women who are knowledge producers and who demand encounter with the truth. Baldwin calls in Sojourner Truth's embodied oration and confrontation with northern audiences in fighting for abolition and suffrage, and he remembers more intimately watching his mother's face as she tried to convey a message to someone who would not hear. As a practice of *rememory*—what Toni Morrison describes as "recollecting and remembering as in reassembling the members of the body, the family, the population of the past"—Baldwin assembles an embodied archive of Truth's and his mother's and Hansberry's study of and confrontation with disavowal.[83] Their facial expressions constitute a record of their study of the person they witness and, as those expressions change and change, tell a story about small, large, familial, and national disavowals and evasions. It bears noting that the hearing Hansberry demands of Kennedy is not an audiological transaction but an epistemological practice. It is an encounter with knowledge. Further, what Kennedy must hear at the summit is not conveyed simply in an aural register—Smith's weeping, rocking, and shaking his head are all forms of articulation within the signed language at the summit.[84]

Hansberry's dramatic writing was predicated on the very idea of compelling listening and sympathetic imagination.[85] She loved playwriting's particular power to sharply dramatize dialogue and conflict—she loved to be, as she explained in one interview, "very selective about the nature of the conversation, . . . to treat character in the most absolute relief . . . so that everything— sympathy and conflict—play so sharply, even a little more than a novel."[86] Hansberry knew that the lines of sympathy, dialogue, and identification she wrought and crafted both emerged from and would be heard within a context of racialized, gendered, and classed structures of power and hierarchy. Hansberry leaves a body of work conceptualizing (among many other themes) the barricades with which white people foreclose self-knowledge and the processes through which white people construct Blackness as a repository of their own projections.[87] As she explained in a 1960 essay, Hansberry understood herself to be writing in a context of U.S. theater in which neither the Black person's body nor their soul was allowed to evoke empathy.[88]

Hansberry intervened at the summit as a playwright who was committed to and held a deep analysis of political transformation. She was, in a way, *directing* at this critical moment. Part of Hansberry's belief as a writer was that strong plays have a lead character, and when she told Kennedy that he needed to listen to Smith, she was insisting that it was *Smith's* account that was the lead line of the meeting. It was his story that had the most consequence and was the most urgent. It was his narrative that would move things politically in that moment. Hansberry and Horne tried to steer Kennedy toward a point of entry of hearing and acknowledging Smith's account, which was the very account in the room that gave Kennedy the most discomfort and which he was the quickest to maneuver away from.

In a retrospective interview eighteen years later with Mike Wallace, Clarence Jones recounted this part of the summit—of Kennedy turning from Smith and Hansberry intervening. As Jones was speaking, Baldwin, for whom this moment in the summit was pivotal,[89] tried to interject, but Jones kept talking over Baldwin. Then precisely as Jones, after searching for the right words, explained that Hansberry stepped in to "*interpret* to the Attorney General, to tell Bobby Kennedy that what Jerome Smith [was] saying [was] not extreme," Baldwin's shoulders, arms, and face relaxed, he gently touched his eyebrow, and his gaze turned downward as he nodded in agreement and softly affirmed "yeah"—as if in relief that Jones had articulated the point Baldwin had been wanting to convey. Indeed, Hansberry and Horne not only demanded Kennedy's attention but also *interpreted* and *translated* the significance of Jerome Smith's experiences for Robert Kennedy because in Kennedy's political world the everyday violence of racial terror did not meet the criteria of "the political."[90]

Smith had, according to CORE historians, "spent more time in jail and had been beaten more often than any other CORE member," and his family had needed to move for their safety.[91] Smith did not only represent himself. As Imani Perry observes, Smith represented the many voiceless Black Americans who were on the frontlines of Black freedom struggles and living in conditions of racial terror and who had, as Smith has put it, "paid a tremendous price." In his reflections about the movement, Smith lifts up its deeply collective nature, noting that for on-the-ground organizers "to face those monsters every day with no cameras rolling, plain ordinary people had to extend their hand and help you get your job done."[92] *This* kind of representation, Perry explains, is what Hansberry meant when she told Kennedy and Marshall that Smith spoke for "twenty-two million Negroes."[93] Hansberry's insistence that Smith's voice was the most important voice in the room emerged from her unwavering conviction that grassroots activists and the Black working class held political significance over and above the Black upper or middle class. When Hansberry pointed the attorney general's attention back to Smith and essentially told Kennedy "you have to listen to *him*, and he represents *us*," this was a refusal of a politics of respectability and an inversion of elite representation. Hansberry was clear about who mattered as leads in Black liberation struggles at that moment and in the future, and she had no illusions that it was the Black intelligentsia.

Three weeks after the summit, Hansberry chaired a fundraising "Rally to support the Southern Freedom Movement" in the Hudson Valley featuring a

"Our sorrowing gaze turns to the other children of God everywhere, suffering because of race and economic conditions... Our word of heartfelt sympathy longs to pour forth into the hearts of each one an expression of human and Christian solidarity". POPE JOHN XXIII

Rally to support the Southern Freedom Movement

SUNDAY, JUNE 16, 3:3 P. M.
TEMPLE ISRAEL, GLENGARY ROAD, CROTON

Chairman: **LORRAINE HANSBERRY,** Author, Raisin in the Sun

Jerome Smith and Isaac Reynolds

Taskforce Organizers of the Congress of Racial Equality, give you a first-hand report from Mississippi and Alabama.

ADMISSION FREE Folk Songs by **JUDY COLLINS**

ATTENTION PARENTS! SUPERVISED PLAY FOR SMALL CHILDREN WILL BE PROVIDED

SPONSORS INCLUDE:

Msg. Charles R. Bidgood
Church of the Holy Name of Mary, Croton
Rev. Frederick Gotwald
Our Saviour Lutheran Church, Croton
Rev. Raoul J. Water
Asbury Methodist Church, Croton
Rabbi Michael A. Robinson
Temple Israel of Northern Westchester, Croton
Rev. Ivan Gossoo
Head of Peekskill Pastors Association
Msg. John M. Harrington
Head of Catholic Charities, Yonkers
Rev. Philip Hurley, S. J.
Catholic Interracial Council of Westchester
Mr. Walter Lawton
Leader of Ethical Society of Northern Westchester

Mr. Lee Culpepper
Head of Unitarian Fellowship, Croton
Catholic Interracial Council of Westchester
Temple Israel of Northern
Westchester, Croton
Senior Youth Group of
Temple Israel, Croton
Judge Seymour Levine
▬▬▬▬▬▬
Mrs. Stanley M. Isaacs
Mr. Bill Chillemi
Mrs. Adolph Elwyn
Mr. George Biddle
Mr. "Buck" Canel

Dr. Mortimer Feinberg
Dr. George Hill
Dr. A. Victor Landes
Dr. Aurelius Semisa
Dr. George Vogel
Senesqua Boating Association
Mr. and Mrs. Robert Northshield
Mr. Harrison Kinney
Mr. and Mrs. Louis Lubin
Mr. and Mrs. Yale Joel
Mr. Louis Rolnick
Mr. and Mrs. Edward Rutledge
Mr. Seymour Waldman

Figure 3.1 Event flyer, 1963. "Rally to support the Southern Freedom Movement." Lorraine Hansberry Papers, Manuscripts, Archives, and Rare Books Division, Schomburg Center for Research in Black Culture, The New York Public Library. (Redaction in original)

"first-hand report from Mississippi and Alabama" by Jerome Smith and two student activists—Gene Young and Barbara McNair—as well as folk songs by Judy Collins and remarks by local civic and religious leaders (Figure 3.1). Funds were slated for SNCC, CORE, SCLC, and the NAACP Legal Defense and Educational Fund.[94] When she introduced Smith at the rally, Hansberry recounted some of the summit proceedings, describing that it was when Smith indicated that "the passion and the absence of patience of a sorely oppressed, native American people is beyond anything that we can sit around and be polite about anymore," and when the attorney general "exhibited some impatience" in response, she was

> feeling free that I was speaking for every single Negro and indeed white ally in that room if there were, [and] I suggested that the Attorney General reexamine his impatience because while there might be in that room some of the celebrated figures of whom we all know, the qualitative change in the struggle for Negro freedom was that we are not remotely interested in the all-insulting concept of the exceptional Negro, we are not remotely interested in any tea at the White House, that what we are interested in is making perfectly clear that between the Negro intelligentsia, the Negro middle class and the Negro this and that, that we are one people and as far as we are concerned, we are represented by the Negroes of the streets of Birmingham. It is in that connection that I asked him, or we asked, that he pay attention to our next speaker who I said is the most important person in this room, Mr. Jerome Smith.[95]

Hansberry's own narrative of her intervention is precious given how little of her own account of the summit exists in the archives. Her comments are infused with her long-standing belief in the shared fate of Black people. She asserted to Kennedy, to everyone at the summit, and again to everyone at the Croton rally, that she and the other Black delegates understood their fate to be bound to the work that was being done on the streets in the South. At the summit, she refused the terms of the elite identifications by which the Kennedy administration would hail her.[96] She announced as point of fact that Smith, and other activists from the southern freedom struggle, represented the position of the delegates in the room. That the other delegates then "closed ranks" around Smith—that they did not discredit his account or disidentify with Smith in order to appeal to Kennedy—mattered to Hansberry in later reflections.[97]

Disavowal as a Gesture: Kennedy's Turn Away

Kennedy's turn away from Smith, and Hansberry and Horne's subsequent intervention, helps to theorize the ways in which disavowal is a *gesture*; it has an embodied shape and weight. Disavowal as a gesture has expression in legal and political realms, and at the summit it could be found in Kennedy's corporeality, in his physically turning away from Smith (whose testimony he read as messy, angry, and counterproductive) and toward what he presumably thought would be a more useful and policy-oriented terrain of engagement. In this move, Kennedy turned toward a more familiar emotional register, in which there was no room for Black suffering, despair, or anger, and away from what Hansberry tells us are pivotal ways of knowing. Indeed, such affective ways of knowing are regularly dismissed or disallowed for Black people, or they are so highly sutured to projections of hyper-emotionality and anti-reason that Black affective expression gets used to delegitimize Black political analysis of what must be done.

Practices of emotional distancing and refusing to hear are practices that sustain and bind white racial identity and hegemonic masculinity. In the U.S., both require excess and anti-rationality to be mapped in racialized and gendered ways onto the bodies of people of color. In this mapping, Kennedy is upheld for citizenship as member and leader of the national body. Smith and other young men of color are figured as "out of control" rather than as loyal to Black people. Kennedy maintains a self-image of rationality, individuated boundedness, and contained composure—all positioned against an image of Smith as nonbounded, falling apart, and overflowing.

Against Kennedy's impatience and rejection, Hansberry laid out a practice of turning *toward* rather than away and, from within this orientation, *hearing*—a practice that anticipates and speaks forward to the Clinton meeting with Yancey and Jones that I examine later in this chapter. What Hansberry wanted Kennedy to hear was not factual information or policy suggestions but testimonies, provocations, and questions that had emotions in them and that could be neither relayed nor heard without feeling. Her insistence that Smith be heard and not dismissed by Kennedy was a refusal to give power to the ways in which white masculinity claims power—power over those bodies deemed excessive, emotional, dangerous, eruptive, and vulnerable.[98] Hansberry interrupted Kennedy's gendered and racialized mapping of feeling/anti-reason onto Smith, rejecting his masculinized, racialized, and classed rules of emotional comportment and elocution and his contorted measurements of reason. She endorsed and centered a young man who was representative of grassroots struggle and who was feminized and discredited for being, in that moment, wounded and emotional and for speaking with a stutter. Kennedy was not hearing Smith; he was not hearing the content or the feelings; and he grew more and more red, tense, and immobile, shutting down and using language that seemed to project his own emotionality onto his interlocutors.[99]

What Kennedy would or would not do, risk or not risk, at the summit was not only about his own person: it was also about himself as a state actor. When Kennedy made moves to defend the virtue and promise of the American state; when he could not hear the message of Smith, Hansberry, or Baldwin; when he rejected outright the concrete action steps suggested by the delegates; he, in a way, *became* the state and from that position understood the condemnation of state and extralegal violence as a personal attack.[100] Kennedy defends a state that cannot, for its own coherence as a racial regime, risk symbolically accompanying Black students in acts of integration in 1963. Kennedy's gesture is a layered archive of individual/interpersonal distancing and institutional distancing, a record of the racialized tonal structures and distance required to participate in and to rise in rank within U.S. political institutions. This is the operation of white disavowal within institutions: racial terror becomes "race relations."[101] The delegates came to the summit to tutor Kennedy on the meaning of freedom in the U.S. but found him antagonistic to witnessing and therefore antagonistic to genuine Black freedom—in this way, he had more in common with Bull Connor than he might have liked. He was unable to use his position to interrupt, explain, or even understand the centrality of racial terror to American governance and sociality.

Refusal and "Failure"

After three hours of effortful work to get Kennedy to hear, Hansberry's final remarks crystallized the impasse of the summit in a way that left it ringing in the room. She was not willing to perform an agreement or a softening of the terms. Her politics of refusal protected the integrity of her and Horne's intervention and marked a break, a refusal to close on a point of false connection. In inverting Smith's comment in her final message to Kennedy, she flipped the script that the meeting was "for" Black people, and she remapped the project of the summit as the work of apprehending the illness of a civilization that could produce the gendered and racialized state violence encapsulated in the photo of police officers pinning a Black woman to the ground, one with his knee on her neck.

Hansberry was invoking a close-up photograph taken during the Birmingham Children's Crusade earlier that month, in which a woman named Ethel Witherspoon is pinned to the sidewalk in daylight, with two Birmingham police offers attempting to restrain her arms, and a third with his knee on her neck and shoulder. The photograph appeared in May and June across the country's largest-circulation Black newspapers and the magazines *Ebony* and *Jet*, but it was notably absent in leading white liberal media outlets, an omission that, as Martin Berger explains, is emblematic of larger patterns of photographic narration of the civil rights struggle in white and Black media in the early 1960s.[102] When Hansberry called in the image at the close of the summit, she summoned a story about racialized and gendered violence and resistance in Black freedom struggles that the white press was busy editing out. And she references a larger body of interpretive, witnessing, and diagnostic work by Black reporters and Black citizens—a larger study of the society that could produce such an image.[103]

Kennedy's failure to hear signaled to Hansberry and others a broader crisis. SNCC press records quote Hansberry describing that "when we left the Kennedy's apartment I had a feeling of complete futility, and as I got on the elevator I wondered if there is any way to make white people in this country understand."[104] After the WGBH-TV interview later that day, Baldwin and Clark spent the evening reconstructing the summit together and concluded that it was a disaster. "Our considered judgment," Clark recalled, "was that the whole thing was hopeless," "that we had made no dent or impact on Bobby," "that there was no chance that Bobby heard anything that we said; and that there was no chance that Jack Kennedy was going to do anything beyond the trite and usual words."[105] Clark thought that whatever rapport had existed had been lost. But then six days later, Lyndon Johnson gave his Gettysburg talk, which, Clark explains,

> contained every single suggestion we made to Bobby Kennedy. . . . We were flabbergasted! And I am convinced that there had to be a taping of that confrontation unless Bobby Kennedy has an extraordinarily photographic mind . . . because they were verbatim things! And almost in sequence. And then in June . . . Jack Kennedy gave that famous civil rights speech of his which contained many of the same ideas.

Clark is referring here to John F. Kennedy's June 10, 1963 televised national address calling for civil rights legislation.[106] The address was opposed by all members of his Cabinet besides his brother, and, notably, framed the question of racial justice as a moral issue, just as the summit delegates had insisted.[107]

Even so, it is unclear precisely what Bobby Kennedy heard at first beyond the level of message.[108] Baldwin explains that Kennedy did not come into the kind of hearing Hansberry had called on him to practice until later experiences and losses gave the words a fuller meaning. And that was not soon enough. Reflecting almost two decades later, Baldwin speculated that "if what we'd been trying to say in that room had been *heard* that day in that room . . . "—and here, Baldwin is signaling a fuller kind of hearing—"I really don't believe that John F. Kennedy would have died . . . as soon as he did. I don't believe that the course America took would have been the same. If the Attorney General and his brother had been able to *hear* what was going on . . . in our country at that moment, we could have altered something which we failed to alter. . . . It was a very, very short time later that the wave of violence we were talking about which was a plague that overtook the entire country."[109] The delegates wanted Kennedy to hear what Baldwin called a "plea to the nation . . . to stop the slaughter of our children" and the delegates' insistence that "we can't afford" to have young people like Smith being beaten.[110] The delegates tried to shake Kennedy from an illusion that anti-Black violence was a superficial political matter to be brokered, they wanted Kennedy to "understand [the] urgency,"[111] to relinquish liberal mythologies of progress, and to stop deferring political action in perpetual delay for what King had sardonically named in his "Letter from Birmingham Jail" the month prior, "a more convenient season."[112]

By Hansberry's, Clark's, and Baldwin's accounts, the interpersonal and political relationships between Bobby Kennedy and the delegates were deeply impacted by the summit—as Clark put it, the "wounds were deep" and the suspicions and hostility toward Kennedy would remain for a long time.[113] Baldwin and Kennedy never spoke again. Clark recalls visiting Hansberry in the hospital in late June, when she vowed to get out of the hospital for two reasons: to see the premier of her play, and to vote against Bobby Kennedy.[114] Clark himself left the meeting with a sense that Bobby Kennedy was an exceptionally insensitive person who personalized issues that were not meant to be personalized.[115] It was not until six years later, when Clark met a very different Bobby Kennedy—and realized Kennedy had grown—that things shifted for Clark.

The summit lived on in different ways in the relationships of the participants and in their political thought. It is important to mark that the appeals circulating at the summit worked in multiple directions and—despite the central objectives of the meeting—did *not* all concern Kennedy. Not at all. For one example, Horne, in her autobiography, explains that she and the other, more senior Black delegates were deeply moved by Smith. Smith was, for her, "the soul of the meeting." He "cut through the fog of statistical arguments" and "thr[ew]" his story "out on the floor for all to see," in a way that made it impossible for

> Mr. Belafonte and Dr. Clark and Miss Horne, the fortunate Negroes, who had never been in a Southern jail, [to] keep up the pretense of being the mature, responsible spokesmen for the race any more. All of a sudden the fancy phrases like "depressed area" and "power structure" and all the rest were nothing. It seemed to me that this boy just put it like it was. He communicated the plain, basic suffering of being a Negro.... We were back at the level where a man just wants to be a man, living and breathing, where unless he has that right all the rest is only talk.[116]

Horne indicates that this shift in identification across social status and across specific embodied locations within Black freedom struggles (e.g., having been in a southern jail, having stood in Jim Crow cotton fields trying to register people to vote) had its own power in the meeting. "Mr. Kennedy was taken aback," she explains, not only by the "naked fury" of Smith but "also, I think, at the response it drew from us."[117]

The intervention at the summit was a part of a robust line of Hansberry's political action, but it was a turning point for Horne, a turn *toward* the grassroots leadership of Smith's generation.[118] After the summit, Horne went home to reflect, and within days, phoned the NAACP to ask how she might go to the South. Her fear of flying, she resolved, would not stop her, nor would she let herself be stopped by her fear that Black people would reject her. In Jackson, Mississippi, Horne met Medgar Evers and witnessed his work, grace, and vulnerability to attack just a week before he was murdered. In August, Horne participated in the March on Washington and in the fall she co-led a fundraiser at Carnegie Hall, filling seats to support SNCC at a time when SNCC was very controversial and ultimately raising $32,000 for the organization.[119]

The very complexity of identifying what the summit achieved—or failed to achieve—demonstrates important dimensions of political appeals. For one, political appeals move forward in incredibly complicated ways, and they can be at work even as those who are summoned may resist their interpellation. They may take hold in fuller meaning at a later time. Into at least late 1964, Bobby Kennedy talked about the summit as if the experience hadn't changed him.[120] The emotional register of the appeal was delayed in being heard—and this has to do with the structures of distancing and disavowal that constitute white identity and, in this case, its intersection with class, gender, education, political power, and related epistemes of knowledge. Part of the political appeal to Kennedy traveled quickly, but the real hearing, according to Clark and Baldwin, happened much later.

The *Longue Durée* of Interruption

In the summer of 2015 and into the following year, activists within the contemporary movement for Black lives held multiple widely publicized encounters with potential Democratic presidential candidates. From Tia Oso's and others' interventions at Netroots Nation to Marissa Johnson and Mara Willaford's action at a Bernie Sanders rally in Seattle to Ashley Williams' action at a Clinton fundraiser in South Carolina, these ruptures of campaign-speeches-as-usual form an archive in the political record to be reckoned with.[121] These actions were highly public and even spectacular in nature.

The meeting between Hillary Clinton and Black Lives Matter organizers Daunasia Yancey and Julius Jones lies among these ruptures of the summer 2015 primaries, but it was staged somewhat differently than the others, in a way that articulates with the 1963 summit. Here, Yancey and Jones met with Clinton not in the middle of a rally or speech, but after a public event, in an overflow room. This is, on the one hand, a somewhat more intimate setting, but the almost eternal repetition of the event—covered on Democracy Now, Comedy Central, and NBC, and the meeting footage viewed over a million times on YouTube—gives it a different quality. Yancey and Jones' intervention with Clinton would, in its recording and circulation, have a wider kind of viewing beyond the room that night. Their questions for Clinton would become an instructive rupture that rippled outward in a long-reaching repetition.

It is a repetition in two senses. First, in the sense that the encounter works within and stretches outward through the repetition of the news cycle—through the uptake and recirculation of the story on multiple outlets and in the life of a video that has been replayed many times. Second, the encounter as an intervention is a repetition of a political practice that has a long history within the Black radical tradition—a practice of interrupting white-dominated political discourse. This is what Jasmine Syedullah has called "the *longue durée* of interruption," the history of Black intervention into the terms of political engagement themselves.[122]

That evening, Yancey (founder and lead organizer of Black Lives Matter Boston, with a background in LGBTQ organizing[123]) and Jones (founder and lead organizer of Black Lives Matter Worchester) traveled to New Hampshire from Massachusetts with fellow organizers only to find themselves unable to enter Clinton's forum on drug policy. They were denied entry on the grounds that the space was filled to capacity but were granted time for a brief semi-private meeting afterward. Yancey and Jones confronted Clinton about her role in lobbying for the Violent Crime and Law Enforcement Bill in 1994 and her role, over two decades, in the domestic and international war on drugs.[124]

Yancey began by telling Clinton that she was an ardent feminist who had long looked up to Clinton, and then she confronted Clinton, explaining that "you and your family have been personally and politically responsible for policies that have caused health and human services disasters in impoverished communities of color through the domestic and international war on drugs that you championed as First Lady, Senator, and Secretary of State." Yancey asked how Clinton felt about her role in that violence and how she planned to reverse it. There are two parts to Yancey's question—*feeling* as a practice of acknowledgment and knowledge production, and then action guided by that feeling and knowledge—action that would undo the violence.

Clinton explained that she "feel[s] strongly" and then performed a kind of innocence through an account of time—claiming that there was a "different set of concerns" in the 1980s and early 1990s and that today, "we have to . . . figure out what will work now." Yancey explained that those policies were not simply outdated but that they "didn't work then, either"; they were violent in the first place, "ripping apart families" and "actually causing death." Conceding that the war on drugs had "consequences"—as "any kind of government action" often does—Clinton defended the bill as having been a response to a crime wave primarily impacting communities of color and poor communities—that the bill was partly *for* Black people and had been requested by some Black leaders. Political scientists Elizabeth Hinton, Julilly Kohler-Hausmann, and Vesla Weaver have unpacked and historicized this claim, explaining that in the early 1990s, Black people's criticism of police brutality; calls for full employment, quality education, and drug treatment; and demands for "*better* policing," not *more* policing, were answered by "selective hearing." Selective hearing has a long and fraught history—legislators responded to nineteenth-century and 1960s Black activists calling for social investment, economic inclusion, and economic redistribution with the same harsh culture of punishment.[125] As Dr. Clark explained in his reflections on the summit, the vestiges of a past during which Black people were subject to everything but acknowledgment of dignity shapes generations of mishearing by state officials and explains the ongoing need to issue urgent appeals.

Clinton urged Jones and Yancey to continue consciousness-raising work but to move toward articulating a comprehensive set of policy proposals. What she misses is that for Yancey and Jones, consciousness raising and policymaking are not mutually exclusive. Jones underscored that "we as a country" and the president must address anti-Blackness as a founding problem in this country and must reckon with mass incarceration as being a part of this longer history rather than as a simple failed policy outcome. Jones then reiterated Yancey's original question. He marked out, as Yancey did, Clinton's historical and political coordinates in relationship to drug policy and mass incarceration, explaining,

> You and your family have been, in no uncertain way, partially responsible [for these policies and outcomes]. Now, there may have been unintended consequences, but now that you understand the consequences, what in your *heart* has changed that's going to change the direction in this country? Like, what *in you*—not your platform, not what you're supposed to say— how do you actually *feel* that's different than you did before? What were the mistakes? And how can those mistakes that you made be lessons for all of America for a moment of reflection on how we treat Black people in this country?

Yancey and Jones were, as Hansberry and Horne were at the summit, parallel rhetoricians deploying a politics of feeling to do political staging work. As Horne repeated Hansberry's point across the summit, Jones returned to Yancey's original question, and together they corralled Clinton toward a turn to acknowledgment.

In prophetic terms, Clinton reflected back what she heard them asking: she said she agreed that there needs to be a "reckoning," using the language of "original sin" to describe slavery. She stopped there and insisted that activists needed a "plan ready to go"—something she could "sell," "because in politics if you can't explain it and you can't sell it, it stays on the shelf." She advised that getting a stadium full of white people to concede, "Oh, we get it, we get it. We're gonna be nicer, okay?" as an outcome was "not enough, at least in my book"—positioning herself as the champion of a bigger vision of politics.

In this fifteen-minute encounter, where Clinton speaks the conventional language of interest politics, Yancey and Jones invoke a politics that is about deeper forms of identification and solidarity that are not bound through national belonging but through an understanding of one's relationship to the violence itself. For Yancey and Jones, the *pathway* into any kind of policy action that will not reproduce but will undo anti-Black violence can only be through grappling with the ways in which Clinton is herself bound to the violence. It is constitutive of her public persona and political power.[126]

Yancey and Jones press Clinton to reflect on how she feels in her heart—underneath the veneer of campaign talk, the glossy rhetoric, and the calculated admissions. Clinton misses that Yancey and Jones were not proposing feelings as an "endpoint." Instead, she misreads their project in which acknowledgment is the precondition of necessary and urgent action. Yancey and Jones want Clinton to be transformed by confronting history. They raise questions of inheritances and responsibility. The task of truly confronting her own relationship to the violence would equip Clinton to enact the form of solidarity—which is actually bigger than solidarity but a kind of responsibility to the violence—that Yancey and Jones press her to inhabit. Without this, Clinton cannot but produce more of the same. When Clinton responds by asking them for a policy proposal, they refuse—because if they give her a plan, they will have preempted the very thing they are trying to induce in her.[127]

Yancey and Jones call Clinton to relate to the questions raised by the contemporary movement for Black lives not as a candidate without history, not as a "representative" of their interests, not as a kind of policy entrepreneur, not on the basis of some abstract moral obligation, but as someone who is in fact quite intimately related through the history of violence itself.[128] They each map out Clinton's historical and political coordinates in relationship to drug policy and mass incarceration. From this site, from this orientation, if Clinton were to actually *be* with her history in that place, she'd find that she is bound to the political questions raised by activists in the movement for Black lives through her historical connection to the very violence they seek to end.

Boundness is the basis on which Clinton should understand her relationship to the movement demands. Partly, this is boundness across time.[129] Where Clinton invokes time as a form of distance ("that was then, this is now") and forges a past of "mistake" in a way that evades responsibility, Yancey's and Jones' questions plumb the relationship between Clinton in 1994 and Clinton in 2015—and insist on the insolubility of these moments.

Acknowledgment

The register of all three of the interventions—the telegram, the interventions at the summit, and the New Hampshire meeting—is prophetic. As I explained in chapter 1, the prophetic is a genre of political language that issues urgent demands for accountability and poetic promises of redemption.[130] Through this powerful vernacular and symbolic structure, actors summon acknowledgment of disavowed realities, and they pose fateful decisions about a collective future. The problem in each case studied in this chapter is not "ignorance" that can be remedied by information or argument. Instead, the problem is what George Shulman calls "a perception of what and who . . . count as real."[131] The confrontation is, then, with *disavowal* rather than lack of information. As prophetic messengers, the summit delegates and Black Lives Matter activists announce the very truths their audience is invested in denying.[132]

The structure of each of these interventions is to press into the space of disavowal and to crowd it out with a different politics. Each of the interventions attempts to "plot a movement from innocence to acknowledgment" through a politics of boundness—to say that Birmingham and Los Angeles are bound together; that the knowledge Kennedy needs and the knowledge that will change him is bound up in Jerome Smith's account of racial violence and an understanding that he (Kennedy) is connected to southern segregationists rather than being an innocent spectator watching from afar; or that Clinton is bound to ending anti-Black violence through her historic relationship to that violence.[133]

The political challenge faced by the activists at the two meetings is not to justify an argument more effectively but to confront a refusal of acknowledgment.[134] Acknowledgment, rather than guilt—or, as Mamta

Motwani Accapadi puts it, "white tears"—is the alternative to innocence.[135] Acknowledgment here does not mean a trite admission or a short-lived performance of recognition: it is a transformative *and* disruptive political project that is the undoing of disavowal. It is to turn toward what has been evaded in life, in social practices, in political conduct, and in history. It is to shift to political responsibility and collective action. The activists engage in a politics of identification by mapping out relationships of ethical obligation and responsibility.

Affect in Black and White

The distance that Hansberry, Horne, Baldwin, Smith, Yancey, and Jones interrupt is a performance against and disavowal of boundness. If Birmingham really were on Mars, and if Birmingham did not reflect the conditions of U.S. cities South *and* North *and* West, white people would not need to constantly perform distance from it.[136] The spatiality of white disavowal is sustained by repeated performance.

In many ways, the intimacy of the interventions by Hansberry, Baldwin, Horne, Smith, and others at the 1963 summit anticipates Yancey's and Jones' 2015 interventions. At the two meetings, the appeals issued to Kennedy and Clinton are made at a disallowed and intimate register—one that is about facing the violence with an emotional honesty that breaks the rules. They wield intimate appeals and call Kennedy and Clinton to be present emotionally with the violence. Clinton's and Kennedy's repeated return to interests, statistics, and policy proposals in the face of the provocations at the summit and the New Hampshire meeting are practices in, as Cory Gooding has put it, "atomizing Black suffering meant to establish a certain kind of distance."[137] Racial politics becomes a series of "calculated events to be navigated but never experienced or inhabited," about numbers rather than about being and beings. Hansberry, Horne, Yancey, and Jones refuse these terms. They use "intimacy" as a register of political engagement to replace the very terms and conditions of engagement that Kennedy and Clinton demand.[138] They use intimacy as an intervention into distance.

At both meetings, emotions and the practice of hearing emotions have an important role—both in their distortion and in their political significance for knowledge. Smith's account, including his emotions, was the crux of what Hansberry and Horne wanted Robert Kennedy to encounter. One needs to *feel* to access critical knowledge for political action. Paradoxically, "emotion-ality"—in a distorted sense—was, in a way, the only thing Kennedy could perceive. Kennedy would not or could not hear the content and the feelings of Smith's testimony, just as he compressed into his own unfelt feelings.

The political praxes of *hearing*, *feeling*, and *turning toward* are practices through which to know boundness. These are haptic and somatic practices in which sensory knowledge has a central role in learning and knowing. The practice of "turning toward" also has a spatial dimension that is about a kind of orientation. Forms of identification themselves are spatially structured, not only in the sense that they are lived in space but also in that they are oriented toward or away from others, from knowledge, from ways of being, and from political questions. Kennedy's turn away from Smith and Hansberry and Horne's effort to get him to turn toward Smith are both somatic and spa-tial practices of orientation. "Turning toward" is a practice through which Kennedy might reorient his sense of self and his relationship to the others in the room and to the work of ending anti-Black violence. Hansberry and Horne ask Kennedy to, as Sharon Krause puts it, "feel with other citizens who are differently placed."[139] Hansberry and Horne press Kennedy as Yancey and Jones press Clinton to be with the reality of historical and contemporary violence. The two events are tribunals of a sort, not a brokering with Black suffering but a public indictment of these public officials.

Embedded in Baldwin's choices in the design of the summit and embedded in Hansberry's interventions at the summit is the contention that the knowl-edge at stake in the meeting—what Kennedy needs to know to make him into the political actor that is urgently needed—is not knowable through reviewing and discussing charts and statistics. In his choice of whom to invite and how to set the tenor of the day, Baldwin privileges the figures of the ac-tivist and the artist at a time when there were growing pressures to divide ac-ceptable roles between "art" and "politics."[140] As Richard Iton has explained, the aftermath of the Cold War saw ongoing attacks on the viability of the artist-activist—attacks issued through state violence and attempts to silence Black activists, attacks upon their mentors, and pressures from other civil rights leaders and elected officials who sought to establish their legitimacy as the most appropriate representatives of Black interests.[141] The summit, as it lives forward today, is a microcosm and critical record of who the artist (e.g., Hansberry) has been against these forces, how she has refused the pressures of the history Iton chronicles. It is a record of what her relationship has been with her collaborators, how she has led her friends who are social scientists, what her relationship is to frontline organizing, and how she is at war with the state. Although intended by Kennedy to be an off-the-record meeting, the summit's life in the newspapers, while partly garbled or embellished, stamped and announced in that moment some of these things.

In the two encounters, there is an impasse between the state officials' language of interests on the one hand and, on the other hand, the project of political feeling and acknowledgment. Clinton misreads the work of feeling and acknowledging harm as presented by Yancey and Jones. In the activists' project, feelings are important for coming into political knowledge and for propelling shifts in identification. Emotions themselves are not the end point. This is an important distinction to make in the contemporary context, in which "feelings-talk" with university administrators, police departments, government officials, or community members can forestall institutional accountability and the redistribution of power and resources. In both moments, however, it would be a misreading to label the activists' interventions as that kind of feelings-talk. None of the activists are interested in sentimentalism. Yancey and Jones, for example, are trying to get Clinton to see that how we feel about past political decisions is what motivates our future action, that if she is going to respond in the right kind of way, there can't be a motivational deficit, an absence of proper affect.[142] In both sets of interventions, feelings don't *precede* acknowledgment—they are indivisible from it and they are a kind of evidence of the knowledge that is needed to address and undo racial violence.

Clinton's misreading is emblematic of how feelings get misread in studies of politics more broadly, as in the bifurcation of affect and reason.[143] As Debra Thompson explains, in western liberal democratic thought, emotions are situated in opposition to rationality and are imagined to be suspect—with emotional displays "symboliz[ing] a loss of control over oneself or a society."[144] The racialized (especially as Black), gendered, and colonial "other" is figured, through projection, as *hyper*-emotional and therefore unfit to govern (to govern others or even oneself)—as opposed to the white male, settler subject who imagines himself to be rational, civilized, and fit for democracy.[145] But emotions are not actually ever absent; they are just handled, used, and known differently. While Black people's emotions are cast as suspect, dangerous, and unreasonable, anger or other "negative" emotions of dominant groups get incorporated into democratic politics.[146]

Yancey and Jones present "feeling" as a pathway into acknowledgment, and Hansberry and Horne present "*hearing* feeling" as a political practice of knowledge production. Both of these practices are what would guide and propel political action. Hansberry's and Horne's practice of "hearing feeling" works to dismantle the reign of white liberal civility discourse. The work to be done from this place then is, as Yancey explains, to *reverse* the violence— not only to end the violence but to change all that it touches in its long reach.

Interlude
"My Friends, These People
Are Our People"

Pat Buchanan's Nostalgic and Demonological Appeals

> My friends, these people are our people. They don't read Adam
> Smith or Edmund Burke, but they come from the same schoolyards
> and the same playgrounds and towns as we came from. They share
> our beliefs and our convictions, our hopes and our dreams. These
> are the conservatives of the heart. They are our people. And we need
> to reconnect with them. We need to let them know we know how
> bad they're hurting. They don't expect miracles of us, but they need
> to know we care.
>
> —Patrick J. Buchanan, 1992 Republican National Convention

Appeals to identification like those issued in the preceding chapters by
Rivera, Baldwin, and Hansberry are never in a vacuum but are always in relationship to a larger field in which competing and even deeply antagonistic
calls—such as calls to white supremacist kinship—are being issued simultaneously. And yet those identificatory appeals issued by Black, brown, queer,
and feminized subjects are so often pathologized as politically retrograde and
inhibitive to politics,[1] while white and masculinized appeals to right-wing
politics, conservatism, liberalism, or cultural traditionalism go unmarked as
interpretive political acts.

One place where this dynamic plays out is in national discourses criticizing
"identity politics." The term "identity politics" carries at least three very different meanings—first, and originally, as a Black lesbian feminist materi-
alist account and set of political practices originating in the 1977 Combahee
River Collective Statement that, as Barbara Smith explains, "grew out of our
objective material experiences as Black women."[2] Drastically reconfigured

If We Were Kin. Lisa Beard, Oxford University Press. © Oxford University Press 2023.
DOI: 10.1093/oso/9780197517338.003.0005

and even demonological meanings have been attached to the term in succeeding decades. Second, then, identity politics came to work as a shorthand
referent a decade later for a set of critiques issued from *within* queer, feminist, and antiracist organizing about single-issue politics.[3] And third—and
by far most dominantly in national political discourse—the term has been
harnessed by conservatives and by elements on the Left to condemn feminist, antiracist, and queer politics, and to disavow their own identitarian
politics.[4] Here, my focus is on this third meaning. As Ruth Wilson Gilmore
explains, "a tiresomely overdeveloped take on leftist politics argues that the
twentieth-century failure of solidarity to endure in the long run should be
laid at the door of something the critics call 'identity politics.' What they
seem to mean," Gilmore translates, "is antiracist politics, or antisexist politics; and often what they really mean, given the examples they choose, is that
Black people or women of all races interrupted and messed up class politics
in favor of 'militant particularism.' "[5] The blaming works through caricatures
and gross misreadings that, as Linda Martín Alcoff explains, render antiracist
and antisexist politics as a kind of "harping" on difference that is "irration-
ally preoccupied with the past" or opportunistically and selfishly focused on
grievances.[6] "Identity politics" is overdetermined, and Gilmore helps name
the phantom that is invoked by detractors yet is, as Alcoff explains, "nowhere
defined" in their narratives.[7] That "something the critics call 'identity politics' "—if we understand those politics to be struggles over identification,
appeals to identification, or political mobilization through and generative
of identification—is in fact something that is actually at work everywhere
on the landscape—though with different stakes and visions.[8] This is to say
that white- and male-dominated liberal,[9] leftist, or conservative analyses are
not less identitarian than the politics they blame—they are just saturated in,
encoded through, and often rendered unknown to political actors themselves through racialized and gendered practices of disavowal.[10] Although
in today's most immediate context, the Far Right has actually become
much more explicit in claiming and advancing its politics as identitarian,
conservatives have, as Jodi Dean explains, so often "displac[ed] attention
from their own activism," insisting on the "naturalness" of their values even
as they politicize those values.[11]

This Interlude turns to a political appeal issued on the Far Right—Patrick
Buchanan's speech at the opening night of the 1992 Republican National
Convention (RNC)—to examine the construction of ideas of white nation-
alist kinship through a web of demonological and intimate political appeals;

to theorize the relationship between the form and the visions of different political appeals; to explore the role of nostalgia and myth-making in claims of a *we*; and to develop an account of struggles over identification that defy formal measures of political "victory" or "failure." Taken together, the speech and its audiovisual record also illuminate important dimensions of tone, volume, pacing, and facial expression in the participatory encounter between Buchanan and his audience.

Author, speechwriter, and conservative commentator Patrick Buchanan was an extremely divisive figure in conservative politics in the 1990s, from his opposition to the Gulf War to his vitriolic attacks on neoconservatism. He had served in the White House as an advisor and speechwriter to Richard Nixon and as communications director for Ronald Reagan. Running for the GOP presidential nomination in the 1992 primaries, Buchanan received nearly three million votes, running on a populist, isolationist, anti-free trade, anti-Wall Street, anti-immigrant, anti-gay rights, anti-affirmative action, anti-abortion, and Christian Right platform, pulling "cultural traditionalists and angry white workers (many Democrats and union members) into his 'Buchanan Brigades.'"[12]

Buchanan's RNC speech worked through themes of political friendship, demonology, familial narratives of the GOP as a political "home," mythologies of shared childhood origins, and yearnings for a "return" to an earlier racialized and gendered political order. He appealed to a reconsolidated whiteness through a practice of party identification and a narrative of white kinship lacking any mandate of distributive justice and deeply invested in forms of white patriarchal masculinity that anticipated and laid the groundwork for Donald Trump's appeals more than two decades later. Particularly through a performance of nostalgia in the second half of the speech, Buchanan appealed to belonging and political community, constructing a past and invoking a longing for that past in order to orient present identification and action.

Politically, Buchanan's RNC speech was significant in the 1990s and, as I will address, remains significant today. Although the speech stood out in 1992 for its controversy—both within and outside the Republican Party—it pulled on enduring demonological tropes that both preceded his address and reach into the contemporary moment in appeals from the Far Right to the liberal Left. Against the backdrop of a changing legal landscape that enshrined social inequality in law, education, and healthcare policy, Buchanan's public proclamations explicitly denounced feminists, LGBTQ people, and people of color—questioning their very humanity and their belonging in U.S. society and urging state and vigilante violence against them.[13] His speech sets the stage politically and historically for chapter 4 because it is emblematic of the identificatory landscape faced by organizers within race and gender justice movements at that moment and across the following decade.

"No Necessary Political Belongingness"

Before turning to Buchanan's speech, I want to pause to consider the relationship between competing political appeals. Stuart Hall's reflections on the process of studying articulations issued by the Right proves immensely helpful here. In a 1989 panel with Homi Bhabha and Jacqueline Rose on the rise and grip of Thatcherism, Hall explained that while the recent political context in British cultural politics "has shaken me politically, . . . it has not shaken me theoretically."[14] He insisted that Thatcherism's ideological reign proves "that disarticulation and rearticulation need not necessarily be directed towards any progressive, humane or socially just end"—that the processes of articulation have "no necessary political belongingness"— and while this may shake or disturb us politically, it "should not disturb us *theoretically*."[15] This is to say that while so many of the *ideas* of articulation, hegemony, or coercion/consent arise from theoretical scholarship and organizing history of the Left, they are not political processes that "belong" to the Left. Identificatory attachments and political visions can be constructed in various political recombinations and, indeed, often in ways that contain quite contradictory elements. Stuart Hall explained facetiously to his audience that "rearticulation is attractive only so long as we think *we* are going to do the rearticulating. When it is we who are rearticulated, we don't like it so much."[16] Hall may have been teasing himself and his interlocutors, but the larger scope of his comments make clear the political stakes of the matter.

At least one figure in Buchanan's closest circle of advisors turned self-consciously to the Left for ideas to advance the political visions of the Far Right, with far-reaching implications given the ways in which Buchanan's own campaigns in the 1990s laid groundwork for the reflowering of explicit white nationalism, misogyny, and antisemitism in the 2016 election.[17] In the early 1990s, the diehard racist and nativist Samuel T. Francis pulled heavily on Italian Marxist philosopher Antonio Gramsci to envision a means by which cultural traditionalists could regain power in U.S. politics and political culture.[18] A figure flagged on the Southern Poverty Law Center's watchlist, Francis had worked for the conservative *Washington Times*—until he was fired for suggesting that neither slavery nor racism was immoral—and then went on to work for Far Right publications. In his 1993 article, "Winning the Culture War," published in the ultraconservative magazine *Chronicles*, Francis advised his readers that "if the cultural right in the United States is to take back its culture from those who have usurped it, it will find a study of Gramsci's ideas rewarding."[19] Francis insisted that there is very little to learn from conservative theory (which would not help, he explained, with challenging dominant authorities—as Francis understood cultural traditionalists to be embattled and suppressed by elite neoconservative/libertarian leadership). In a deeply ironic identification, Francis described the fight by those who espouse "egalitarian, homophile, feminist, multiculturalist, and socialist agendas" and are "punished, intimidated, [and] terrorized" by establishment media, as being most like the battle that must be fought in an archconservative crusade against not only neoconservative elites but also against those "egalitarian" political communities.[20] Francis recommended taking from the Left the practice of consciousness-raising to raise awareness about how "traditional American culture is being subverted and destroyed."[21] Francis called for a return to domination—for cultural traditionalists to regain their "rightful position as the dominant and creative core of American society."[22] When Buchanan invokes a culture war, then, we should hear an unnamed Gramscian referent. Battles over identification are sometimes being understood *theoretically* in related terms by political actors who have fundamentally antagonistic political visions.

The study of identificatory appeals requires distinguishing between the form and function of the appeals on the one hand and their political investments and visions on the other. It will not do to collapse the landscape of identificatory appeals into a pluralist portrait—as if there are simply "different appeals" that on equal footing constitute a diverse political landscape. Nor will it do to erect a lexicon or framework that obscures the ways political appeals are connected discursively, politically, and theoretically. Different appeals are not only connected in the sense that some competing claimants are trying to summon the same people. They are tied to each other because they make political claims *in relationship* to each other—indeed, often *against* each other—while struggling for different futures. When, as I will explore in chapter 4, the grassroots feminist, antiracist, and LGBTQ liberation organization Southerners On New Ground (SONG) was founded in 1993, it was founded in large part to fight the kinds of political visions and projects articulated in Buchanan's 1992 speech.[23] SONG co-founders had extensive experience organizing against the Right in their campaigns across the 1990s. Identificatory appeals must be theorized within and across these lines of contestation and struggle.

A War for the Soul of America

The events in Houston leading up to the 1992 RNC included a series of protests and counterprotests at local abortion clinics as well as the standing-room-only God and Country Rally, an event organized by the Christian Coalition featuring Vice President Dan Quayle, conservative political commentator Oliver North, and the fervent antifeminist Phyllis Schlafly (lead organizer of the STOP ERA campaign in the 1970s and Eagle Forum chairwoman).[24] Seven ACT UP and Queer Nation protestors were arrested after infiltrating the Jerry Falwell Christian Action Network Luncheon.[25] On the opening night of the convention, a march outside the Astrodome organized by ACT UP and Queer Nation to protest government inaction on HIV/AIDS was met with charging cavalry in full riot gear. Although the scale of Houston's militarization in anticipation of the RNC was kept at a low profile, the Texas National Guard stood poised to mobilize 2,500 troops on the streets within sixteen hours, armed with M-16 rifles, shotguns, .45-caliber pistols, and more than 1,000 hand and smoke grenades. The Rice University football stadium was slated as a staging area if forces were committed, and city buses would be taken over for military transportation.[26]

On the opening night of the convention, Pat Buchanan addressed a 17,000-person audience of delegates and media representatives in the Houston Astrodome, with many in attendance wearing business suits and neon baseball caps or red cowboy hats decorated with antiabortion stickers (distributed by the Eagle Forum at the God and Country Rally) and brandishing "Buchanan Brigade" or "Bush/Quayle" posters.[27] The audience's energy was exhilarated and rowdy, like fans at a college football game. At the podium, Buchanan appeared a bit taken aback by the roar of cheers, then chuckled. He greeted the audience, "What a terrific crowd this is, what a terrific crowd," and assured his own followers that "we may have taken the long way home, but we finally got here to Houston."[28] The crowd cheered. "The first thing I want to do tonight," Buchanan opened, "is to congratulate President George

Bush, and to remove any doubt about where we stand. The primaries are over, the heart is strong again, and the Buchanan Brigades are enlisted—all the way to a *great Republican comeback victory in November!!*" The camera cut to Barbara Bush nodding in approval—a visual cue that helped to perform a reconciliation between Buchanan and the president—then panned out so that the crowd looked like a sea.

Buchanan celebrated, at length, the legacy of Ronald Reagan and outlined George Bush's qualifications to serve as president based on his military experience and antiabortion politics. He defined Bush's legitimacy as a leader contra Bill Clinton—whose agenda, Buchanan described, was "unrestricted abortion on demand," "homosexual rights," and opposition to private school vouchers, and whose "lawyer-spouse" was a champion of "radical feminism." He mocked the Clintons and vice-presidential running mate Al Gore ("Prince Albert") as out of touch with Americans and set on steering America far to the left and away from its core values. Throughout the speech, the audience regularly pulsed into stadium-wide chants—"Pat! Pat! Pat!" and "Go, Pat, Go!"—cheering readily at each of Buchanan's prompts and often, as if frenzied by their own volume, cheering far past Buchanan's cues to quiet down so he could keep speaking.

Buchanan then changed his tone, thanking his supporters for their loyalty during the primaries, announcing he wanted to "speak from the heart to the three million people who voted for Pat Buchanan for President," and promising to never forget the "honor you have done me." Then, with the authority of "believ[ing] deep in my heart," he linked those three million people with the Republican Party, assuring them that the "right place for us to be now, in this presidential campaign, is right beside George Bush." He described the GOP as a "home" and positioned himself and the Brigades as wayward children who need to "come home." He performed his own return, insisting that "this Party is our home and we've got to come home to it. And don't let anyone tell you different." The camera frame captured a wide view of the audience facing Buchanan on stage, where his face was magnified on two large screens framing the podium.

Buchanan then ratcheted up the stakes of the election beyond a conventional political calculus of representation and interests, warning his listeners that the election is about "more than who gets what." Instead, he explained, the election was about national political identification: "It is about who we are. It is about what we believe and what we stand for as Americans." Buchanan called upon the imagery of a crusade, naming a "religious war going on in this country . . . a cultural war, as critical to the kind of nation we shall be as the Cold War itself. For this war is for the soul of America." Finally, Buchanan spelled out the lines of friend and enemy, with "Clinton and Clinton . . . on the other side, and George Bush . . . on our side. And so to the Buchanan Brigades out there," Buchanan called, "we have to come home and stand beside George Bush."

In the second half of the speech, Buchanan pivoted away from mocking the Clintons, touting Reagan's and Bush's military credentials, and claiming an apocalyptic struggle, toward more solemn and intimate tones of nostalgia, precarity, and loss. He turned to tales from the campaign trail, where he had collected "memories that are going to be with me the rest of my days." At this point, the rowdy crowd in the Astrodome became very quiet. In the quiet, Buchanan described meeting workers at the James River Paper Mill in Groveton, New Hampshire, who were "under threat of losing their jobs at Christmas." Buchanan recounted that none of the men would say a word to him as he shook their hands, until one "looked up and said . . . 'Save our jobs.'" Buchanan described meeting a legal secretary who ran up to him at an airport on Christmas day, weeping because she had lost her job and was about to lose custody of her daughter. Buchanan paused and explained to the crowd slowly and almost wistfully:

> My friends, *these people are our people.* They don't read Adam Smith or Edmund Burke, but they come from the same schoolyards and the same playgrounds and towns as we came from. They share our beliefs and our convictions, our hopes and our dreams. These are the conservatives of the heart. They are our people. And we need to reconnect with them. We need to let them know we know how bad they're hurting. They don't expect miracles of us, but they need to know we care.

At the very end of this passage, the quiet audience clapped earnestly and somberly. Buchanan described the "tiny town" of Hayfork, California—a community "under a sentence of death" because a federal judge had set aside protected habitat for the endangered spotted owl, "forgetting about the habitat of the men and women who live and work in Hayfork." He then pivoted away from the image of small white towns toward the specter of the 1992 Los Angeles rebellion, ultimately using the rebellion as a metaphor for his professed war to save "the soul of America." Notably, given his vitriolic anti-immigrant rhetoric across the previous years and months, Buchanan included "the brave people of Koreatown" as connected, albeit ambiguously and contingently, to the *we* he had crafted in his speech. They "took the worst of those L.A. riots," Buchanan explained, "but still live the family values we treasure, and . . . still deeply believe in the American dream."

Buchanan's identified his heroes as the "young fellows" of the 18th Cavalry, "who had come to save the city of Los Angeles" from "the mob," and described their M-16-armed response as "force, rooted in justice, and backed by moral courage." Buchanan's final bid was a pronouncement that like the troopers who "took back the streets of Los Angeles, block by block, . . . we must take back our cities, and take back our culture, and take back our country. God bless you," Buchanan ended, "and God bless America!" The crowd roared. Buchanan traveled to the two corners of the stage to give a thumbs up and to greet the audience with his hands held out in victory fists, before departing from the stage.

Demonological Appeals

Over the months prior to the RNC, Buchanan had been verbally bashing George H. W. Bush on the campaign trail for raising taxes, for the loss of U.S. industry jobs, for his foreign policy platform, and for being out of touch with "forgotten Americans." He dramatized ongoing tensions between the populist Right and the mainstream Right. "Pitchfork Pat," as he was sometimes called, presented himself as a working-class representative of labor, donning a tweed cap and fashioning himself as a scrappy working-class Irish-American candidate against "King George" Bush's wealthy WASP New England pedigree.[29] He attacked Bush's manhood and class background and painted the contest leading up to the RNC as a football match between a Catholic parochial school and Washington, DC's professional team.[30] Buchanan's attacks on Bush were so vitriolic that he almost was not permitted to speak at the Convention. Bush operatives had sought Buchanan's endorsement in July—after he had dropped out of the race—but were extremely reluctant to grant Buchanan his demand for a primetime speaking slot at the RNC in exchange for his support. Ultimately, though, Bush's team concluded that for the sake of healing internal divisions in the party, a Buchanan endorsement outweighed the risks of the deal.[31]

After the prior months of enmity, Buchanan walked his followers toward identification with Bush during his RNC speech. In a sharp pivot from his campaign speeches, Buchanan withheld his scathing economic critiques of Bush and GOP elites, shifting all the blame for America's economic problems to Democratic social policy (e.g., environmental and social welfare programs) and presenting a list of conservative Christian social values as uniting a *we* under the banner of the Republican Party. To be clear, this was a bid for specific terms of unity rather than a statement of fact. Indeed, in the days after the RNC, some Republican moderates would condemn Buchanan's divisive declarations, including his pro-life and anti-gay statements.[32] But in steering his antiestablishment Brigades to identify with and rally behind Bush, the blue-blooded establishment candidate, Buchanan presented a formulation— collapsing the economic impasses between Republican elites and blue-collar workers, blaming Democrats for white working-class grievances, and heralding conservative social values as unifying, all through a combination of nostalgic intimate appeals and images of conquest—that would have an enduring legacy over the coming decades.

The opening of Buchanan's speech performed a public amending— rewriting his earlier condemnations of Bush as being a simple matter of disagreement while in the same breath pivoting toward a list of shared values, including school choice, traditional marriage, keeping women out of military combat units, and supporting strict constitutional interpretation. His appeal reformulated the inside and outside of a Republican Party *we*, rearranging the boundaries between friend and enemy so as to try to steer the Buchanan Brigades toward Bush. At the center of this part of his appeal is the figure of the Republican Party as a "home." When he assures members of the Buchanan Brigades that the GOP is their home and instructs them to not "let anyone tell you different," he is in a way acknowledging that competing claims have been and will be made and urging his listeners to ignore them.

Identifications are defined as much by their "inside" as they are by their remainder. Whereas in Sylvia Rivera's speech (chapter 1), the lines of "inside" and "outside" were drawn across and through the crowd assembled in Washington Square Park (in her account, the people in the park were tied to her *and* were becoming the enemy), Buchanan crafted an imagined community against a raced/gendered/queer/effeminized/feminist *other* outside the walls of the Astrodome. He invoked an idea of shared vulnerability to cultural changes brought on by a collection of gendered, queered, and racialized others—including the "environmental extremists who put birds and rats and insects ahead of families, workers, and jobs"; radical feminists who wanted women in combat units; the "homosexuals" and their allies who wanted to undo the sanctity of marriage; those that would permit "the raw sewage of pornography" to destroy America's moral fabric; liberal Supreme Court judges; and the "rioting mob" in Los Angeles, which was coded as Black. All these figures are the "monsters" in Buchanan's demonology. This creation of monsters is, as Michael Rogin has demonstrated, an enduring feature in countersubversive American political culture. Indeed, Buchanan's demonological symbolism—his inflation, stigmatization, and dehumanization of political foes through raced and gendered terms—stands squarely within a larger countersubversive tradition in the U.S., a discursive tradition that trades in misogynist and white supremacist demonology to construct the specter of a multiheaded menace that is configured as mutually exclusively from a sanctified we.

Buchanan's claims "soar[ed] above the real," as Rogin has put it, replacing the world he claimed to represent with a coded parade of subversives and terrorists.[33] The historical fact of the sadistic beating of Rodney King by Los Angeles police officers was replaced by the specter of a rioting mob, itself a long-standing symbol in U.S. political culture that inverts and disavows histories of white mob violence and racial terror against Black people.[34] Demands to end diverse forms of intrafamilial and structural violence were replaced by the specter of feminists and gay people busy unraveling God-given social structures and moral codes.[35] The blame for rural suffering was placed on Al Gore and environmentalists rather on global markets, short-term profit imperatives, and the workings of what Ruth Wilson Gilmore has called "the antistate state"—a structure of organized state abandonment of welfare provision together with intense occupation by state power.[36] Buchanan invoked and condensed all these figures, drawing them together in his speech as if they collaborated in a coherent and unified threat to America's material and moral survival.

Buchanan forged the links in this associative chain through metaphor and monstrous spectacle. The suturing of the feminist and "the homosexual" was a very particular pairing being conjured by the Right in the 1990s, a kind of monstrous coupling at the nexus of battles over marriage that would only increase across the decade, fueled in part through a proliferating network of conservative institutes and think tanks addressing marriage. As Priscilla Yamin demonstrates, marriage was *the* political institution through which conservatives challenged several major political legacies of the 1960s, including in their efforts to roll back policies for race and gender equality, dismantle New Deal and Great Society programs, and reaffirm heteronormativity.[37] For the GOP and conservative activists, marriage associatively linked feminists, the Black poor, and gays and lesbians in a narrative of precipitous national decline. As a political project, "protecting marriage" united Republicans and centrist Democrats in calls for a return to two-parent, heterosexual, and monogamous families as the basis of American political culture and as defined against pro-choice organizing, no-fault divorce policies, the welfare state, and queer visibility and activism.[38] In a Moynihan-inflected framing, conservative political leaders linked the Los Angeles uprising to the erosion of traditional marriage, with Dan Quayle explaining, for example, that the "lawless social anarchy which we saw [in Los Angeles] is directly related to the breakdown of family structure."[39] The 1992 election was also fought in the wake of the Commission on Pornography's Meese Report, ordered by Reagan and published in 1986, from which several commissioners would go on to head the conservative think tanks Focus on the Family and the Family Research Council.[40] At this time, anxieties about cultural decay and pornography were articulated in environmental terms as a kind of toxic waste, with Reagan explaining that if the government can locate and inventory the "worst hazardous waste sites in America . . . [t]hen it was about time we did the same with . . . pornography."[41]

Having invoked a multiheaded monster, Buchanan painted a "titanic struggle" between forces of good and evil—figured through a spectacle of danger, on the one hand, counterpoised with Reagan and Bush's redemptive militarism and religious appeals to Christian morality on the other. His appeal worked through a process in which, as Rogin explains, the demonologist splits the world in two, attributing magical, pervasive power to a conspiratorial center of evil.[42] Those who would constitute the *we* of the Buchanan Brigades and the GOP are figured as the benign center, with all malignancies placed outside its borders. His appeal thus also works through what Elisabeth Anker calls "melodramatic political discourse," or stories that position the nation-state as a virtuous and innocent victim of villainous action.[43] As Anker argues, melodramatic narratives are significant because they work to reformulate political discourse and transform the political fields they depict.[44] "In the name of describing a centralized, apocalyptic battle," to use Rogin's words, Buchanan "was trying to create one."[45] The culture war in Buchanan's enunciation would primarily be sited *within* national borders—rather than the melodrama being played out with a demonized foreign country.

The scale of the identificatory terms in the first half of the speech were thus articulated through militarized, epic, nationalist, and fraternal vocabularies.

Buchanan's imagined *we* was incoherent without the consolidating specter of threat. In the first place, the binding of the people who made up the Buchanan Brigades—many of them Democrats and union members—to each other and, secondly, to Republican Party elites was constituted almost entirely by their imagined *differentiation* from others, and through generous injections of sentiments of belonging invoked through a language of shared values, references to "the heart," calls to "come home" to the Republican Party, and descriptions of "our people." Buchanan thus set up a threatening *other* as the foil of shared identification—but his work was not done because he still needed to bind that *we* together.

Nostalgia, Origins, and Constructing a White Kinship Imaginary

The crux of Buchanan's political appeal falls in the middle of the speech when Buchanan shifted to themes of intimacy and nostalgia. When he pivoted to "tales from the campaign trail that will be with [him] all his days," he primed his audience for a more intimate identificatory appeal through his tone and pacing, and by invoking themes of suffering and vulnerability. At this point, in a sweeping change of affect, the rowdy and almost uncontainable audience—an audience that had been clapping, yelling, chanting, laughing, waving signs, high-fiving, and talking with neighbors—grew still and quiet. People gazed, fixated on Buchanan, some with their mouths open, and almost no one commenting to their neighbors during these two and a half minutes (Figure Int.1). Whereas Buchanan's earlier demarcations of *us* and *them* required very little labor to be received and were met with what seemed like instant con-currence, here the sutures were not so quickly cognizable—they took time to evaluate and integrate. The terms of the hailing were not obvious or seamless, needing the slower pace of Buchanan's shift to themes of sorrow and despair.

Buchanan appealed to his audience in Houston to identify—on some level—with the white blue-collar workers facing unemployment in northern New Hampshire and vice versa. New Hampshire's economy had been hit very hard by the recession in the early 1990s, with twelve banks closing in 1991, a collapse in the housing market, and a tripled unemployment rate.[46] In Buchanan's political appeal, white misery—as figured by the plight of the paper mill workers and the unemployed secretary—was, as Tiffany Willoughby-Herard has put it, fashioned into something meant to be

Figure Int.1 Stills from "Pat Buchanan 1992 Republican Convention Address," C-SPAN, August 17, 1992.

understood as unnatural to whiteness and therefore an object of sympathy for white elites and semi-elites.[47] These appeals work, as Willoughby-Herard explains, to cultivate white citizens' political obligations to each other, and to "[naturalize] white kinship and white nationhood as the political extension of white kinship."[48] Like all forms of political identification, white political identifications must constantly be rearticulated. In August 1992, in the wake of Reaganomics—with the felt effects of deindustrialization, the transfer of industry overseas, and rising national rates of unemployment—it was *not* "inevitable," as Joseph Lowndes and Joel Olson have explained in deconstructing the backlash thesis, that white working-class people would come into alignment with GOP elites.[49] Buchanan had leaned heavily on the New Hampshire story across the campaign trail—at times recounting the fact that the workers were waiting in line for a free Christmas turkey, or that the day after his visit, newspaper headlines had announced a papermill company opening in Mexico.[50] Across the narratives, Buchanan presented the workers as silent, emasculated, and miserable. His story evokes feelings of "intimate association" or a sense of responsibility across class lines that would bolster white fraternity—but a fraternity that would not require any redistribution of power.[51] It is an instrumental sympathy—one that works to bind white people together in an idea of kinship in which the white working class and the white poor remain disposable.

When Buchanan describes the silent "tough, hearty men" about to lose their jobs, he evokes the threat of a failed white working-class masculinity. While the paper mill workers' silence toward Buchanan could be interpreted either as shame or as a refusal to engage Buchanan, in either case their economic precarity is married to their victimhood as aggrieved "makers" in Buchanan's populist appeal. Buchanan draws on enduring discourses of producerism in U.S. political culture, long associated with whiteness and masculinity. As Joseph Lowndes and Daniel Martinez HoSang explain, producerist ideology in the U.S. has historically posited "not an opposition between workers and owners but a masculine, cross-class assemblage connecting factions of the elite with poor whites . . . in opposition to those cast as unproductive and threatening," including, according to this framework, bankers and speculators, people who were enslaved, and Indigenous people.[52] Producerist politics have always retained elements of racialized demonization, from Andrew Jackson's anti-Black and anti-Indigenous politics, to the anti-Chinese campaigns of the 1880s, to the exclusion of Black workers from New Deal programs.[53]

When Buchanan assures the audience in the Astrodome that "these people are our people," and that even though they may not read Edmond Burke or Adam Smith, they come from the same playgrounds and towns, he anchors his appeal in a mythology of shared origins and a vision of the future. In defining the *we* inside the Astrodome as those who read Burke and Smith, Buchanan names as settled a set of shared investments in conservative intellectualism, cultural traditionalism, Christian conservatism, and capitalist enterprise. The "conservatives of the heart"—such as the paper mill workers in New Hampshire—are both lauded for their conservative sensibilities and paternalistically figured as unlettered and without intellectual pursuits. He establishes their belonging and virtue in their victimhood.

Buchanan's nostalgic invocation of childhood schoolyards and playgrounds should be understood as a thinly veiled longing for pre–*Brown v. Board* spatial histories of racial segregation. His memories of childhood leisure do not directly name but are constituted and haunted by histories of both school segregation—a preeminent site of struggle in civil rights battles[54]—and park segregation fought through youth activist sit-ins and numerous legal battles over public accommodations and named in King's "Letter from Birmingham Jail," Gordon Parks' documentary photojournalism, and other key civil rights era texts.[55]

Buchanan calls his listeners to find pleasure in the memory of a segregated white and Christian small-town Americana. Buchanan's longing for towns rather than cities or urban spaces articulates a 1950s isolationism, located geographically and culturally far away from and positioned against urban connotations of people of color, unassimilated immigrants, non-Christians, cosmopolitanism, and diasporic connections to global politics.[56] He invokes a past era in which life is imagined—for this *we*—to have been simple, natural, and right. This should be understood as Buchanan idealizing a social structure characterized by Jim Crow legalized segregation and racial violence and by 1950s heteropatriarchal household structures not yet—as the Right thought of it—"ruined" by feminists and LGBTQ people.[57] Buchanan's appeal to his listeners to *return* to those schoolyards and towns, and to reimagine a *we* from that mythical origin, works affectively through what Jeanne Scheper calls the "nostalgic grotesque," or a desire to return to retrograde practices and inhabit the racist-sexist past.[58] Nostalgia, as Svetlana Boym explains, is both a sentiment of loss and displacement and a romance with one's own fantasy.[59] Utopian nostalgia tends to be collective—a yearning for a past Common Place—but it works through co-opting and building on the personal. In this form of nostalgia, exile from the mythic past is a definite fall from grace, and the dream is to rebuild the world as it was.[60]

Buchanan's nostalgia rescales a national community to an intimate origin story. As Benedict Anderson explains of imagined communities, members will never know most of their fellow members, "yet in the minds of each lives the image of their communion."[61] The image of communion at the same playground is a fiction, a mythology of deep and long-term familiarity, neighborhood ties, and remembrance. The nostalgic, as Boym puts it, "reinvents her or his own imaginary affective geography that does not coincide with any scientific maps."[62] Despite any actual geographical histories to the contrary (because, for one thing, the RNC delegates and viewers hailed from across the United States), Buchanan called white Christian Americans into an idea that their origins were in small-town Middle America. Together, he explained, they are the true Americans, the inheritors of conservative cultural values and the protectors of America's future even if twentieth-century party politics had led them astray from each other. Buchanan's intimate appeal works through a performance of political memory—invoking a *we* of the past and potentially the present through inventing something that *we* can remember together. White mutual identification is painted as a return to a natural origin rather than a serially constructed political phenomenon or a serially discovered potential vulnerability.[63]

Buchanan asked the Houston crowd to witness "them"—the people in rural New Hampshire—and to "let them know" their suffering is registered. Working-class white people were never directly addressed in the speech, nor were they ever addressed as though they were in the stadium. Indirectly, Buchanan narrates their class experience for them, explaining who they are by virtue of who they are vulnerable to and, in doing so, enlisting a notion of class wounds. Buchanan's appeal across class lines did not contain a political mandate for economic redistribution—that the paper mill workers "don't expect miracles of us, but they need to know we care" neatly sidestepped the economic questions raised by the mill worker's message to Buchanan to "Save our jobs." To craft a shared identification between GOP elites and working-class white people, Buchanan omitted his own structural argument enunciated earlier on the campaign trail about the paper mill workers' lost jobs and the relationship between NAFTA, international financialization, and economic depression in rural areas. Although during the months prior he had attacked Bush's economic and trade policy, the need to endorse Bush that night in the name of party unity made it impossible to openly spell out his alternative from the podium—for example, to call for tariffs—and so he instead called for compassion.[64]

Buchanan's description of Hayfork presents white working-class communities and resource-extractive industry as a kind of endangered species eclipsed by the protection of nonhumans by fanatical environmentalists in a town whose very name evokes historic populist imagery. The workers of Hayfork and Groveton together with the residents of Ellijay, Georgia, at the start of the speech are figured as belonging to a "virtuous middle" bound together politically, economically, and culturally. The narrative of the virtuous middle dates back to the Jacksonian era and has been articulated across twentieth-century speeches by George Wallace, Spiro Agnew, Richard Nixon, and Buchanan through the language of "Middle Americans," "forgotten Americans," and the "Silent Majority."[65] While political pundits have treated this Silent Majority as a self-evident constituency, it is instead a rhetorical assertion and an attempt to craft a shared form of political identification. As a political narrative, its emergence and evolution can be historically traced, as can its pivotal role in the realignment of the Republican

Party in the mid and late twentieth century through terms of racial resentment, a Manichean storyline of "who hates who," white producerism, and
rebranded class politics—away from the image of the party of the rich to the
party of the working and middle class.[66] The Silent Majority posed a virtuous
middle in opposition to civil rights activists, Nixon praising the former in
his 1968 campaign as the "non shouters" and "the non demonstrators."[67] As
Lowndes explains, although Nixon won by a landslide in 1972, having pulled
in white Southerners, urban ethnics, union members, and others from the
Democratic coalition, Watergate prevented Nixon from cementing this
Silent Majority.[68] Ongoing tensions in the GOP between populism and economic conservatism and George H. W. Bush's elite associations put the GOP
coalition under strain and left elements of the Silent Majority ripe for recom-
bination in 1992. It was into this fray that Buchanan issued his white populist
appeals, with his symbolic incorporation at the RNC performing a kind of
party reconciliation.

As a speechwriter for Nixon, Buchanan was in fact one of the rhetorical
architects of the Silent Majority.[69] It was through the terms of this identification that Buchanan built the Buchanan Brigades, and it was a modified
version of this narrative (because he could not that evening bash Republican
elites) that structured his RNC appeal. In a decidedly producerist imaginary, the virtuous middle is imagined to suffer between (northeastern) establishment elites above and a "mob" of campus radicals, "criminals" (coded
as Black), and immigrants from below.[70] In Buchanan's RNC speech, the
Clintons, Al Gore, and delegates of the Democratic National Convention
were figured as the snobby elites out of touch with this virtuous middle
(on the campaign trail he included Bush and other Republican elites in this
group), while the "mob" in Los Angeles, the "homosexuals," and those that
would consume the "raw sewage of pornography" constituted the specter of
a criminal underclass.

Buchanan's nostalgic appeal reverberates in Donald Trump's 2016 call
to "make America great again" (MAGA). A revivalist nationalist slogan
with roots in Reagan's 1980 appeal "let's make America great again" and
Buchanan's "make America first again," MAGA pulls upon the mythic and
the real—summoning on the one hand a fictitious industrial heyday when
("deserving") Americans were purportedly better off economically, just
as it simultaneously traffics an explicit desire to return to an *actual* time of
legal segregation and a time before the women's movement of the 1960s and
1970s.[71] In this latter sense, MAGA beckons a return "to that era, *as it actually*

existed, with its racist and sexist hierarchies wholly intact."[72] MAGA's nostalgic grotesque is packaged within familiar white supremacist appeals and calls to violence, with a misogynistic bluster that steers far from any reference to childhood unless it is to call opponents "pathetic babies."[73]

Buchanan's speech also reveals the ways the alchemy of demonological and intimate appeals to white kinship is distinctly gendered and racialized, with the feminized sentimentality of nostalgia—including images of home, childhood, and precarity—sandwiched between masculinized calls to a cultural war; first in a crusade against effeminized Democrats; and lastly in a crusade for "law and order" in Los Angeles. Buchanan cannot forfeit the register of nostalgia because it does critical work in summoning people affectively into his *we*, but to protect his (and his listeners') image of white masculinity, he must package that nostalgia within calls for war.

Identification Against

Invoking the Los Angeles rebellion through the specter of "the mob," Buchanan called in the latest version of a long-standing and defining national discourse about "irrational" and "pathological" Black political action.[74] In Buchanan's description, the Los Angeles rebellion was rendered wanton, senseless, monstrous, perverse, maniacal, and unstoppable by anything other than the threat of death. In the backdrop of his references to the Los Angeles rebellion was the war on drugs and related discourses through which white America imagined the city as a racialized space of riot and violence.

Partly, Buchanan did not have to name "the mob" as Black because in national discourse, the Los Angeles rebellions were already thoroughly saturated with tropes of Black criminality and framed as "riots." And partly he could not do so, in the sense that the terms of political discourse in the early 1990s made it somewhat of a political liability to explicitly name race.[75] In the increasingly coded rhetoric that was a hallmark of the culture wars, liberal multiculturalism, and racialized antistatism of the 1980s and 1990s, the language of "culture" was firmly substituted as a proxy for race.[76] Across his speech, Buchanan articulated many of the terms of the culture wars that would be waged across the next decade. A year prior to the RNC, Buchanan himself had been at the fringes of what Kimberlé Crenshaw and Gary Peller have described as a broad national outrage or a wide congruence of interpretation, on some level, after the video of the LAPD's beating of Rodney

King was broadcast on national television.[77] At that moment, the moderate white Right was increasingly defining itself against explicit white suprema-cist discourse. As Crenshaw and Peller explain, open condemnation of the beating gave more moderate conservatives an opportunity to perform an op-position to clear-cut racism and thereby make claims that their opposition to affirmative action was not linked to issues of racist ideology.[78] In contrast, Buchanan invoked the rebellion to fasten an anti-Black populist animus to an anti-immigrant animus as he ratcheted up his nativist appeals on the campaign trail that summer. Following the lead of Daniel Stein at American Immigration Reform and following the lead of Sam Francis, he blamed immigrants and Black people for the civil unrest.[79] By the time of his RNC speech, however, he was using more coded language.

Buchanan's inclusion of Korean Americans as members of a political *we* can be read as an attempt to manage national discourses about the Los Angeles rebellion and to brandish long-standing political rhetoric of "Black criminality" within contemporary terms of acceptable coded language. The *we* of the larger speech was, in a way, made more securely white with its ges-tural incorporation of a 1990s multiculturalist rhetoric that traded in anti-Blackness and the tentative and conditional inclusion of an Asian-American/immigrant *other* whose belonging was contingent on their performance of the "family values *we* treasure" (emphasis added), their resolute commit-ment to the American dream, and, most importantly, their vulnerability to "the mob."[80] Written for a "contentious electorate unable to understand itself in any terms other than race" as Toni Morrison has put it, the speech was all the more saturated by race in its un-naming of race.[81]

Reading Buchanan's speech at the Houston Astrodome today, it is haunted by another rupture in U.S. race politics: Hurricane Katrina and its aftermath. While George H. W. Bush was president during the Los Angeles uprising, his son would be president at the time of Katrina and preside over the catastrophic failures in federal response. In the first weeks of September 2005, the Houston Astrodome housed 25,000 evacuees.[82] The dome floor was filled with thousands of cots, and the large scoreboard flashed messages from families seeking news of their loved ones—a digital record of displace-ment, loss, and efforts to find one's kin. There is a stark contrast between Buchanan's *us* inside the Astrodome in 1992—defined largely through identifying *against* Black people—and representations of the Black post-Katrina *them* in the Astrodome thirteen years later. In Buchanan's terms of friend/enemy, the events are almost photographic negatives of each other.

After touring the dome with her husband on a campaign to ameliorate criticism of the federal response to the hurricane, Barbara Bush explained notoriously in an interview that "what I am hearing, which is sort of scary, is they all want to stay in Texas. . . . And so many of the people in the arena here, you know, were underprivileged anyway, so this is working very well for them."[83] Drawing on long-standing tropes of anti-Black racism, Bush's comment transmogrifies evacuees into a *them* that is parasitic, miserable, and unwelcome, just as she positions (white) Texans as the true victims and Houston as a city in danger of being overrun. Here, again, representations of Black people in the white imagination work through transforming a scene of dispossession, displacement, survival, and the impacts of structural racism into a fantasy lexicon of Black criminality and narratives of white martyrdom and white vulnerability.

Political Failure

In political science, one of the few places where political identification is reckoned with as a dynamic site of political contestation is in the area of party identification, tracked by scholars through questions about party affiliation, issue framing, and changing voting patterns. Part of the story of this chapter, though, is that when cracked open, primaries, elections, and bids to call people into political parties are about so much more than party identification per se. The primaries leading up to the RNC and the RNC events themselves, for example, were animated by competing claims about American national identity, about the possibilities of race and gender justice or the entrenchment of racial and gender domination, about people's imagined obligations to each other across lines of race and class, and about how to remember the past or envision the future. These are all attempts or bids—and those that do not "win" nonetheless often live on in longer-reaching chains of articulation.

When asked in 2013 if he thought he was on the "wrong side of history" in the context of the fight for marriage equality, Buchanan laughed, apparently unoffended, affirming, "I *am* on the wrong side of history! I don't mind being a loser. Look, if you looked at my career, I don't mind being a loser."[84] Buchanan's bids for the GOP nomination in the 1990s were dramatic electoral failures. Not winning a single primary on the 1992 campaign trail, Buchanan refused to pull out of the election until the very end despite pressure from the GOP.[85] Buchanan ran for the GOP nomination again in 1996, and then ran with the Reform party in 2000. Electoral loss was not the same as "failure" in Buchanan's understanding of politics and change. In a 2017 interview about the groundwork his own campaigns laid for Donald Trump and the rise of white populist nationalism in the 2016 election, Buchanan explained, without regret, that "the ideas made it. But I didn't."[86]

In the case of his 1992 run for the GOP nomination, Buchanan's formal political loss was not, in terms of identificatory appeals, a total failure. Buchanan's task at the 1992 RNC was partly to reorient his followers—to draw people into identification with a Republican Party led by Bush—but his appeals would also work to shape the meaning/agendas of conservative identifications. As noted earlier, Buchanan had demanded the promise of a primetime slot at the RNC in negotiations with the Bush campaign for his endorsement.[87] Buchanan used the RNC speech together with his campaign trail speeches to advance a political vision. This is why winning the Republican nomination itself was not, in his mind, the sole purpose of his campaign. Rather, he understood himself in that campaign and in subsequent campaigns to be engaged in a struggle over conservative forms of identification—he was in a fight over what it meant to be conservative in the post-Reagan era.[88] Buchanan's failure at winning the nomination, followed by his incorporation at the end of the GOP primaries, provides a kind of foundation for the GOP's performed redemption—in rejecting and absorbing Buchanan, the Republican base could unashamedly embrace the virtue of white masculinist producerism.[89]

In a 1996 essay, Samuel Francis bemoaned that Buchanan did not risk an even greater electoral loss for the sake of advancing his political visions.[90] He critiqued Buchanan for diluting his political position by conceding to the GOP and endorsing their candidates. Francis would have far preferred Buchanan to suffer an even more fantastic electoral defeat rather than dilute or compromise his radical positions. Buchanan's time, Francis insisted, had not yet come, but without standing by his most radical messages, its arrival would only be stalled. Buchanan's and Francis' accounts articulate some of the ways in which the power of political appeals to identification is not confined to whether those appeals enjoy immediate uptake. Instead, political actors make attempts—and they may well know that they will likely lose the formal political bid (e.g., in an election, initiative, or referendum) but have in mind a longer timeline, knowing that over time what may seem to be unwinnable bids can coalesce into a new "common sense," a new (racialized and gendered) political order.

4

"Igniting the Kindred"

Southerners On New Ground's Family Values

> We vision a world where the triple shift factory worker and the drag
> queen at the bar down the block see their lives as connected and are
> working together for liberation.
>
> —Southerners On New Ground

In the fall of 2011, a coalition of grassroots organizations anchored by
Southerners On New Ground (SONG) joined a statewide campaign against
North Carolina's Amendment One, a proposed state constitutional amendment that would prohibit the recognition of same-sex marriages and civil
unions. SONG leadership was reluctant to enter the fight—seeing other
campaigns as building better wins and meeting wider needs of LGBTQ
people at the intersection of racial, economic, and gender justice[1]—and yet,
as then-co-director Caitlin Breedlove explained, SONG found that in North
Carolina this "was the fight our people were in."[2] On May 8, 2012, the polls
came in at 60 to 40 in favor of the amendment, leaving the coalition in a spe-
cious defeat. Later that day, SONG prepared and circulated a response in
the form of a three-minute film, "The Day After Amendment One . . . OUR
WIN IS BIGGER!" in which they flipped their political loss into a political
win. In the short film, a bright beat pulses in the background and a single
SONG organizer at a time speaks, standing on a city street that is lush with
green foliage. Each speaker testifies to the significance of so many North
Carolinians having come out to claim their LGBTQ neighbors and community members during the course of the campaign.[3] At the end of the clip,
SONG's then-senior strategist Kai Lumumba Barrow claims the campaign's
enormous win in advancing a statewide as well as national dialogue beyond

If We Were Kin. Lisa Beard, Oxford University Press: © Oxford University Press 2023.
DOI: 10.1093/oso/9780197517338.003.0006

"gay rights" and advancing a multi-issue queer politics that drew people across lines of difference into an understanding of shared liberation. Barrow points into the camera and directly addressed the architects and supporters of the Amendment One campaign: "You know what? This amendment *made that possible, helped that process,* so THANK *YOU.*" While the electoral defeat was certainly felt by organizers, the film is important because it signals how SONG conceptualized the campaign itself, as being not only—or even primarily—about the vote but also about the forms of identification forged through the fight. SONG lost the electoral campaign, but they had secured, by their account, a larger kind of win.

SONG had been founded almost twenty years earlier, in 1993, as a two-fold intervention: first, into the increasingly elite, white, and assimilatory tone that was consolidating under the growing nonprofitization of national LGBTQ politics and, second, as a challenge to anti-LGBTQ organizing by the Christian Right, especially in communities of color and rural communities. Centrally, SONG insisted on the co-constituted relationship of LGBTQ liberation and racial, gender, and economic justice while resisting competing political projects that would split Black and LGBTQ, immigrant and LGBTQ, rural and LGBTQ, or working-class and LGBTQ forms of political identification. SONG also was founded as a distinctly southern organization, self-consciously anchored in a place shaped by histories of slavery and genocide as well as the long civil rights movement and traditions of resistance. Today, SONG has a membership base of approximately 1,300 people,[4] works across twelve states in local and regional campaigns in the U.S. South, and is nationally involved in the Movement for Black Lives and immigrant justice organizing.

Since SONG's inception, organizers have drawn heavily on themes of intimacy in their identificatory appeals—especially through their use of kinship language (e.g., language of familia, family, and kin) and in their language of "our people"—which they credit to Ella Baker. SONG organizers conceptualize the group as a southern "kinship organization" in a fight for "beloved community" against rural abandonment, homophobia, transphobia, ableism, gender and racial violence, and against the use of the South as a "testing ground" for right wing campaigns.[5] They have conceived their vision against the conservative "family values" politics of the 1990s (which reach into the contemporary moment), and against the normative family ideals that have dominated marriage equality politics in the early twenty-first century. SONG, as Ruth Wilson Gilmore has put it, has "renovate[d]" themes of kinship and "[made them] critical."[6]

In this chapter, I read excerpts of oral histories and original interviews with SONG co-founders and recent leaders alongside selections from SONG's writings and political education materials in order to examine how SONG conceptualizes what is at stake in their work to shape forms of political identification. I demonstrate not only that SONG organizers invoke the concept I call *boundness* in their appeals but also how critical the concept of boundness is to advancing a multi-issue queer politics of shared liberation. Identificatory projects such as those by Sylvia Rivera and STAR (chapter 1), Black Lives Matter activists (chapter 3), and SONG never operate in isolation but respond to and intervene in a wider political landscape—including, in SONG's case, a landscape shaped by the Right's identity politics emblematic in Buchanan's 1992 culture wars speech (see Interlude). SONG's archive brings this field of political contestation into sharp relief. When SONG organizers describe being in a multidecade "struggle over the Soul of the LGBTQ movement," they are articulating a fight over the ethical and emotional orientations of LGBTQ forms of political identification and the shape of the politics contained therein.[7]

LGBTQ politics have been the crucible in which many of the terms of U.S. politics have been forged. Whether in the ways that homonationalism, as Jasbir Puar explains, has been mobilized in justifications of U.S. foreign policy, militarism, and Islamophobia; in debates about the need for an expanded or smaller role for government vis-à-vis bodily integrity and reproductive justice; in the suturing of rights and healthcare access to marriage status; or in the use of gayness as what Roderick Ferguson has called an "alibi" for housing dispossession and the racialization of urban space, LGBTQ politics has been a cipher for both progress and incorporation.[8] The wild swings in national politics over how to manage and contain what is, as Mattilda Bernstein Sycamore puts it, "revolting" about LGBTQ politics drive so many of the political debates of our time.[9] The fact that dominant LGBTQ politics have, in Cedric Robinson's words, "smuggled in" the logic of assimilation and the ethos of respectability and have traded away the most radical components of the movement has not been lost on LGBTQ grassroots organizations that have origins and goals in antagonism with the neoliberal management of the post–civil rights era.[10] When contemporary SONG organizers describe that in the early 1990s SONG was "founded to ignite The Kindred to fight the right wing" they invoke in singularly prophetic terms a latent and potent political community awaiting activation, and yet the body of their work attests to the labor that goes into hailing and mobilizing that community.[11] In this chapter, then, I both track the emergence and salience of conceptualizations of boundness in SONG's organizing and demonstrate how boundness is operationalized in the mutual articulation of political imaginaries between SONG members and the movements that SONG co-creates as part of a community of mutual aid.

"Igniting the Kindred"

In 2007, SONG began explicitly issuing identificatory appeals through a kinship framework at the same time that it began its work rebuilding its base and shifting to becoming a membership organization. SONG leaders often cite the regional experiences of Hurricane Katrina as having a deep impact on their organizing strategy. In the wake of Katrina, as organizers watched the state turn its back on the region, co-founder Suzanne Pharr asked SONG, "What would we have wanted to have in place when Katrina had hit?"[12] SONG leaders resolved to prioritize building a large regional network of well-trained organizers who had strong political relationships. They began building up their base through listening campaigns, organizing schools, and in-person recruitment across the region.[13]

Since that time, *kinship* as a rubric for shared identification appears in SONG lexicon as "kin," "fam," "familia," and "beloveds." In 2007, the two new co-directors, Paulina Helm-Hernández and Caitlin Breedlove, used the phrase "Igniting the Kindred" within a logo that featured a heart surrounded by flames, with the bold shading of a woodcut print and a form that evokes the tin heart pendants, *milagros*, offered to patron saints in many Mexican cities and appearing in Chicanx cultural production in the United States (Figure 4.1).[14] The flames and the language of "igniting" presents SONG's kinship not as domesticated but as having a fiery charge. SONG's 2010 tagline built on these themes of kinship by drawing on the language of home—"Building a Political Home Across Race, Class, Culture, Gender & Sexuality."[15]

"The Kindred" is an articulation of how people are related to each other as a political family. It is a narrative of belonging against the ways in which queer people have been pushed out of families, places of worship, and communities of origin, and it is a narrative of belonging against the devaluation of Black

Figure 4.1 SONG logo in "Igniting the Kindred: A National Council Convenes to Work on the SONG Organizing School," 2007. Courtesy of Southerners On New Ground.

and Brown lives, poor people's lives, rural lives, southerners' lives, and queer and trans lives. SONG's shared identifications assert value and recognition— not from the state but from each other. SONG announces that its people are valued, cherished, and worthy of political action.[16]

In a 2014 interview, Serena Sebring, who at the time was SONG's North Carolina field organizer, discussed the affective and ideological work achieved through SONG's notion of political kinship. She explained how important it has been to her and others to have SONG as a family, because so many queer people are

cast out or separated from our families of origin, or at least feel unsupported by them in living our lives. And so to have a set of people that say "yes, we are family" . . . it's that it's a shared condition is important. I think also it's a political term. I think about the way the state and the Right sort and discard families that don't meet particular definitions—to say "here's one that's bigger than you *ever* imagined, with more people than you could *ever* sit around your dining room table at Thanksgiving. We'll be understanding our relationships to each other in spite of and outside of whatever your definition is"—is very political.[17]

Sebring first names an experience of exclusion from families of origin and a yearning for belonging and recognition. But instead of turning toward the state to remedy this loss (i.e., in a form of identification *with* and desire for the state[18]), SONG creates conditions for and forges practices of turning toward each other. This is an important departure from mainstream LGBTQ politics, which in the 1990s increasingly pursued state recognition and acknowledgment. In radical queer and trans critiques of mainstream state-focused goals—ranging from the incorporation of LGBTQ people into the military, marriage politics, family law (adoption), and hate crime legislation—these aims are challenged as forms of incorporation that are a part of state reproduction.[19]

To read SONG's kinship politics carefully requires distinction between, on the one hand, the pursuit of legal or state recognition, and, on the other hand, a politics of mutual or self-recognition that explicitly does *not* turn to the state.[20] In recent decades, scholars and activists have explained how state-recognition politics make social movements easy to co-opt and incorporate and have demonstrated how state recognition is twinned with forms of destruction.[21] Here, however, I want to bring back in a different account or genealogy of recognition that is about mutuality. This is the kind of recognition that Ruth Wilson Gilmore references when she insists that "organizing is always constrained by recognition," meaning that organizing is constrained by whether people can recognize and identify with each other and with a political agenda in some way.[22] This kind of recognition is a matter of political identification or the processes through which people, as Gilmore puts it, "contingently produce their individual and collective selves."[23]

In Sebring's account cited above, SONG's primary system of receiving recognition is a form of self-recognition, from *within* its constituency. These recognition politics are hyper local, regional, and relational. It is not that SONG organizers don't engage the state at local or national levels (they do make demands on the state)—but they do not go to the state for a sense of belonging (as I show later in this chapter, they sometimes hail state agents, but it is through a more intimate politics that attempts to summon shifts in identification). In the second half of the passage, Sebring shifts to a different voice and speaks directly *to* the state and to the Right. "In spite of and outside of" how the state and the Right define valid relationships, valid family structures, and who is worthy of connection and care, Sebring declares that SONG's family will be in relationship to each other *as a political act*. It is worth noting that SONG's kinship practices have powerful resonances with STAR's recognition politics. Even as Marsha P. Johnson and Sylvia Rivera made demands on the state to change pressing conditions of disposability and premature death—from frontline activism for Intro 475 to protesting in front of the Albany State House for the repeal of anti-gay legislation and to demand housing and employment protections—STAR's daily praxis of community care was not animated by a longing for state incorporation.[24]

To be sure, it is a complicated move for SONG to invoke familial language in their work, given the history of how family has been leveraged as a rhetorical and ideological tool and how, as Tiffany Lethabo King has put it, as an "institution and episteme," family has functioned as a foundation of social hierarchy and an organizing logic of control and state power.[25] There is an extensive literature that attests to these dangers. Particularly important for this study on identificatory appeals, Patricia Hill Collins, Duchess Harris, and others have shown how family as a *political idea* works to naturalize and depoliticize social relationships within a hierarchy, how it is marshalled in expressions of racialized state power, and how groups avowedly fighting for racial and gender justice have often used familial discourse in ways that uphold intragroup hierarchies.[26] A look at feminist movement history makes this readily apparent, including where white feminists' invocations of sisterhood belied their own failures to be in sustained and substantive antiracist (and cross-class) solidarities.[27] Women of color feminists have also challenged deployments of familial language in Black, Chicano, and other nationalist movements where that language has obscured and upheld gendered and sexual hierarchies.[28]

To be clear, the question in this chapter is not a normative one about whether familial language *should* be harnessed as a political vocabulary; it is instead a question of how this language works within intimate appeals and what it reveals about the registers through which people come into forms of identification. Rather than a politics organized around expanding the definitions of *family* in the eyes of the law, SONG reworks complicated themes of family and even marriage to summon people into alternative political visions. For SONG, family works as an intragroup vocabulary, a language of political appeal and mutual recognition.

Part of what becomes apparent is that familial language is quite potent for organizing people. Collins suggests that it is worth seeing if the idea of family may be "reclaim[ed]"—"recast" in intersectional terms "in ways that do not reproduce inequality"—and used for feminist and racial justice projects.[29] Richard Rodríguez excavates queer Chicana/o/x reformulations of *la familia* as a site of resistance to racial and economic discrimination and heteropatriarchal kinship formations.[30] Ruth Wilson Gilmore recounts that when she asks students what forms of power-difference couplings are not structured by vulnerability to premature death (as racism is), her students always suggest "family"; and while, Gilmore explains, "we debate how and why different kinds of contemporary families are structured as they are, and to what extent patriarchy is still a family rather than state affair" and "how the concept of family defines normative sexuality, there's something in the answer to work with."[31] As Gilmore explains, in the context of capitalism, divisions between home/work and private/public constitute the normative limits to particular kinds of conflict, and political breaches in those limits generate new possibilities for social movements.[32] When SONG activists experiment with the political use of kinship, they work at this juncture.

Against national discourses on the Right (e.g., family values) and nationalist discourses of LGBTQ movement politics (e.g., marriage equality politics), SONG renovates and redeploys notions of *family* as a renewed and reignited political concept for feminist and antiracist LGBTQ movement work. This is to say that the Right does not get to have exclusive hold over meanings of family. Family as a site of meaning making is ground that is not ceded.

One of the ways in which SONG repurposes and, as José Muñoz puts it, "critical[ly] recycl[es]" themes of family to forge forms of political identification is through their radical family narratives rooted in social movement history.[33] SONG continuously lifts up "radical lineages"[34] of movement elders, including Bayard Rustin, Audre Lorde, Stonewall activists, Leslie Feinberg, the Combahee River Collective, Kitchen Table Press, Street Transvestite Action Revolutionaries (STAR), and Ella Baker. Movement ancestors and loved ones are highlighted in SONG's convenings (e.g., Queer South Revival, Gaycation, Out South, and Bayard Rustin Retreats), their deaths are mourned in SONG writings, and their memory is called in on altars at SONG gatherings (Figure 4.2).[35] SONG's list of movement ancestors represents

Figure 4.2 Altar at Queer South Revival, 2018. Photograph by Stef Bernal-Martinez. Courtesy of Southerners On New Ground.

individuals and collectives dedicated to multi-issue movement work—these are intersectional practitioners who were theorizing the concept before intersectional theory was named as such. These lineage narratives fortify SONG's own multi-issue activist commitments and claim a line through movement history in which LGBTQ people who are poor and working class, immigrant, people of color, and/or rural have been erased or distorted.[36] SONG co-founders and senior strategists have been on staff into the 2010s and have maintained—on into the current moment—a strong presence in SONG retreats, political education programs, oral history projects, celebrations, member group organizing, and direct action campaigns (Figures 4.3 and 4.4).[37] Part of SONG's power lies in these ties across multiple generations of SONG leadership, which works as a kind of raft across the last part of the twentieth century and the first part of the twenty-first century, sustaining and transporting critical movement technologies and multi-issue frameworks *through* a time of the professionalization of nonprofits, the narrowing of LGBTQ movement formations into single-issue refrains, and the splicing of economic and race politics in movement analyses.[38]

In SONG, kinship as a political concept is also saturated with regional nuance and meaning. Kinship, especially as a Black and southern legacy of

Figure 4.3 SONG co-founders and recent co-directors at Southerners On New Ground 25 Year Celebration Reception, Creating Change conference, January 25, 2018. *Left to right:* Mandy Carter, Roberto Tijerina, Paulina Helm-Hernández, Caitlin Breedlove, Mab Segrest, Mary Hooks, Pam McMichael, and Pat Hussain. Photograph by Angela Hill. Courtesy of Southerners On New Ground.

survival and resistance, does not exclusively signify blood-level relationships but invokes intimate networks of othermothers, adoptive families, outlawed connections, and webs of mutuality and care. As former SONG membership director Kate Shapiro explained, SONG's identity as a kinship organization is often unintelligible to organizations outside of the region or to funders, but SONG "know[s] a lot about kinship networks—that's how we've gotten this far! That's how we've been fighting white supremacy for generations. We didn't invent this . . . we do shit differently here because we have a different set of conditions and a different sort of legacy that we can draw on."[39] In fact, the temporality of fighting "for generations" is not happenstance, because these particular articulations of boundness are designed to be organized, like kinship networks, as going on in time and space across and far beyond (both in the future and past) the lifetimes of individual members or activists. SONG understands *kinship* to be capacious enough to account for many ways of being connected without reproducing property relations.[40] SONG's

Figure 4.4 Suzanne Pharr, Pat Hussain, and Mandy Carter (speaking) at SONG's Out South convening, December 6, 2014. Courtesy of Southerners On New Ground.

identification as a kinship organization also intervenes in the split between (depoliticized and homonormative) "social" and (impersonal) "political" LGBTQ spaces.[41]

SONG repurposes kinship language in ways that pull on and rework national discourses of marriage equality politics. In the wake of multiple federal court decisions in 2013–2014, SONG has explicitly claimed gay marriage as a win—insisting, as Serena Sebring put it, that the victory "does not belong to white gay men alone," and affirming that the marriage victory is a testament to organizing by many queer people of color and rural people.[42] SONG accounts for and acknowledges how marriage equality wins have meant some concrete protections for many of their people. But SONG activists do not rest on that laurel as though the win announces equality; instead, they pivot toward the ongoing state violence faced by people of color and challenge LGBTQ people across the U.S. with the charge that "we cannot pretend this is the final win."[43] Importantly, SONG's 2013 statement to their membership base in the wake of the overturn of DOMA and Proposition 8 issued such a political articulation. SONG named recent Supreme Court rulings (impacting affirmative action, the Voting Rights Act, and the Indian Child Welfare Act) as having made many of our lives worse; insisted that "we still have so much work to do together as LGBTQ people"; and invited people to "join us in Marrying the Movement until every LGBTQ person has full dignity, safety, and liberation."[44]

The second part of their statement was a one-and-a-half-minute video, *Marry the Movement*, which was covered in *Colorlines, HuffPost,* and *The Nation*.[45] In the video, SONG repurposes marriage as a concept and proposes that people "marry the movement"—that they pledge themselves with a deep, abiding, and lived commitment to social justice movement work. The film features SONG members and co-founders dressing up for a commitment ceremony (tying bowties, buttoning shirts, styling hair, putting on earrings, helping each other with makeup) and talking and laughing with each other. The audio text layers music and voices of SONG members completing the statement, "I'm married to a movement that..." with descriptions of the kind of movement they will commit their lives to. The movement they outline is one that "fights for a world where every queer and trans kid goes to a school which treasures them and validates their existence," that "fights for every LGBTQ person to have good food to eat and a safe place to sleep," and where "I can love across language and borders." It is a movement that "ties your freedom to my freedom."

The camera turns to a bowl of rings, with hands reaching in one at a time to pick one out (Figure 4.5). Instead of wedding rings representing a singular

Figure 4.5 Still from *Marry the Movement,* 2013. Produced by Southerners On New Ground, directed by Sowj Kudva. Courtesy of Southerners On New Ground.

moment of romantic practice that binds one person to one person, SONG's bowl of rings is a reminder of and a call for plural and ever-expanding ethical relationships.

SONG uses a critically reappropriated image of gay marriage as a tool to hail people to identify with a multi-issue LGBTQ movement rather than with state recognition. Marriage is a potent and saturated metaphor for LGBTQ politics in this era, one that carries, for many LGBTQ people, a powerful affective charge of celebration and victory. SONG critically reworks the tropes and iconography of gay marriage to renegotiate national debates about the role of state recognition in LGBTQ politics. SONG organizers are not aiming to reconcile those critiques, but to reorient the meaning of marriage equality campaigns as a warm-up for more expansive campaigns in the future, and to leverage a statement about movement-building that centers multi-issue LGBTQ politics.

LGBTQ Identification and Disavowal

In a 2014 interview, Caitlin Breedlove explained that today "we're looking at a time in history where more people are out in this country . . . than ever before, and yet it's a real question how those people will be politicized."[46] That is, the broader political impact of increasing numbers of people who are out as LGBTQ cannot be certain because the political commitments of LGBTQ identifications are not fixed. What will be their political priorities, their orientations of care and obligation? What will those identifications mean to adherents and, taken collectively, what will that mean for the intersection of LGBTQ politics with race, gender, class, and transnational politics?

The political meaning of LGBTQ forms of identification has been a central target of SONG's work since its inception in 1993. The kernel for SONG took shape that year at the Creating Change conference, an annual LGBTQ conference organized by the National Gay and Lesbian Taskforce (NGLTF). There had been several disruptions to business as usual for the conference that year. For one thing, it was the first time the conference was held in the U.S. South. Many attendees from outside the region balked at the prospect of traveling to the South (organizers received phone queries about whether there were airports and roads in the region) and to North Carolina in particular, where the white nationalist Republican Senator Jesse Helms had just been re-elected for his fourth term in office. The 1993 conference was also the first year Creating Change held a preconference workshop on race, class, and gender. Intersectional and transnational analyses were centered in conference keynotes by Urvashi Vaid and Mab Segrest who focused on the very matters (NAFTA, welfare, deindustrialization, white supremacy) that were being so earnestly disavowed by many NGLTF members.[47] SONG co-founder Suzanne Pharr explained that these multiple disruptions "caused great upset, particularly among guys, who were walking around saying 'What the hell does this have to do with my gay freedom?' "[48] SONG co-founder Pat Hussain described white gay people storming out of the plenary, cussing and complaining, "I can't believe I wasted my money coming here!"[49] Pharr reflected:

> We knew it was a problem before we went in, but we really recognized it then, after there was so much controversy: how badly we needed to get people off single-identity politics, at least in the South, and to get LGBT people to take on race, class, and gender, in addition to LBGTQ identity. And we saw that was not all that was needed. We needed to get the historic civil rights organizations to take on homophobia as well.[50]

At the time, national LGBTQ politics were becoming increasingly professionalized and articulated through white and middle-class terms, with same-sex marriage rising as the central campaign.[51] In this moment in the early 1990s—with the AIDS crisis in full swing; anti-gay state ballot initiatives recently rolled out in Oregon and Colorado; the downsizing of state assistance through demonological tropes of "welfare queens";[52] widening gaps in wealth and wage equality; and attacks by the New Right that framed Black people, gay people, feminists, and non-Christians as endangering "the soul of America"—the meaning of "gay politics" was up for debate: *What does it mean to be gay in this moment? What politics is an LGBTQ identity connected to and beholden to?*

Mandy Carter, Pat Hussain, Pam McMichael, Mab Segrest, and Suzanne Pharr all attended the conference—leading workshops as a part of a Fight the Right Organizing Intensive and a Southern Organizing Intensive conference track—and they recruited Joan Garner soon after the conference. They founded SONG in January 1994, with Pat Hussain and Pam McMichael as the first two co-directors and the other four co-founders forming the original board.[53] The co-founders each came to SONG with extensive backgrounds in racial, economic, and gender justice organizing at local, regional, national, and transnational levels. A group of three Black women and three white women who were out as lesbians or dykes, the co-founders identified their political commitments as grounded in Black feminist theory and the grassroots movement theory and history of southern freedom struggles.[54] Combined, the co-founders held an extraordinary level of expertise as the foundation from which they built their collective political analysis and strategy. Their organizing backgrounds and political orientations were the very ground on which they developed SONG's political visions and their calls into a politics that would hold together antiviolence organizing, anti-Klan work, economic justice organizing, anti-imperialism, regional and national LGBTQ and antiracist feminist organizing, and lesbian feminist cultural production. Concerned about the rise of single-issue politics and the serious pushback they were witnessing against multi-issue politics, the co-founders came together and created SONG to respond to the political moment.

SONG began building their organization with a deliberate sense of pacing. Pat Hussain explained that she approached SONG's founding with the philosophy that "some things we need to do so urgently that we need to slow down. You can't have a first meeting again. Once you've had that first meeting, and everyone in the room is white, and/or male . . . there's no backing up from that. The table has been set, and everyone else is a guest. Not an author. Not a founder. A guest."[55] SONG's core leadership reflected and modeled the relationship-building that the co-founders thought was needed both in the region and on a larger scale in multi-issue political organizing.[56] Hussain and McMichael explained to their membership base that "in looking to shift the way we work together, SONG is staffed by an inter-racial team of co-directors and also has an inter-racial board. This is no easy task. We trip over barriers that are centuries old and learn how to keep moving forward."[57] In an interview, Hussain explained that even though she had "done work" and Pam had "done work,"

> that's a whole different thing from having to talk to someone of a different race every day concerning work and working out strategies and who's going to do what, when, and how. . . . We hit bumps in the road. It became a teaching moment. First, learning for us, and then teaching. That if we, as people who had been around the block a time or two, cannot find our way through what just happened, or didn't happen, then . . . where's the hope that it can ever happen? We learned to live with discomfort. How to move into it, and then through it. And it became a part of the model . . . don't back

away from the conversation. Maybe you decide not to have it right then, maybe you do, but not to ignore things that come up. And see where you are, to approach it honestly but not to [back] away.[58]

Hussain theorizes "learn[ing] to live with discomfort" as a model that does not seek, necessarily, to find resolution but cultivates a capaciousness for being in relationship through conflict. Co-directorship meant a daily practice of negotiation, especially given the organization's tiny size in its early years (with just the two co-directors as paid staff).

At the time of SONG's founding, the U.S. South was being wracked by what the founders called the "divide and conquer" politics of the Right. They were especially concerned with the conceptual division being produced on a national level between LGBTQ and Black politics and about the ways economic restructuring was impacting the U.S. South and the Global South. The founders developed what they called a "dual injection strategy" to push LGBTQ organizations to take on issues of race and economic justice and to push historic civil rights organizations like the Highlander Center and the Center for Democratic Renewal to take on LGBTQ issues.

In the early 1990s, right-wing Christian groups produced two films, *Gay Rights, Special Rights: Inside the Homosexual Agenda (GRSR)* and *The Gay Agenda: The Report*. The Traditional Values Coalition produced and sold thousands of copies nationally and sent free copies to all members of Congress and to Black churches especially in cities poised to pass anti-gay ballot initiatives.[59] *GRSR* argued that to grant LGBTQ people rights would undo the protections of the 1964 Civil Rights Act; and the film featured Black, Latina/o, and Asian American people rendered as spokespeople describing LGBTQ people as pathological, sinning, and ontologically separate from communities of color.[60] Mandy Carter documented the white conservative Christian funding behind campaigns to screen *GRSR* in Black churches to "recruit" and "court" people of color to vote for anti-gay ballot measures.[61] In a countermobilization against these films and against related campaigns by the Christian Right, one of SONG's first campaigns involved traveling widely to lead discussions in Black churches with the teaching documentary *All God's Children*, which features African American community members, pastors, and leaders claiming LGBTQ people as family and as belonging to their communities.

SONG also labored from the beginning to articulate LGBTQ politics as bound to transnational and regional questions about the economy in the context of increased deregulation, a shrinking social safety net, and racialized and class-charged scapegoating. Social theorists have noted how the divide that appeared in the 1980s that conceptually separated economics/ class from race/gender/sexual politics became more entrenched in the 1990s, but SONG leaders worked hard to maintain a connection between the two in their organizing.[62] One of SONG's earliest actions was to join the Immigrant Workers Freedom Rides—intentionally choosing, as Mandy Carter put it, something "that wasn't just about being gay" to broaden the scope of the politics that "count" as gay politics.[63] In the mid-1990s, SONG developed a participatory and popular education workshop on the economy and traveled widely across the South to offer the workshops (see Figure 4.6).[64] In 1996, SONG took a delegation of conference attendees from the Creating Change conference in San Diego to Tijuana, Mexico, for a political education workshop that included meeting with factory workers to learn about NAFTA, factory working conditions, and border politics.[65]

In these and other campaigns across the 1990s, the SONG founders deliberately set out to shape what racial and economic politics were contained within LGBTQ identifications.[66] This unheeded history is critical as an alternative lineage of organizing that resisted state pressure to structure the nonprofit system around extra-economic forms of identity and that was simultaneously internationalist and rooted in a U.S. southern context.[67] This lineage demonstrates how boundness may be enacted through the very conceptualization and practice of movement work. SONG has refused to leave out economics or to parse out forms of identity in their appeals, insisting on the boundness of what have so often been articulated as separate "sectors" in activist work, and advancing an account of mutually constituted liberation.

"Our People Are Worth the Risks"

Although "kinship" as a frame was not introduced until 2007, SONG has invoked the language of "our people" from its earliest work into the contemporary moment. In a 1994 essay published in the feminist journal *The Sojourner,* Suzanne Pharr invoked this language to intervene in dominant interpretations of a conflict in Ovett, Mississippi, where a women's retreat center, Sister Spirit, had received death threats and had found their property vandalized after local Baptist ministers learned that the center was owned by lesbians.[68] Framed, as Pharr described, as "the dykes against the

Figure 4.6 Workshop Flyer, "The Economy and Lesbigaytrans Liberation," 1996. Courtesy of Southerners On New Ground.

bigots," the conflict gained national attention—the attorney general sent in federal mediators and the event was covered by Oprah Winfrey, *20/20*, and Larry King. In her essay, Pharr explains that "as a lesbian, I have strong identification with the women of Sister Spirit, and as a woman from a low-income rural Southern family, I identify with the working-class people who make up Ovett. They are both my people."[69] Here, Pharr performs her own political identifications with the lesbians at Sister Spirit and with her own family as a claim against the split identifications presented in national discourse, suturing together the very groups being depicted as mutually exclusive.

Twenty years later, in its intensified immigrant justice organizing in the early 2010s, SONG used the framing "Our People Are Worth the Risks."[70] In July 2014, after a year of actions in collaboration with #Not1More and direct action at ICE detention centers, SONG authored a letter to the Congressional LGBTQ+ Equality Caucus signed by twenty-six organizations outlining a series of demands for queer and trans undocumented people and deportation detainees and for the separation of ICE from local law enforcement.[71] SONG also collaborated with the Los Angeles–based organization "Familia: Trans Queer Liberation Movement" to stage a sit-in in the caucus office in Washington, DC to pressure caucus members to attend to the demands of the letter. While national LGBTQ politics were fixated on marriage equality, the previous two years had witnessed historically unprecedented levels of immigrant deportations, building up after two decades of heightened border militarization and the escalated criminalization of immigrants.

On first blush, the caucus sit-in could be understood as a tactic for winning short-term political demands. However, interviews with participants reveal that the sit-in also functioned as a series of identificatory appeals and as a challenge to the presumption that LGBTQ politics are about marriage equality but not about immigrant justice. The sit-in illuminates the multiplicity of identificatory appeals at work in one place and time as well as the triangulations actors use to map relationships across differences in power.

Of the six queer and trans activists participating in the sit-in, two members of the group had U.S. citizenship status and four did not. Additional SONG and Familia staff and members were present to lead negotiations with the caucus, video and photo document the sit-in, and provide other support. The direct action participants sat in the caucus lobby, loudly singing Spanish translations of classic civil rights movement songs.

Serena Sebring, SONG's North Carolina field organizer, was among these six sit-in activists. Sebring, who identifies as a queer Black feminist mother, organizer, activist, and educator, described her relationship to her fellow direct action participants and explained her identificatory appeal to the congressional representatives: "I was there in this kind of anchor role, like: I'm a U.S. citizen . . . so these Congresspeople *know* that's their job to represent me. And so from that positionality to be able to say: '*These are my people*, and you need to listen to *them*.'" Sebring recounted that she entered the action ready to confront the caucus representatives, explaining that she was prepared for arrest and that there was

> nothing that [the police/security] could do that would make me turn around and that is maybe singular in my life in terms of a moment . . . outside of the law, unbound by it, unbound by what we're "supposed" to do . . . to say "I just *won't* be moved—you will *have to* listen to me, you will *have to* recognize that"—they were LGBT folks also—"so, you will *have to* recognize our connection because I won't let you forget it."[72]

In this passage, Sebring offers an account of the triangulation of identificatory claims and appeals that articulates in certain ways with Sylvia Rivera's triangulation between the park and the prison in chapter 1. This triangulation is a practice of using one's own location as an intermediary space from which to call people with more power into a reoriented identification and a shift in their sense of responsibility. In these triangulated appeals, the claimant herself embodies the suture between, in Rivera's case for example, the brothers and sisters in jail and the brothers and sisters in the park—with Rivera herself as the messenger. More than the messenger, though, Rivera performs the embodiment and boundness of the two positions she attempts to suture as she stands in the park, testifying to experiences of imprisonment and police violence. While Rivera did not use the nation or U.S. citizenship in her 1973 appeal, Sebring begins by staking a position that is spatial and political in relationship to the congressional representatives, first as a documented citizen of the United States. From this political position, Sebring claims identification with her fellow direct action participants who are undocumented and asserts her connection and responsibility to them as "[her] people." Sebring then stakes a second basis of identification for the congressional representatives, summoning the representatives into recognizing a mutual connection as LGBTQ people. Different than Rivera's call, then, Sebring's multivalent appeal is issued in a two-part form, and it is within the shell of her call as a citizen/constituent that she issues a second call as a queer person in a way that attempts to circumvent and change the very terms of their formal relationship—to go from being a citizen enacting a sit-in to being queer kin reminding others of their connection. Sebring's countercall is issued within the casing of a partly sanctioned call (sanctioned as an appeal by constituents to their representatives but unsanctioned in its form as a sit-in). In contrast with these two registers of relationship—one legal, and one as a form of boundness—she articulates her connection to her fellow sit-in activists at a single register. Sebring calls the Congressional Equality Caucus representatives to recognize the people in the sit-in as "their people," and to take political action from *that* orientation.

The sit-in also transformed Sebring's relationship with the other direct action participants. Sebring describes being "the receiver of some relational organizing at the sit-in" by an activist from Familia

> who I had not met before and who is a monolingual Spanish speaker and I'm a monolingual English speaker—she was in solitary confinement and had suffered tremendous hardship and violence in her home country, Mexico, before she came here, but I didn't know any of that. Five hours into the sit-in, [she] decided she wanted to tell me her story, . . . and Salem, who's also on [SONG] staff, is an interpreter. So, she just leaned in, caught my eyes and . . . unloaded this history of the past three years of her life. Horrible trajectories of violence, state violence, isolation, and then coming to this country where she'd only been for a few months and was already organizing—she wasn't even an organizer where she was before. Understanding the story with her looking in my eyes and Salem's interpretation made it impossible for me to do anything other than understand her as my people, understand her as part of what I'm responsible for . . . to make that relationship really clear . . . I was *sure* organized by [her] that day, I will *not* forget it.[73]

Just as Sebring was appealing to the Equality Caucus representatives, she explained that she was being "organized by" her fellow activist; she was being called into a kind of identification rooted in responsibility for each other's safety, well-being, and liberation. Five hours into the sit-in, in a loud and charged space (Paulina Helm-Hernández leading negotiations with the Congressional Equality Caucus while nearby congressional offices were threatening to phone the police), the fellow activist leaned in and shared her account with Sebring. In Sebring's telling, the testimony was not autobiographical as an isolated narrative—but was, as Sebring heard it, an identificatory appeal that established their relationship moving forward. In the midst of a multiplicity of affective registers and identificatory projects at work in the one space, this appeal functioned to build a political relationship across what Sebring noted were differences in language, racial and gender identity, immigration history, and citizenship.

The formal outcome celebrated on SONG's website was the letter they secured the next day from the Equality Caucus written to President Obama. The letter became the official archive of these historic events, marking the outcome as a win in the realm of representational politics, but a review of interview accounts sheds light on a different register that shows the action was also about producing transformed political actors who have transformed relationships. It is this objective—a shift in identification, a shift in understanding self and relationship to others—that is less legible or measurable than securing a letter to the president but is nonetheless central to SONG's identification politics.

Earlier that year, SONG issued a "Coming Out of Exile" statement to their membership base, articulating SONG's choice to take an active role in #Not1More campaigns. Unlike most LGBTQ organizations in the late twentieth century, SONG had from the time of their founding understood immigrant justice politics to be central to LGBTQ politics. While their contemporary work builds on this legacy, they must rearticulate their commitment to multi-issue work against the tide of single-issue politics, within the contemporary context and with new membership. To connect their historical LGBTQ work to contemporary immigrant justice organizing, SONG explained in their statement that that

> Lesbian, Gay, Bisexual, Trans and Queer people understand a good deal about being pushed into the shadows to suffer and die because of who we are and where we sit in any given moment of political history. We know what it is like to long to be reunited with our loved ones, and we know what it is like to live in fear as we walk down the street. While our realities can be different, the hounding, caging and exiling of immigrant people is either our reality because *we are* LGBTQ undocumented people or because it reverberates with the homophobia and transphobia that haunts our lives.[74]

As Shana Redmond has explained, because of the ways gestures of equivalency erase and displace critical particularities, it is a complicated claim to say that one experience of being in the shadows can be used as a resource to understand another experience of being in the shadows—but I suggest that SONG's appeal must be read within the larger archive of their work that lifts up and attends to those critical particularities.[75] Here, SONG navigates the complex task of invoking embodied experiences to map lines of boundness across different but related structures of violence. SONG offers an account of "the shadows" as linked sites of disposability, fear, isolation, and vulnerability, and asserts a *we* that encompasses SONG members with different social identities and social locations, who together "know" fear in public spaces. Their statement maps constellations of yearnings—invoking experiences of being estranged from families/communities of origin due to homophobia, transphobia, economic precarity, transnational migration, and deportation. This yearning is presented not as an equivalency but as a potential resource for SONG members who are not immigrants to identify with people who have been separated from families or communities of origin through transnational migration, deportations, and border militarization.[76] In the next part of the statement, SONG explains that the #Not1More campaign has "captured the hearts" of SONG's members and leadership, and that this is not surprising given the campaign's Shutdown ICE actions, its unrelenting prioritization of undocumented people, and its *"coming out spirit."* SONG condemns the nearly two million deportations under the Obama administration, using familial language to reread the statistic: "This number does not represent two million anonymous or hypothetical lives, but two million of ourselves, our family members, and our people" or two million "precious loved one[s]."

Third Space and World-Making Work

In 2016, SONG announced their desire to acquire an acre of rural land in the South as a sanctuary and a place "to gather, to regroup, to dream and scheme, to touch the earth and clay and water, to pray, to experiment."[77] In this era dominated by new modes of digital organizing, being together in person remains central to SONG's practices of identification and political organizing.

In their early years and today, SONG gatherings can be understood as sites of what Deborah Gould calls "collective world-making"—spaces where participants interact and "produce sentiments, ideas, values, and practices that manifest and encourage new modes of being."[78] As "world-making" projects, SONG convenings are sites where group identification is produced, enacted, embodied, practiced, and negotiated. In the 1990s, co-founders very deliberately set up the conditions for world-making as integral to the organization's methodology and visionary practices. In an early article, Hussain and McMichael reflected that in pulling together participants for SONG gatherings they would "pay specific attention to the composition of the group in terms of race, class, gender and geography so that our group reflects the diversity of communities and does not contribute to the isolation of individuals who could feel tokenized."[79]

Social movement scholars understand movements to be sites where identities are constructed, negotiated, and performed in social practice.[80] Actors in a movement space can produce "figured worlds," or assemblages of socially produced and culturally organized activities through which people create new understandings and sensibilities about themselves and others.[81] Figured worlds are potent sites in which to forge and incubate new identifications. Debra Minkoff argues that especially in cases of geographic and social isolation, organizations can play an important role in convening people and facilitating collective identification.[82] SONG convenings are a place to build and practice identifications.

SONG's 2014 Gaycation retreat—its annual membership retreat—is an example of SONG's world-making projects. That year, SONG convened more than one hundred members from across the region at a rustic Girl Scout camp outside of Savannah, Georgia.[83] People traveled from Virginia, Louisiana, North and South Carolina, Mississippi, Alabama, Florida, and Kentucky to attend. Their weekend events included an elder's storycircle in which SONG elders told stories of political organizing and movement work; a political-music history dance party curated and emceed by Pat Hussain; a membership meeting where participants filled out a large map of the South with notes on state-based issues and action campaigns; and breakout groups to discuss SONG's base building and regional anticriminalization and immigrant justice campaigns. Additional events included a water balloon fight, a twerking competition, and workshops led by SONG members on topics including planning a contingent for the 50th anniversary Selma march, talking about "Sex in the South," and learning how to make screen prints. The common room was decorated with large paper lanterns, rainbow-colored *papel picado* banners, an altar, SONG swag, musical instruments, and brightly colored tablecloths. Members were warmly addressed as "SONG fam" and "dangerous homosexuals." New SONG members became acquainted with longerterm members over meals, during dish shifts, in icebreaker games, and in facilitated political conversations.

SONG's world-making work is often embodied/in person (as in convenings like Gaycation but also at the annual Bayard Rustin Retreat, OutSouth, protests, or the physical space of the SONG office), and it is also a project tied to political imagination. In their organizing schools beginning in 2009, SONG has explicitly used a concept of "third space," which they credit to Black revolutionary thinkers and Xicana and Indigenous writers and organizers and which they introduced for many years using Patrisia Gonzalez's poem "Dreaming of Guatemala."[84] SONG defines the third space in relationship to first and second space:

> We live externally in the first space: the space of capitalism, the space of McDonalds, the space of trade and stealing within this country. As activists, we often also live in the second space: the space of resisting and pushing back on oppression—the space where we do anti-racist work, anti-sexist work—the space where we oppose something. The third space is the space of creation, invention, innovation, and birth. It is the space where we dream a new world, with new words that are shaky on our tongues. It is an exhilarating and scary space. Some would liken it to standing on the edge of a great cliff. It is easier to not go to this space, but we believe it is the space that we need to survive.[85]

What distinguishes the second space and third space is defined less by tactics, as might be presumed, than by a kind of political orientation. The second space is defined by an opposition-based politic in which activists focus their work *against* racism, sexism, homophobia, and economic injustice. As an orientation, the third space looks toward an unknown but transformed world. It dreams beyond "present reality and reaction" toward a space of possibility.[86] The task is to dream, invent, and bring this new world into being. SONG's third-space work *defines* their second-space work such that SONG comes to second-space work from a place of vision.[87] The third space also incubates the forms and practices of identification used in political work—SONG's articulations of boundness and kinship appeals are third-space inventions.

The concept of third space has shaped and animated SONG's organizing schools since SONG's rebirth in the early 2000s. In addition to curriculum on social movements, direct action organizing, and participatory democracy, SONG political education programming has drawn on dance, art, music, and magical realist poetry in their political imagination practices in order to develop organizing strategies.[88] SONG's account of third space has resonances with Lani Guinier's, Gerald Torres', and Derrick Bell's use of magical realism to cultivate an expansive political imagination around racial identification and the possibilities of social transformation; Gloria Anzaldúa's "kneading" into being a new story of the world and new maps of relationality; Robin D. G. Kelley's account of the Black radical imagination and his insistence that the significance of freedom dreams—the desires and hopes of people who have fought for change—far exceeds the dismissive evaluation of whether movements "succeeded" in realizing their visions; José Muñoz's account of queer futurities; and political imagination practices and world making embedded in Afrofuturistic literary production.[89]

SONG conceptualizes its work as traveling between and working within both second and third spaces—as in their contemporary Black Mamas Bail Out Actions to free Black mothers and caregivers from prison, a project pursued from within a longer-term vision of prison abolition.[90] For SONG, the Black Mamas Bail Out Actions lie within a tradition established by ancestors of "buying each other's freedom." SONG calls people into an opportunity to free each other; to take up the collective responsibility to free Black mothers; to enter a long-term fight to end money bail, abolish modern systems of bondage, and build alternatives to policing; and to be bold and unapologetic in advancing a pro-Black agenda. SONG thus enacts the second-space work of fighting to end money bail with a third-space approach. They create physical spaces of beauty (with flowers, banners, and welcoming committees) for Bail Out Action sites, they orient present action in a "mandate set forth by our ancestors," and they build a *we* that is skilled up in abolitionist praxis (see Figure 4.7).[91]

"To Multiply Political Preoccupations"

SONG lies within a lineage of political thought and organizing that troubles dominant historiographies of racial justice in the late twentieth century. As Roderick Ferguson explains, what gets obscured in the dominant narrative of the fragmentation and co-optation of racial justice movements in the 1970s and 1980s into the early 1990s is the burgeoning rearticulation of antiracist

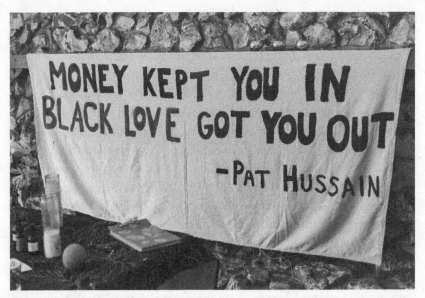

Figure 4.7 Banner, Gaycation, 2019. Photograph by Emily Metzguer. Courtesy of Southerners On New Ground.

politics by Black feminist and other women of color and queer of color organizations. With the emergence of women of color feminisms, the very definition of antiracist politics expanded, using, as Ferguson puts it, "racialized gender and racialized sexuality to multiply political preoccupations" and to "broaden political identifications." The "universe of antiracist opposition" grew to hold issues of domestic violence, nuclear proliferation, welfare rights, rape prevention, childcare, labor exploitation, apartheid, war, environmental justice, reproductive justice, and lesbian feminism, among many other issues. Indeed, one of the signature features of antiracist articulations during that period is how deliberately women and lesbians of color pushed the boundaries of what counted as race-based politics.[92] So rather than "fragmentation," this rearticulation generated vibrant sites of action for antiracist politics.

In their regional, internationalist, and multi-issue movement work, SONG's collaborations with other organizations far exceed dominant conceptualizations of coalition as limited-term collaborations based on a "coincidence of interests."[93] Their work illuminates deeper registers of appeals to identification and their long-game work of forging the meanings of forms of political identification. To be clear, even when groups forge more limited-term, transactional, or what María Lugones calls "epistemically shallow" coalitions, that story, too, is far more about political identification than dominant accounts allow.[94] It is just that in those formations, actors may be issuing more siloed ideas of identity and interests. They are practicing a different kind of politics of identification, issuing more narrow ideas of who constitutes the *we,* what are their interests, and on what basis they will work with others.

Part of what becomes clear in SONG's archive is that the endeavor to shape identifications is itself a political project, one that exceeds dominant notions of political campaigns (e.g., winning an election, passing legislation, or increasing representation). In their campaigns against prevailing forms and emergent boundaries of political identification—especially against identificatory appeals issued by the Far Right, within mainstream LGBTQ politics, and within historic civil rights organizations—SONG has staged interventions both from *within* claims to community (as in claiming relationship with Equality Caucus representatives) and from the *outside* in clear positions of political enmity (as in their work fighting the Christian Right). Through intimate appeals, they have attempted to rescale vertical relationships of power into horizontal ones, have fought competing projects that would produce disidentifications between LGBTQ and Black or immigrant politics, and have summoned into mutual identification people who might, in other articulations, be figured as disparate and disconnected. Within its membership base and in ways that reach far outward, SONG constructs a form of shared identification that centers specific relationships to contemporary and historical racial and economic violence while advancing an account of mutually constituted freedom.

Conclusion

"Remember That Feeling Because It's the Same Cage"

Appeals to Boundness

> Racism operates by constructing impassable symbolic boundaries
> between racially constituted categories, and its typically binary
> system of representation constantly marks and attempts to fix and
> naturalize the difference between belongingness and otherness.
>
> —Stuart Hall, "New Ethnicities"

The day after Barack Obama issued his November 2014 Executive Actions
on Immigration, which created a ranking system to prioritize deportation
actions and expanded DACA, Not1More Deportation campaign director
Marisa Franco appealed to the immigrant justice community to resist the
terms of the president's pledge to target and deport "felons, not families."[1]
Over the previous year, #Not1More had become a hub of cultural and legisla-
tive organizing against the criminalization, incarceration, and deportation of
immigrants. In her statement, Franco argued that the framework of "felons
not families" must be challenged because when political leaders talk about
"felons," "they are talking about people who are part of our community, and
part of our family." She refused Obama's positioning of "felons" as the source
of social problems. But she also critiqued the criminal justice system itself,
refusing to allow contemporary conditions of mass incarceration to "settle"
into the backdrop and exposing the carceral system as a structuring feature
of our political, social, and economic world.

Franco appealed to forms of resistant identification rooted within a
larger political movement and its organizing practices—including work by
#Not1More, SONG, and Familia. In issuing this kinship appeal in the wake
of the executive actions, Franco intervened in a process by which value is

If We Were Kin. Lisa Beard, Oxford University Press. © Oxford University Press 2023.
DOI: 10.1093/oso/9780197517338.003.0007

granted to some immigrants through criminalizing others. She maintained a claim on political community against logics of racialized carcerality, disposability, and assimilation. In the United States, as Lisa Cacho explains, social value is articulated against the rightlessness and social death of criminalized people.[2] In this system of relative value and disposability, marginalized communities are recruited to participate in each other's devaluation and to identify with the state, with whiteness, and with power. In order to gain certain political wins, the broader immigrant rights movement is summoned to disidentify with those immigrants and nonimmigrants who are incarcerated or have criminal records.[3] In a speech the previous summer at the Not1More Deportation March in Washington, DC, Franco had envisioned the day when the movement would win their campaign against deportations, telling the audience, as one listener recalled it, that "*when* we win, I want you all to remember what it feels like in your heart to have your people in deportation, in detention centers, and in deportation proceedings."[4] She then asked people to think about people in prison and jails and to "remember that feeling because it's the same cage." Looking forward in time to when they would win their fight—when concerns about state violence may be resolved for some people— Franco anticipated and tried to preempt a forgetting. She attempted to avert the pattern in which a community, upon gaining a measure of political power or protection, turns to defend or ignore state violence against others.

Five months later, #Not1More issued two statements in solidarity with the Baltimore uprising that pushed back against immigrant and Latinx disidentifications with Black protestors in the wake of Freddie Gray's murder. At the time, mainstream news coverage of the uprising pathologized and roundly condemned Black protestors, displacing attention from Gray's death and fixating, in a haunted arithmetic, on property damage.[5] In one of the statements, Franco explained that "people do what we need to do to survive. We cross borders and police lines," and she marked that "the second guessing of tactics combined with the silence coming from the immigrant rights community and Latino community is noted and must change."[6] Part of her intervention was into a longer political history of immigrant disidentifications with Blackness and the construction of immigrant belonging "on the backs of Blacks" and through a "lesson of racial estrangement," as Toni Morrison elucidates.[7] In explaining that "we cross borders and police lines," Franco pairs border crossings and public forms of demonstration as strategies for survival and freedom—the necessity of both produced by oppressive conditions, and both involving risk of physical danger, incarceration, assault, and death—and she proposes that this pairing offers a mutual legibility against dominant political narratives. Her calls reverberated through the Letters for Black Lives project—an open letters project initiated by Asian Americans and Asian Canadians and also penned from within Dakota, Latinx, Russian, Nepali, and Hmong communities—in which activists issued through familial claims (e.g., "Querida Familia," or "Dear Family") a series of intergenerational interpretive bids to identify with rather than against the contemporary Movement for Black Lives.[8] Their bids hinge immigrant or Indigenous liberation historically and contemporaneously to Black freedom struggles.

Franco's statements are, together with the primary appeals studied in this book, a part of a larger archive of intimate appeals issued "against the grain of power," to borrow María Lugones' phrase.[9] Franco reads the executive action and the Baltimore uprising in a practice of what Lugones calls "witnessing faithfully and . . . conveying meaning against the oppressive grain," a practice of interpretation that moves one "to act in collision with common sense, with oppression."[10] These appeals are multidirectional, traversing horizontally and vertically. They call people not into tactical orientations but into reoriented relationships. Identificatory appeals are interpretive political acts. I conclude *If We Were Kin* by exploring the fantasies that bracket certain patterns in the study of political identification and then reflecting on what is at stake in appeals to boundness and the freedom dreams called forth in intimate appeals.

Fantasies of Identification

A deep tension in political identifications is that their production is both constrained and constructed. To drop either of these features from theoretical and empirical analyses poses significant problems. On the one hand, when forms of identification are thought to be a "given"—fully constrained or predetermined—we are left with overly mechanistic accounts of politics, including explanatory narratives about "backlash" as well as the interest group framework that in many ways underpins the discipline of political science.[11] What gets evacuated in these accounts is the contingency and indeterminacy of the political world, the enormous and ongoing labor invested in fights over identification, and, most importantly, the possibility of rearranging structures of power.

On the other hand, an idea that identification is totally up for grabs—that its constructedness makes it available to rework in any way, by anyone, with total freedom from the past—is a fantasy that fails to account for the durability of whiteness, for example, or the structural inheritances of any given political moment, or the constraints of appeals issued against pulls of assimilation. What gets lost here is that the cognizability, reception, and uptake of appeals and practices of identification are constricted by ideological norms and material history. As seen in Sylvia Rivera's fight to get to the stage (chapter 1), multiple meanings of identification are not competing on even ground—certain interpretations have more historical, institutional, and ideological backing.

Ultimately, identifications and disidentifications are not, as dominant accounts would tell us, foregone conclusions or "natural" discords. They are not discrete, fixed, or arranged in a permanent constellation, describable with concrete and reliable tags to track and quantify. Nor are forms of identification completely floating, unconstrained or unencumbered by historical foundations. They are simultaneously moored to historical formations and they are unstable.[12] The study of identificatory appeals requires careful attention to the relationship between the contingency/malleability and the constraints of the field of appeals and the ways appeals are issued within and across institutionalized hierarchies of power.

Within and against these constraints, political actors like Rivera, Hansberry, Baldwin, and SONG organizers exploit the instability of forms of identification and work (through language, organizing, and performance) to forge forms of identification. They call out to their interlocutors, summoning them as the subjects they want them to be. Many actors, like Baldwin and Rivera, do not present their appeals as proposals. They instead invoke forms of identification as a point of fact, invoking them as already in existence but disavowed, distorted, or forgotten. Others—like Ella Baker asking, "Who are your people?" and María Lugones asking, "Who are our own people?"—issue their appeals in a pedagogy that points to ways in which we might consciously choose and take responsibility for our identifications.[13]

As Franco's appeals mark, questions of identification are critical to the ethical and political imperatives raised by conditions of racialized violence and premature death. Certain practices of identifications themselves are part of the fabric of what produces, sustains, and institutionalizes racialized and gendered violence. These identifications and disidentifications work through what Lugones calls "arrogant perception" within a context in which racial violence constitutes the moral landscape of whiteness and the nation.[14]

As a site of study, political identification beckons us to explore the *we* of politics in ways that defy dominant accounts of "interests," resist ideas of stable groups, challenge conceptualizations of coalition as a "confederation of discrete formations,"[15] exceed party politics, and track something that is related to but ultimately different than solidarity.[16] In these sites of conflict, it is not discrete groups that are "failing" or "succeeding" in solidarity or coalition. Instead, the meanings and boundaries of specific identifications themselves and the relationships of those "groups" are being constantly negotiated, rearticulated, and reconfigured. Identificatory appeals ask and answer the question of how people imagine themselves politically in relationship to each other, and what political visions flow from there. These appeals contain mandates—signaling what kinds of politics one is beholden to ("this is who 'we' are and so this is what we should do"). Identificatory appeals are performative political acts with political implications that are both epistemic and material.

Appeals to Boundness

As Stuart Hall explains in this chapter's epigraph, "racism operates by constructing impassable symbolic boundaries between racially constituted categories." This book has explored the contestations of and calls to boundness across these boundaries. These calls reconfigure rubrics of "belongingness and difference." They are not calls for a kind of coalition that would maintain notions of discrete groups but instead are appeals to deeper forms of identification, meant to produce transformed subjects who have transformed relationships. What is at stake in this politics of boundness is a rejection of the atomization of social/political life that is produced through white supremacist ideology and its codification in and through political institutions. Partly, boundness is enunciated through an account of how conditions of violence are co-constituted across racial (and gendered, classed, and colonial) lines. We can hear this, for example in Patrisse Cullors' narrative of eating dinner as a young person at her classmate's home in Sherman Oaks where she and her friend's father realized that they knew each other, or that he knew Cullors' mother—that he was actually her family's "slum lord . . . the very same man who allowed my family to subsist without a working refrigerator for the better part of a year."[17] Cullors plumbs the encounter to theorize the relationship between wealthy and white Sherman Oaks and her own neighborhood of Van Nuys. She theorizes the hyperpolicing aimed to prevent any "spillover of us, the others, the *dark* others" into Sherman Oaks from neighboring communities, explaining that

> [w]e, our poverty and our music and our different foods and our reminders that they, the residents of our pretty adjacent neighborhood, were wealthy only at our expense, could not seep into the neat white world of Sherman Oaks. Of course that's not what they said, that they didn't want to be reminded of what it took to keep themselves rich.[18]

The very conditions that enabled her friend's family dinners in Sherman Oaks—including her friend's father taking (having) the time to ask Cullors about her day and her dreams—was likewise constituted by the impossibility of family dinners in Cullors' own home, where her mother worked three, sometimes four, jobs and could never be home in the evenings. We can hear echoes here of Elsa Barkley Brown's insistence that

> [m]iddle-class white women's lives are not just different from working-class white, Black, and Latina women's lives. . . . middle-class women live the lives they do precisely because working-class women live the lives they do. White women and women of color not only live different lives but white women live the lives they do in large part because women of color live the ones they do.[19]

Barkley Brown insists that to look at difference is not enough, but we must grapple with the "relational nature" of difference.[20] In appeals to boundness, these relationships become part of the substrate for constructing the ethical orientations of forms of identification.

An account of the co-constitution of conditions of violence can be heard in Audre Lorde's question of "who labors to make the bread we waste";[21] in Frederick Douglass hearing the wailing of enslaved people within the "national, tumultuous joy" of the Fourth of July;[22] or in Sylvia Rivera's account that gay liberation is *constituted by* her and other street queens' activism, political visions, and their absorption of state violence. It is in Melanie Yazzie's reflection that as Native and Black communities have worked to reveal the violence that upholds the U.S. nation-state, what has become clear is that "even though we're racialized in very different ways, the ways that power works and how the violence works on our bodies and in our communities is always related and co-constituted with these other structures of power and other ways that power operates."[23] In ways that exceed the boundaries of the human and that travel across continents and time, such an account is in W. E. B. Du Bois' testimony of the ivory trade—his being able to see and hear the murder of a mother elephant "far away over miles and years," in imperial London, where men played the *Moonlight Sonata* on "lovely keys chipped from her curving tusks"—keys that were covered in blood and emanated the shrieks of her pain and her death.[24] The blood on the keys was unseen by "the society darling" or "the great artist," and Du Bois reminds his reader that this violence is gratuitous, that "neither for the keys nor the music was the death of the elephant actually necessary"—but *these* are the kind of keys that are coveted and that constitute the daily fabric and soundscape of bourgeois and elite imperial life.[25]

An account of boundness and shared freedom is in June Jordan's memory of bringing one of her college students to help another in a moment of great danger. One had survived alcoholism in her family, and the other was currently in danger from her partner's alcoholism, and Jordan writes about walking behind them down the hall at the end of their visit, watching the young Irish woman and the young South African woman "hugging each other, and whispering and sure of each other" with the felt sense that "it was not who they were but what they both know and what they were both preparing to do about what they know," Jordan writes, "that was going to make them both free at last."[26]

Appeals to boundness advance an account of "freedom with," and they aim to shape political subjectivity at a deep level. This "freedom with" entails responsibility to the past, to each other's freedom, and to ending conditions of violence that are configured as being *far away* even as they may be as close as Sherman Oaks and Van Nuys—or as close, as Baldwin says, as Birmingham and Los Angeles, which is to say there is "not one step" between them. Boundness—as a kind of mutuality, as a way of understanding emotional and ethical responsibility, and as a way of understanding political inheritances (how, as James Baldwin has put it, "we carry [history] within us"[27]) is deeply at odds with western individualized ideas of negative freedom, ideas of self-interest, linear time, the cordoning-off of places, and other practices of disavowal. In a form of interpretive violence, appeals to boundness are often misheard and distorted as an oversimplified dissent rather than as calls to-ward reoriented relationality.[28]

How are identificatory imaginaries generated and brought into being? The appeals issued in this book by Rivera, Baldwin, Hansberry, Horne, Yancey, Jones, and SONG are resistant and imaginative. Their interventions contain descriptive accounts of the disavowals embedded in white racial identity, American national identity, gay assimilation politics, and incorporative forms of identification within immigrant rights movements. Simultaneously, their appeals deeply reconceptualize the boundaries between self, the world, and people's connections to each other.

If what Robin D. G. Kelley calls "freedom dreams" contain visions of what the world could look like and *feel* like, if they contain ideas of how we could move and be, one key part of those dreams concerns how we may be in political relationship with each other.[29] The appeals centered in this book generate and call people into sharing an idea of what freedom is—and herein lies the intimacy of the calls. In doing so, these appeals open political space—they open horizons of emancipation, transformative webs of belonging, and new terrains of politics.

Notes

Introduction

1. Ella Baker in Barbara Ransby, "Quilting a Movement: Real Movements for Social Change Need Many Grassroots Leaders—Not One Charismatic Politician," *In These Times*, April 4, 2011; and Ransby, *Ella Baker and the Black Freedom Movement*, 27.
2. Baldwin, "On Being White . . . and Other Lies," in *The Cross of Redemption*, 169. In this way, the identification he invokes fundamentally requires a risk or "dying" of the former self, as Ernesto Martínez has put it. See Martínez, "Dying to Know," 783.
3. Tarso Luís Ramos, correspondence, April 15, 2021.
4. Tarso Luís Ramos, Keynote address, Rural Organizing Project, Madras, Oregon, June 3, 2017.
5. On the rise in these kinds of organizations, see Hardisty, *Mobilizing Resentment*; Pharr, *In the Time of the Right*; Zeskind, *Blood and Politics*; and Chacón and Davis, *No One is Illegal*.
6. See Lowndes, "Response to Shane Hamilton's Review," 380; HoSang, *Racial Propositions*, 12; and Hall, "Who Needs Identity?," 441. In political science, political identity is typically harnessed as a category of analysis to ask questions about political mobilization, state recognition of identity groups, how political behavior works as a function of identity, or about the implications of "identity-based movements" for democratic politics.
7. Hattam and Lowndes, "The Ground Beneath Our Feet," 204; Hattam, *In the Shadow of Race*, 2–3.
8. Brennan, "Essence Against Identity," 94; Koné, "Transnational Sex Worker Organizing in Latin America," 96; Hall, "Who Needs Identity?," 16–17; and Hattam and Lowndes, "The Ground Beneath Our Feet," 204.
9. Hall, "New Ethnicities," 41.
10. Gilmore, "Forgotten Places and the Seeds of Grassroots Planning," 42.
11. Hall, "New Ethnicities," 441; Gilmore, "Forgotten Places," 43–44.
12. Gilmore, "You Have Dislodged a Boulder," 12, 24, 26.
13. Gilmore, "Forgotten Places," 55.
14. Brennan, "Essence Against Identity," 94.
15. Hooker, *Race and the Politics of Solidarity*, 33.
16. See Baldwin, "On Being White . . . and Other Lies" and Menzel, "Generations of White Women's Violence Stop Here." White racial identity is constituted through the construction and exclusion of a racialized other—but as Devon Carbado explains, this exclusion functions as a type of inclusion within a national racial order. See Carbado, "Racial Naturalization," 637. As I discuss in chapter 2, the boundaries of

racial difference were made (and are remade) through physical/sexual violence as well as through policing affective bonds and identification. See Sharpe, *Monstrous Intimacies,* 3; and Stoler, *Haunted by Empire,* 13. See Jasmine Syedullah and Rae Leiner's account of care work in liberation organizing in the context of converging global crisis in their article, "Take a Moment to Ask Yourself, If This Is How We Fall Apart?," 25–26.

17. Lugones, *Pilgrimages/Peregrinajes,* 143; Hames-García, *Identity Complex,* 22.

18. In *Pilgrimages/Peregrinajes,* Lugones anchors her theorizations of deep coalitions in women of color feminist philosophy, understanding Audre Lorde as the preeminent theorist of coalition (p. 30).

19. DiPietro et al., *Speaking Face to Face,* 3.

20. Lorde, *Sister Outsider,* 139.

21. Hong, *Death Beyond Disavowal,* 5, 77.

22. See Michael Hames-García's discussion of Lugones' question in *Identity Complex,* 34. See Shana Redmond on "identification with" sliding into "identification *as*" in a series of "violent displacements" ("As Though It Were Our Own," 20, 24–25, 31–32); and see Saidiya Hartman on white abolitionist identifications that substituted the self for the other (*Scenes of Subjection,* 19–20).

23. As I explain in chapter 1, the converse of identification is disidentification as a kind of disavowal, or a process in which people turn away from and refuse identification with others. This is different than disidentification in the Muñozian sense, which I explore further in the next chapter.

24. Brennan, "Essence Against Identity," 94; Beltrán, *The Trouble with Unity,* 168; Hall, "Who Needs Identity?" 16.

25. Rogers, "David Walker and the Political Power of the Appeal," 213; and Woodly, *The Politics of Common Sense,* 10, 13.

26. See Lani Guinier and Gerald Torres on interpellation and the making of racialized subjects in *The Miner's Canary,* 87–88.

27. Hall, "Who Needs Identity?," 19 (first italics added to quotation); Beltrán, *The Trouble with Unity,* 80. Forms of political identification are forged through articulation, or a process of making a unity of different elements that are not necessarily connected. What appears to be a "unity" of discourse or identity is really the articulation of distinct elements that could be rearticulated in alternative ways. See Hall cited in Slack, "The Theory and Method of Articulation," 115.

28. Collins, "Like One of the Family," 5.

29. King, "Black 'Feminisms' and Pessimism," 70; Collins, "Like One of the Family," 5; Stoler, *Haunted by Empire,* 2, 4, 13–14; Burlein, *Lift High the Cross,* 109, fn99; McClintock, *Imperial Leather,* 357; Yamin, *American Marriage,* 85–91; and Rodríguez, *Next of Kin.* My thinking is also indebted to Khanum Shaikh's theorization of intimate geographies and power in her essay "Intimate Critique."

30. Threadcraft, *Intimate Justice,* xi; Sharpe, *Monstrous Intimacies,* 3; Collins, "Like One of the Family," 12; and Stoler, *Haunted by Empire,* 2–3.

31. Collins, "Like One of the Family," 5. See also Kathi Weeks, "Down with Love: Feminist Critique and the New Ideologies of Work," Verso blog, February 13, 2018.

32. Berlant, *The Queen of America*, 3–5, and Berlant, "Intimacy: A Special Issue," 283. Other scholars have demonstrated how the intimate sphere of sexual, reproductive, and household relations functions as a site of empire and domination. See Stoler, *Haunted by Empire*; Shah, *Stranger Intimacy*; Pascoe, *What Comes Naturally*; and Lowe, *Intimacies of the Four Continents*, 198–199, fn55. See Lowe on the colonial history and political economy that has constituted the conditions for liberal notions of the intimate sphere, 57. On political appeals to love in the public realm, see Maxwell, "Queer/Love/Bird Extinction," 684–685.

33. In chapters 1, 2, and 4, actors invoke kinship in particular as a political idea that contains entailments of how one ought to be treated. I thank Melvin Rogers and Alaí Reyes-Santos for engaging on this point. See Reyes-Santos, *Our Caribbean Kin*, 2–3, 6. See also Beltrán on the rhetorical use of *hermanidad* in Latinx social movements as signaling a kind of unalienated belonging and recognition. Beltrán, *The Trouble with Unity*, 77–79.

34. Shana Redmond, discussion, December 1, 2016.

35. This includes work in the field of political theory. For challenges to the naturalism of this approach, see Beltrán, *The Trouble with Unity*, 162–164; Hall, *The Hard Road to Renewal*, 111; Lowndes, *From the New Deal to the New Right*, 157; and Mathiowetz, *Appeals to Interest*, Introduction.

36. Beltrán, *The Trouble with Unity*, 162–164.

37. Black feminist scholarship on linked fate complicates this narrative—see Cohen's account of a "qualified linked fate" (in which the needs of Black LGBTQ people and Black people living with AIDS and HIV are not seen as representative of "Black interests") in *Boundaries of Blackness*, xi; Simien, "Race, Gender, and Linked Fate," 529–550; and Lopez Bunyasi and Smith's "Do All Black Lives Matter Equally to Black People?" See also Reed, *Stirrings in the Jug*, 46; and García Bedolla, *Fluid Borders*, 178.

The concept of boundness is not a parallel concept to linked fate. The two concepts have different theoretical contexts, the latter emerging to describe (with certain limitations, as examined by the scholars listed above) patterns in African American political decision-making, and the former traceable as a political idea in movement spaces, including in appeals across racial lines and speaking centrally to conditions of racial violence and ideas of freedom that exceed the realm of electoral politics. In political life, appeals to both linked fate and boundness make claims on identification and belonging.

38. Beltrán, *The Trouble with Unity*, 11–12, 127, 163; and Sánchez and Pita, "Theses on the Latino Bloc," 44–45, 48–49.

39. For richer conceptualizations of coalition, see Lugones, *Pilgrimages/Peregrinajes*, ix, 26; and "On Complex Communication," 76; Cohen, "Punks, Bulldaggers, and Welfare Queens," 481–482; Keating, "Building Coalitional Consciousness," 86; and Chávez's introductory chapter in *Queer Migration Politics*.

40. Lowndes, "Response to Shane Hamilton's Review," 380; HoSang, *Racial Propositions*, 12.

41. Hall, "Cultural Identity and Diaspora," 22; Beltrán, *The Trouble with Unity*, 9.

42. Marso, *Politics with Beauvoir*, 7.

43. Lowndes, *From the New Deal to the New Right*.

44. Harris, Opening Remarks, *From Colorblindness to White Nationalism?: Emerging Racial Formations in the Trump Era,* UCLA, March 3, 2017, youtu.be/VKHu1laaOZQ. See also Kelley, *Freedom Dreams,* 9.

45. Morrison, *Playing in the Dark,* 5–6.

46. Cristina Beltrán, Roundtable comments, WPSA Annual Meeting, April 14, 2017.

47. For warnings about cynical and purely transactional solidarity politics, see Naber quoted in "Roundtable on Anti-Blackness and Black-Palestinian Solidarity," *Jadaliyya,* June 3, 2015; and Willoughby-Herard, "More Expendable than Slaves?," 507, 511, 514. On solidarity, see also Pulido, *Black, Brown, Yellow, and Left,* chap. 6.

48. Southerners On New Ground, "Our History," southernersonnewground.org.

Chapter 1

1. Darnton, "Homosexuals March Down 7th Avenue," *New York Times,* June 25, 1973. There were likely between 12,000 and 18,000 participants. On narratives of movement origins, see Armstrong and Crage, "Movements and Memory."

2. The audiovisual and photographic record of the 1973 CSLD events suggests that while many participants were people of color or white women, the majority were white gay men.

3. "Question of Equality Show; Interview with Sylvia Rivera," Tape 112, transcript, 7, Testing the Limits records, NYPL; Rivera, "Queens in Exile," in *GenderQueer,* 82; and Tape 2888, Martin B. Duberman Papers, NYPL.

4. I am using "trans" here as a broad term to include people who at the time may have referred to themselves as transvestites, transsexuals, street queens, drag queens, or crossdressers.

5. Rogers, "David Walker and the Political Power of the Appeal," 2.

6. Rogers, "David Walker and the Political Power of the Appeal," 7.

7. The footage is available in part in the 2015 PBS documentary series *The Question of Equality: Out Rage '69,* youtu.be/uuTNXnQA-ww, and at vimeo.com/465965641.

8. Tourmaline explains that for over a decade she "dove into living rooms and libraries," interviewing people who knew Rivera and Johnson, and "frequently fac[ed] down anti-black transphobic violence just to get in an archive's door." In a commitment to Johnson's and Rivera's multidimensionality and to trans and gender nonconforming people today, Tourmaline's praxis has been to "share everything I could get my hands on" and, in recent years, to create film portraits, as in her film *Happy Birthday, Marsha!* (2018, co-directed with Sasha Wortzel) that represent ancestors in their beauty, power, realness, and glamour. See Tourmaline, "Reina Gossett on Transgender Storytelling, David France, and the Netflix Marsha P. Johnson Documentary," *Teen Vogue,* October 11, 2017; Tourmaline, "Sylvia Rivera 10 Year Memorial," *The Spirit Was,* February 18, 2012; Sessi Kuwabara Blanchard, "Marsha P. Johnson's LGBTQ Legacy Is About How She Lived Her Life, Too," *Vice,* August 20, 2018; "Our March Cover Stars," *Out,* February 12, 2019; and Eva Reign, "These Filmmakers Are Making

Sure Marsha P. Johnson's Legacy Lives on Forever," *them*, August 21, 2018. See also Ashley Farmer, "Archiving While Black," *The Chronicle Review*, July 22, 2018.

9. The printed record of Rivera's and STAR's work is spread between multiple archival collections of gay activists and movement organizations at the New York Public Library, the LGBT Community Center, and the Lesbian Herstory Archives. The dispersal of and gaps in STAR's archive tell a story about the printed/audiovisual record of trans and gender nonconforming people who had unstable housing and who were cash poor. STAR, for example, had limited or no access to recording devices (e.g., videocameras or cameras) or the tools for producing or physical space to retain printed materials. Even so, the record shows that STAR did use print culture to disseminate their political ideas and demands, to recruit people, and to stay abreast of and to participate in debates in gay politics (for one reference about STAR's desire to direct the production of *Come Out!* see Danskey et al., *The Come Out! Reader*, 11). Much of what remains in the formal archive is a narrowed sampling of STAR's appeals—tending to (but not exclusively) representing STAR's appeals to and conversations with white and middle-class gay activists/organizations. STAR members' multivocal and multivalent appeals endure *despite* the fissures and scatterings of the formal archive, and endure in the stories, photographs, filmmaking, and ongoing activism of people who participated in and knew STAR.

10. "Sylvia Rivera," Eric Marcus Papers, NYPL.

11. For Rivera's account of her childhood, see Tape 2887, Duberman Papers.

12. "Question of Equality Show," Tape 112, transcript, 2, and Tape 111 transcript, 15; "Sylvia Rivera, Edit 2B," 4, Marcus Papers.

13. GAA was formed in January 1970 as a single-issue organization. Rivera began at GLF, then went to GAA and became involved in their direct action campaigns, then returned to GLF after GAA failed to support the Weinstein protests. See "Question of Equality," Tape 113 transcript, 1–2; "Sylvia Rivera," Marcus Papers. See Reverend Kennedy's account of being chased by the cops with Rivera at the Stonewall uprising; "Reverend Goddess Magora Kennedy, 81," notanothersecond.com/stories/reverend-kennedy/.

14. Cohen, *Gay Liberation Youth Movement*, 109.

15. Tourmaline, "Rapping with Marsha P. Johnson," February 24, 2012; *Pay It No Mind: Marsha P. Johnson*, directed by Michael Kasino, Redux Pictures, 2012; Tourmaline, "Reina Gossett on Transgender Storytelling"; Tourmaline, "Sylvia Rivera and Marsha P. Johnson's Fight to Free Incarcerated Trans Women of Color Is Far from Over," *Vogue*, June 29, 2019.

16. Stephan Cohen explains that "for Rivera, 'gay' meant non-heteronormative (or 'queer' in today's lexicon), crossing sexual and gender boundaries to include lesbians, gay men, and transvestites, as well as street youth who had participated in Stonewall." See Cohen, *Gay Liberation Youth Movement*, 91, 109.

17. Rivera and Johnson founded STAR in the wake of a five-day sit-in occupation and police confrontation at New York University's Weinstein Hall. The occupation itself was initially formulated as a protest against NYU's decision to ban gay dances but grew into a larger series of demands. What became STAR began as "Street Transvestites

for Gay Power," then "Street Transvestite Actual Revolutionaries," then "Street Transvestite Action Revolutionaries." Rivera and Johnson circulated leaflets at the occupation and co-organized a march two weeks later with GLF to deliver a series of demands to NYU—including "(1) a space for a 24-hour gay community center, to be controlled by the gay community . . . (2) open enrollment and free tuition for gay people and all people from the communities NYU oppresses . . . (3) all NYU students, employes [sic], and faculty have the right to be openly gay, without fear of retaliation by NYU"; community-controlled childcare centers, universal access to community-controlled healthcare, and broad demands for the end of homophobic practices at Bellevue Psychiatric Hospital. See Rivera, "Queens in Exile," 81; "Scenes," and "Gay Demands!," Weinstein Folder, Box 94, Arthur Bell Papers, NYPL. For Roderick Ferguson's analysis of the NYU occupation, including the ways it employed movement tactics from Black revolutionary struggle, see *One-Dimensional Queer*, 23–29.

18. STAR marched with their banner, Rivera arm in arm with organizers from the Young Lords Party. Feinberg, "Street Transvestite Action Revolutionaries," *Workers World*, September 24, 2006; Tape 2888, Duberman Papers; and Enck-Wazner and Morales, *The Young Lords*, ix, 241. I thank Parissa Clark for sharing resources on this historical context.

19. "Question of Equality," Tape 112, transcript, 13.

20. "Memo to Dear Fabulous Eben, January 18, 1971," Prison Reports Folder, Box 94, Bell Papers; and *Gay Flames* no. 10 (February 12, 1971), 1.

21. On their demonstration against job discrimination, see "Stop Job Discrimination," Intro 475-Miscellany Folder, Box 91, International Gay Information Center (IGIC) Collection, NYPL; and *Gay Flames* no. 10 (February 12, 1971), 6. On STAR's participation in the Community Center and college campus presentations see Cohen, *Gay Liberation Youth Movement*, 130, 137–138, 144–145. On the Albany protest see Diana Davies Photographs, NYPL Digital Collection, digitalcollections.nypl.org/items/510d47e3–572c-a3d9-e040-e00a18064a99.

22. Feinberg, "Street Transvestite Action Revolutionaries." See also Stryker, *Transgender History*, 86–87.

23. Tape 2886, Duberman Papers.

24. Tape 2888, Duberman Papers.

25. "Randy Wicker Interviews Sylvia Rivera on the Pier," vimeo.com/35975275.

26. Tape 2888, Duberman Papers.

27. The building lacked heat and plumbing, but STAR members fixed the boiler themselves and rigged up plumbing using a series of hoses. Tape 2888, Duberman Papers. Bob Kohler, a close friend of STAR, also helped with the building. When Bubbles Rose Lee failed to deliver the rent payment, their landlord threatened violence if they did not vacate. See "Sylvia Rivera," Marcus Papers.

28. Tourmaline, "Rapping with Marsha P. Johnson."

29. Miss Major Griffin-Gracy interviewed by AJ Lewis, oralhistory.nypl.org; Tourmaline, "Happy Birthday Marsha 'Pay It No Mind' Johnson!," *The Crunk Feminist Collective Blog*, June 27, 2013; Tourmaline, "Sylvia Rivera and Marsha P. Johnson's Fight"; Stanley et al., *Trap Door*, xvii; Lewis, "Trans History in a Moment of Danger," 60–62; Osorio,

"Embodying Truth," 154; Sylvia Rivera Law Project, "Who Was Sylvia Rivera?," srlp. org/about/who-was-sylvia-rivera/; and Cohen, *Gay Liberation Youth Movement*, 93, 161.

30. As Johnson observed in one interview, while STAR was popular, it was not a given that all street queens identified with or participated in STAR. In explaining the challenges of building STAR's membership base, Johnson reflects how it was "hard to get in touch with transvestites" and that some "don't . . . care about a revolution." Tourmaline, "Rapping with Marsha P. Johnson."

31. Ferguson, "On the Specificities of Racial Formation," 46.

32. Cohen, *Gay Liberation Youth Movement*, 155.

33. See "Morris Kight," Making Gay History podcast; and "Washington Square Park Galla [*sic*]," Folder 2, Box 1, Rudy Grillo Collection, National History Archive, LGBT Community Center.

34. The pattern persists today, as Stonewall veteran and activist elder Miss Major Griffin-Gracy attests, in enduring gay Stonewall nostalgia that excises trans political action. See "Trans Oral History Project: Miss Major on Stonewall," youtu.be/O8gKdAOQyyI; and Dunham, "Out of Obscurity," 93.

35. "Gay Pride Week & Christopher Street Liberation Day '73 Calendar," and "Lesbian Pride Week Calendar," Folder 2, Box 1, Grillo Collection; and Shepard, "Sylvia and Sylvia's Children," 126.

36. "Question of Equality," Tape 112, transcript, 6–7; and Tape 2888, Duberman Papers.

37. Rivera quoted in Shepard, "Sylvia and Sylvia's Children," 127. In a 1994 interview, Rivera recounts that she was beaten up on her way to the stage by emcee Vito Russo on instruction of the CSLD Committee Grand Marshal Jean DeVente. See Rivera, "Question of Equality," Tape 112, transcript, 8.

38. Rivera, "Ya'll Better Quiet Down," vimeo.com/465965641; and *The Question of Equality: Part 1 Outrage '69*.

39. Rivera's specific use of language of "brothers and sisters" at the CSLD rally is both related to and a departure from her 1972 appeal in the pages of the *Come Out!* periodical (vol. 2, no. 8) that "transvestites [are] your half sisters and half brothers of the Revolution." In my reading, Rivera's concept of half-siblings in 1972 is less a claim of step-siblinghood than it is part of a lesson to cisgender people about gender identity. See also Johnson's 1973 CSLD march sign "Free Our Half Sister Bambi" reprinted and discussed in Cohen, *The Gay Liberation Youth Movement*, 120, 142, 144, and see Cohen on STAR's graphics, 118–119.

40. Rivera, "Ya'll Better Quiet Down."

41. Deborah Vargas, "Queer of Color Critique and Jennicet Gutiérrez's Interruption," American Studies Association Annual Meeting, November 18, 2016.

42. See Angela Davis and Gina Dent on prison as a border in "Prison as a Border," 1236–1237.

43. Ferguson, *One-Dimensional Queer*, 1.

44. "GAY POWER—WHEN DO WE WANT IT? OR DO WE?," Weinstein Hall/NYU/Sit-In Folder, Bell Papers. For Bebe Scarpi's comments on the statement, see Cohen, *The Gay Liberation Youth Movement*, 152.

45. Yasmin Nair, "Why I Won't Come Out on National Coming Out Day," October 9, 2008, yasminnair.com. See also Conrad, ed., *Against Equality*, 6.

46. Lushetich, *Interdisciplinary Performance*, 179; and Sedgwick, *Epistemology of the Closet*, 61.

47. Nero, "Why Are the Gay Ghettos White?"

48. Martel, *The Misinterpellated Subject*, 7, 12; and James Martel, conversation, September 3, 2017.

49. Martel, *The Misinterpellated Subject*, 125, 162, 270.

50. Lida Maxwell, Discussant comments, APSA Annual Meeting, September 2, 2018.

51. Tiffany Willoughby-Herard, correspondence, February 23, 2018.

52. Rivera, "Ya'll Better Quiet Down."

53. Stryker and Bettcher, "Introduction," 9; and "For Immediate Release," Queens Liberation Front Folder, IGIC Collection. On Rivera's participation in women's liberation, Black liberation, and peace movements, see "Question of Equality," Tape 111, transcript, 15; and Feinberg, "Street Transvestite Action Revolutionaries." On Johnson's interactions with Daughters of Bilitis and her account of the relationship between trans and non-trans gay sisters, see Tourmaline, "Rapping with Marsha P. Johnson." See also Abelson, "Already Feminists."

54. Bettcher, "A Conversation with Jeanne Córdova," 286; Stryker, *Transgender History*, 102–105; Abelson, "Already Feminists," 47–48; and Thuma, *All Our Trials*, 85.

55. Clendinen and Nagourney, *Out for Good*, 167, 169–170.

56. Rivera, "Queens in Exile," 82.

57. "Question of Equality," Tape 114, transcript, 15–17.

58. "Jean O'Leary Speech at Gay Rally," LoveTapesCollective, vimeo.com/236308070. In an interview two decades later, Rivera reflected on her difficulty remembering the details of O'Leary's speech despite her usual ease in accessing and recounting stories of her past. She explained that it was "something . . . I blocked out of my mind for years," but said she knew O'Leary's general position—they had been on several panels together in activist spaces, Rivera recounted, "and her thing was that I was, that drag queens always [insulted] women." See "Question of Equality," Tape 113, transcript, 11, and Tape 114, transcript, 12. The LFL's anti-trans organizing and the abandonment of trans protections from central movement demands continued after the 1973 parade. Several months later, O'Leary delivered a list of demands to the CSLDC including the "total exclusion of all transvestites" from the 1974 parade and beyond. LFL threatened to "boycott the parade entirely and encourage all women to do likewise" if their demands were not met. According to one account, O'Leary read the demands to the CSLD Committee and "stomped out of the meeting" immediately afterward. See "Goodwin Loses NY Parade Post," Folder 4, Box 1, Grillo Collection. For some of O'Leary's reflections decades later, see "Jean O'Leary-Part 1," *Making Gay History: The Podcast*.

59. Thuma, *All Our Trials*, 24. See also Law, *Resistance Behind Bars*, 71–72; Gómez, "Resisting Living Death at Marion Federal Penitentiary," 65–66; Oparah, "Maroon Abolitionists," 296; and Berger, *Captive Nation*, 7–8. On the revolutionary political analysis built within and across prison walls in these (and other) decades, see Joy

James' introductory chapter as well as the collected essays in *The New Abolitionists* and *Imprisoned Intellectuals*.

60. Kunzel, "Lessons in Being Gay," 15.

61. Kunzel, "Lessons in Being Gay," 11; Tourmaline in "Sylvia Rivera Law Project Teach-In at OWS," BCRW Videos, vimeo.com/102272079.

62. Díaz-Cotto, *Gender, Ethnicity, and the State*, 39–40, 45, 58fn91, 58fn94.

63. Tourmaline in "Teach-In at OWS"; Kunzel, "Lessons in Being Gay," 11; and Teal, *The Gay Militants*, 305.

64. Stanley et al., "Queering Prison Abolition, Now?," 115.

65. Reddy, *Freedom with Violence*, 4, 12–15.

66. Shulman, *American Prophecy*, 3, 5.

67. Shulman, *American Prophecy*, xiv, 5.

68. Jasmine Syedullah, conversation, May 21, 2017.

69. Osorio, "Embodying Truth," 155.

70. Muñoz, *Disidentifications*, 9, 12, 31. Muñoz's conceptualization of disidentification is grounded in Norma Alarcón's theorization of "identity-in-difference."

71. I thank Bonnie Honig for engaging on this point.

72. "Question of Equality," Tape 111, transcript, 13–14.

73. Hooker, *Race and the Politics of Solidarity*, 7, 10, 111; and Lebron, *The Color of Our Shame*, 139.

74. Shulman, *American Prophecy*, 8, 247.

75. The meeting was convened at a temporary building while the Center was being renovated. Caitlin McCarthy (Archivist, Lesbian, Gay, Bisexual & Transgender Community Center), correspondence, October 29, 2018.

76. Rivera, "Sylvia Rivera's Talk at LGMNY," 120.

77. Rivera, "Sylvia Rivera's Talk at LGMNY," 120.

78. Rivera, "Sylvia Rivera's Talk at LGMNY," 120, 122.

79. Baldwin explained of his return to the U.S. in 1957 that "everybody else was paying their dues, and it was time I went home and paid mine." See Baldwin, "No Name in the Street," in *The Price of the Ticket*, 475.

80. As George Shulman explains, jeremiads make infidelity a key political trope. See also Shulman's brief discussion of Isaiah's angry lament that "I have nourished and brought up children and they have rebelled against me" (*American Prophecy*, 8).

81. Rivera, "Sylvia Rivera's Talk at LGMNY," 120.

82. "Sylvia Rivera at Black Pride in Ft. Green Park 2001 from Market This!," vimeo.com/38227391; and Rivera, "Queens in Exile," 81.

83. Douglass, *Great Speeches by Frederick Douglass*, 27, 33. See also Shulman, *American Prophecy*, 16.

84. Rivera, "Queens in Exile," 80.

85. The bill had originally been introduced and defeated by a council vote in 1974. John Goldman, "N.Y. Passes Gay Rights Bill After 15-Year Debate," *Los Angeles Times*, March 21, 1986; and Scarpinato and Moore, "Sylvia Rivera."

86. Shepard, "Sylvia and Sylvia's Children," 125.

87. "Question of Equality," Tape 114, transcript, 10; and Tape 2890, Duberman Papers.

88. Rivera, "Sylvia Rivera's Talk at LGMNY," 120; Kennedy, "Intro 475 Deal Collapses," Intro 475-Correspondence Folder and "Won't Be Sacrificial Lambs," Intro 475-Miscellany Folder, Box 91, IGIC Collection; and "Question of Equality," Tape 114, transcript, 11.

89. Scarpinato and Moore, "Sylvia Rivera"; and Schindler, "HRC Alone in Eschewing No-Compromise Stand," *Gay City News*, October 4, 2007.

90. Rivera, "Sylvia Rivera's Talk at LGMNY," 120. See also "Question of Equality," Tape 114, transcript, 12.

91. Osorio, "Embodying Truth," 155.

92. Rivera, "Queens in Exile," 53; Rivera, "Question of Equality," Tape 112, transcript, 7–8; Stryker and Bettcher, "Introduction," 9. See Viviane Namaste on the spatial politics of gay male establishments in which drag queens are "relegate[ed]" to and "tolerated" only when *on* the stage. Namaste, *Invisible Lives*, 10–11.

93. Rivera, "Sylvia Rivera's Talk at LGMNY," 121.

94. Rivera, "Sylvia Rivera's Talk at LGMNY," 121.

95. Rivera, "Question of Equality," Tape 112, transcript, 8.

96. Rivera, "Queens in Exile," 82.

97. Brewster in "L039A 1973 Gay Pride March and Rally Original Unedited 4 of 4," LoveTapesCollective, vimeo.com/331483480. I have used he/him pronouns for Brewster following Scarpinato quoted in Douglas Martin, "Lee Brewster, 57, Style Guru for World's Cross Dressers," *New York Times*, May 24, 2000. For Rivera on Brewster's intervention at the rally, see Tape 2888, Duberman Papers; and "Question of Equality," Tape 112, transcript, 6.

98. To be clear, Rivera's account of debt is different than an account of origins. In a 1994 interview, Rivera specifies that "drag queens did not start the gay movement. Drag queens were part of the beginning of the gay movement. . . . I give the drag queens credit for being front liners after the gay movement started." Rivera does not posit drag queens as fixed in the beginning of a linear narrative of gay citizenship. She refuses historiographies that relegate drag queens to the past, refuses being commemorated as an expired political actor, and demands that the gay liberation movement reorient its politics in the present. See "Question of Equality," Tape 114, transcript, 15.

99. Tourmaline, "Sylvia Interview," vimeo.com/24188213.

100. "Question of Equality," Tape 114, transcript, 13.

101. Letter from Lee G. Brewster, Folder 2, Box 1, Grillo Collection.

102. "Question of Equality," Tape 112, transcript, 7.

103. Scarpinato and Moore, "Sylvia Rivera."

104. Rivera recounts that she moved to the piers a week before the 1995 Pride parade. See "Randy Wicker Interviews Sylvia Rivera on the Pier." On her residence at Transy House, see "Sylvia Rivera: A Tribute," youtu.be/ybnH0HB0lqc; and Martohardjono, "Changing House," youtu.be/cAdc-D8iZtI.

105. Phillips and Olugbala, "Sylvia Rivera: Fighting in Her Heels," 327; Shepard, "Sylvia and Sylvia's Children," 128; and Shepard, "From Community Organization to Direct Services," 100.

106. Rivera, "Queens in Exile," 83; and "Sylvia Rivera Restarts Street Transvestite Action Revolutionaries," youtu.be/5ijUM7rnFmA.

107. "Sylvia Rivera: A Tribute." See Dean Spade on how, despite lobbying and activism by trans communities in New York state, and despite appeals to the Empire State Pride Committee, SONDA excluded protections for gender identity discrimination and protected only sexual orientation. Spade, "Fighting to Win," 48. In 2019, New York State passed the Gender Expression Non-Discrimination Act.

108. Rivera's speech has also been adapted into a short film, "Hallå, kan ni lugna ner er!" by Conny Karlsson Lundgren and the Swedish feminist performance troupe Kvalitétsteatern. Tedjasukmana, "Ya'll Better Quiet Down," *Video Activism 2.0*, February 11, 2018.

109. Alexandra DiPalma, "The Independent Filmmaker Working to Fight Erasure," *Vice*, September 11, 2018; Stanley et al., *Trap Door*, xvi; Stanley, *Atmospheres of Violence*, 3; and Crenshaw and Ritchie, *Say Her Name*. See Eric Stanley's important warning about the neoliberal incorporation of Johnson's and Rivera's radical and "ungovernable" histories (*Atmospheres of Violence*, p. 3).

110. Different footage of the speech appears in *The Question of Equality: Part 1 Outrage '69*.

111. Conversation with archivists at the Lesbian Herstory Archives, March 7, 2018.

112. Tang, "Contemporary Art and Critical Transgender Infrastructures," 379–380.

113. Tourmaline, Twitter, April 17, 2017. Janet Mock explains how Tourmaline has created conditions for identification through reinstating relationships with movement foremothers, "reintroduc[ing] our [generation] to ourselves by uncovering/recentering trans women of color revolutionaries." See Janet Mock, Twitter, October 7, 2017.

114. Tourmaline has explained her social movement practices of dwelling with elders and ancestors whose lives have created "imprints on the world"—and of grounding political imagination practices in these intergenerational relationships. Tourmaline in Toshio Meronek, "On Trans Day of Remembrance, the Personal Gets Political," *truthout*, November 20, 2016.

115. Tourmaline, "this week vimeo took down the Sylvia Rivera 'y'all better quiet down' speech i uploaded in 2012 b/c of 'copyright issues,'" Twitter, April 17, 2017.

116. Tape 2888, Duberman Papers.

117. "Randy Wicker Interviews Sylvia Rivera on the Pier."

118. See, e.g., "Sylvia Rivera: A Tribute."

119. James Martel, Discussant comments, WPSA Annual Meeting, March 30, 2018.

120. Lida Maxwell, Discussant comments, APSA Annual Meeting, September 2, 2018.

Chapter 2

1. Epigraph is from Baldwin, "An Open Letter to My Sister Angela Y. Davis," in *Cross of Redemption*, 259. On Baldwin's stay in London the previous fall, see Leeming, *James*

Baldwin, 288–289. On the history of the West Indian Students' Centre see Clover, "Dispersed or Destroyed."

2. James Baldwin in Horace Ové, James Baldwin, and Dick Gregory, *Baldwin's N——* (my redaction, see note 85) (London: British Film Institute, 2004).

3. In the eighteenth and nineteenth centuries in the United States, race as an idea was preeminently attached to the body. Across the twentieth century, the framework of race as a social construction was developed in response to and against ideas of race as biological. The social construction framework has primarily focused on the formation of race through discourse, cultural representations, political processes, and institutional structures. See Painter, *The History of White People.*

4. See Roberts, *Killing the Black Body,* 6; Alcoff, *Visible Identities,* 108–111; Young, *On Female Body Experience,* 18; and Desireé Melonas, "A New Material Defense of Mindfulness," WPSA Conference, 2019 and forthcoming work.

5. Sharpe, *Monstrous Intimacies,* 29.

6. Stewart and Richardson, *Maria W. Stewart, America's First Black Woman Political Writer,* 40 (also quoted in Collins, *Black Feminist Thought,* 4); Wells-Barnett, *Southern Horrors;* and Richardson, "A Black Woman Speaks."

7. Stoler, *Haunted by Empire,* 13; and Sharpe, *Monstrous Intimacies,* Introduction.

8. McBride, *James Baldwin Now,* 2; and Bruyneel, *Settler Memory.* For Margaret Mead's and James Baldwin's debate on this matter, see *A Rap on Race,* 69. Also, see Douglas Field concerning the ways Baldwin's public role was circumscribed by contemporary gender and sexuality politics. Although Baldwin was in some significant ways sidelined by civil rights activists on account of his sexuality in the late 1950s and early 1960s, by the mid-1960s, Baldwin came under increasing attack by a new generation of radical Black American writers. Silences in his essays and speeches around gender and sexual orientation must be read in this context. See Field, "Looking for Jimmy Baldwin," 464.

9. Collins, "It's All in the Family," 63.

10. Iris Marion Young argues that "what we call categories of gender, race, ethnicity, etc. are shorthand for a set of structures that position persons." See Young, *On Female Body Experience,* 18. Lived body experiences make up the patterns of how structures position people (and mete out death, displacement, violation, or protection), but they do not constitute essential categories themselves. Baldwin attends to the structural and cultural manifestations of racism while refusing essentialized racial categories. See also Baldwin, "White Man's Guilt," in *The Price of the Ticket,* 410.

11. In addition to the texts examined in this chapter, see, e.g., "Encounter on the Seine: Black Meets Brown" (1950, 39); "Many Thousands Gone" (1951, 76–77); "Stranger in the Village" (1953, 89); and "In Search of a Majority" (1960, 234), all in Baldwin, *The Price of the Ticket.* See also Baldwin's "An Open Letter to My Sister Angela Y. Davis" (1971); and Baldwin and Buckley, "Debate: Baldwin vs Buckley."

12. On Baldwin's use of the first-person plural—the racially ambiguous "we"—see also Balfour, *The Evidence of Things Not Said,* 36.

13. Marshall, *The City on the Hill from Below,* 220n6, 224–225n71.

14. See also McWilliams, *A Political Companion to James Baldwin*; and Turner, *Awakening to Race*.
15. Shulman, *American Prophecy*, 136–140, 163; Marshall, *City on the Hill from Below*, 24, 142–161.
16. Glaude, *In a Shade of Blue*, 15.
17. Baldwin invoked boundness with both Black and white audiences, often in layered forms of address. At the West Indian Students' Centre, Baldwin's audience was primarily Black, but his address allowed white people to "listen in," as George Shulman puts it. Likewise, Baldwin's open letter to his nephew positions white people to "overhear" his account of whiteness and the meaning of integration. See Shulman, *American Prophecy*, 214; and Marshall, *City on the Hill from Below*, 156.
18. Spillers, "Mama's Baby, Papa's Maybe," 77; Sharpe, *Monstrous Intimacies*, 28; and Willoughby-Herard, "Let Me Introduce You."
19. Lugones, *Pilgrimages/Peregrinajes*, 131–132.
20. As Jared Sexton argues, what is at stake in white anxieties about racial mixing is the coherence of racial categories themselves and the (failed) project of achieving whiteness as a "securable identity." Fixation on purity and antimiscegenation is best understood as a "quest for racial being" and a "performative reiteration of racial whiteness." See Sexton, *Amalgamation Schemes*, 222, 224–225.
21. Lugones, *Pilgrimages/Peregrinajes*, 131–132.
22. Lugones, *Pilgrimages/Peregrinajes*, 130–132.
23. Balfour, *Evidence of Things Not Said*, 11; and Leeming, *James Baldwin*.
24. For more on this context, see Klinkner and Smith, *The Unsteady March*; Dudziak, *Cold War Civil Rights*; Singh, *Black is a Country*; Melamed, "The Spirit of Neoliberalism"; and Joseph, *Dark Days, Bright Nights*.
25. *The Price of the Ticket*, directed and produced by Karen Thorsen (San Francisco, California Newsreel, 1990).
26. Balfour, *The Evidence of Things Not Said*, 12.
27. Balfour, *The Evidence of Things Not Said*, 12.
28. Baldwin in Ové et al., *Baldwin's N———*.
29. Holland, *The Erotic Life of Racism*, 6. Giulia Sissa, discussion, January 12, 2018.
30. "White Man's Guilt" first appeared in *Ebony* magazine as a part of a 1966 special issue "The White Problem in America."
31. Baldwin, "White Man's Guilt," 412.
32. Baldwin, "White Man's Guilt," 412–413.
33. Giulia Sissa, discussion, January 12, 2018.
34. Stewart and Richardson, *Maria W. Stewart*, 39–40.
35. Douglass, *Narrative of the Life of Frederick Douglass*, 4.
36. Richardson, "A Black Woman Speaks," 6; and "Thus a Woman Speaks," youtu.be/_ii8kwAKw4g.
37. Collins, "It's All in the Family," 65; Edwards, *Charisma*, xix; Gilroy, *Small Acts*, 192–207; Rodríguez, *Next of Kin*, 6–7, 11.
38. Sharpe, *Monstrous Intimacies*, 2, 21–23; Scheper, *Moving Performances*, 170.
39. Spillers, "Mama's Baby, Papa's Maybe," 70.

40. Spillers, "Mama's Baby, Papa's Maybe," 74. See also Morgan, "*Partus sequiter ventrem*," 1, 14.

41. Spillers, "Mama's Baby, Papa's Maybe," 76.

42. Spillers, "Mama's Baby, Papa's Maybe," 74.

43. Stoler, *Haunted by Empire*, 13, 16, 26, 43.

44. Stoler, *Haunted by Empire*, 13.

45. Balfour, "Vexed Genealogy," 171.

46. Balfour, "Vexed Genealogy," 176.

47. See Balfour, *Evidence of Things Not Said*; Field, "Looking for Jimmy"; Shulman, *American Prophecy*; and Marshall, *City on the Hill*.

48. Leeming, *James Baldwin*, 214.

49. See also Balfour, *Evidence of Things Not Said*, 129.

50. Baldwin, *The Fire Next Time*, 64.

51. Baldwin, *The Fire Next Time*, 65.

52. Baldwin, *The Fire Next Time*, 68–69.

53. Baldwin in Clark, *The Negro Protest*, 11; Baldwin, *The Fire Next Time*, 59.

54. Baldwin, *The Fire Next Time*, 71.

55. Baldwin, *The Fire Next Time*, 81.

56. Baldwin, *The Fire Next Time*, 63–64.

57. Baldwin, *The Fire Next Time*, 79.

58. Baldwin, *The Fire Next Time*, 72.

59. Baldwin, *The Cross of Redemption*, 137.

60. Glaude, *In a Shade of Blue*, 12; Glaude, *Begin Again*, 92.

61. Baldwin, *The Fire Next Time*, 83.

62. Baldwin and Mead, *A Rap on Race*, 221.

63. "Malcolm X, James Baldwin and Leverne McCummins Discuss the Position of the Black Muslims," *WBAI*, April 25, 1961, Pacifica Radio Archives.

64. Baldwin, *The Fire Next Time*, 83.

65. Shulman, *American Prophecy*, 163.

66. Shulman, *American Prophecy*, 112, 154; Marshall, *City on the Hill*, 130, 142–154.

67. Shulman, *American Prophecy*, 133.

68. Baldwin in Ové et al., *Baldwin's N———*.

69. See also Turner's discussion of Baldwin on the Voting Rights Act of 1965 and the Civil Rights Act of 1964 in *Awakening to Race*, 95.

70. Baldwin, *The Fire Next Time*, 94. Hansberry invokes this question in a 1961 panel with Baldwin and Langston Hughes, titled "The Negro in American Culture." Transcript in *Cross Currents* (Summer 1961), 222, Lorraine Hansberry Papers, Schomburg Center for Research in Black Culture. See also Balfour, *Evidence of Things Not Said*, 145n37.

71. See Turner, *Awakening to Race*, 98.

72. Baldwin, *The Fire Next Time*, 94.

73. Baldwin in "Malcolm X, James Baldwin, and Leverne McCummins."

74. Baldwin Ové et al., *Baldwin's N———*.

75. See also Holland, *The Erotic Life of Racism*, 19.

76. Baldwin, *The Fire Next Time*, 9–10. See Marshall's reading of this passage in *The City on the Hill from Below*, 152–154.

77. "Malcolm X, James Baldwin and Leverne McCummins"; and Ové et al., *Baldwin's N———*. On this kind of racial justice struggle as an "exceptional, even transcendent, calling" see Marshall, *City on the Hill from Below*, 130. On Baldwin's letter to his nephew, see Marshall, *City on the Hill from Below*, 152–156.

78. Baldwin, *The Fire Next Time*, 8.

79. Baldwin, *The Fire Next Time*, 10.

80. When Juliet Hooker explains that the question of "'What kinds of obligations do citizens have towards one another and why?' cannot be answered without also asking 'Who are my fellow citizens?'" this matter of the *we* of solidarity puts us squarely on the map of political identification. See Hooker, *Race and the Politics of Solidarity*, 25. On the race, labor, and internationalist politics of the word *solidarity* in U.S. political culture, see Roediger, "Making Solidarity Uneasy."

81. As Juliet Hooker explains, so often in contemporary political theory, solidarity is imagined to rest upon shared national identity, a formation that enshrines the settler violence of the U.S. state and disavows that in the U.S. context, race trumps nationality (i.e., nationality does not unify a solidaristic *we*). See Hooker, *Race and the Politics of Solidarity*, 25, 34, 40. In complicated ways, Baldwin's identificatory appeals marshal U.S. racial history and national identity together.

82. Baldwin, "The Creative Process," in *The Price of the Ticket*, 318.

83. *Take This Hammer*, directed and produced by Richard Moore, National Education Television, 1963, diva.sfsu.edu/collections/sfbatv/bundles/187041. On the removal of critical footage from the final program, see "The Making of *Take This Hammer*," diva.sfsu.edu/collections/sfbatv/bundles/210522.

84. Baldwin in Moore, *Take This Hammer*.

85. In quoting Baldwin, I do not spell out "the n-word" because of the word's connection to violence and death. I thank Tiffany Willoughby-Herard and Jeanne Scheper for their insights. See Patricia Hill Collins on ethics of accountability, in *Black Feminist Thought*, 284–285.

86. Baldwin in Moore, *Take This Hammer*.

87. Baldwin et al., "John Brown's Body," 264; and Baldwin, *The Fire Next Time*, 97.

88. Baldwin, *The Fire Next Time*, 96.

89. Martínez, "Dying to Know," 783–784; Mills, *The Racial Contract*, 18; and HoSang, *Racial Propositions*, 270.

90. Mills, *The Racial Contract*, 18. As Mills explains, the Racial Contract is a non-ideal contract made between white people, who are "the people who count" and the "people who are really people" within the unnamed and taken-for-granted political system of white supremacy (p. 3).

91. Martínez, "Dying to Know," 783.

92. Baldwin in Thorsen, *The Price of the Ticket*.

93. Baldwin, "On Being White . . . and Other Lies," in *The Cross of Redemption*, 167–168.

94. Baldwin, "On Being White . . . and Other Lies," 169. On this moral choice, see Turner, *Awakening to Race*, 102. See also Linda Martín Alcoff's discussion of "choice" in

white racial identity, and her account of the dimensions of social identity categories that limit the elasticity of choice. *The Future of Whiteness*, 40, 60.

95. Baldwin, "White Man's Guilt," 410.
96. Baldwin in Thorsen, *Price of the Ticket*.
97. Thorsen, *Price of the Ticket*; Leeming, *James Baldwin*, 256; and Baldwin et al., "John Brown's Body," 263.
98. Baldwin, "An Open Letter to My Sister Angela Y. Davis," 259.
99. Baldwin et al., "John Brown's Body," 264.
100. When Baldwin invokes "hair straight like an Indian" to describe his uncle's hair and his uncle passing as white, Baldwin is trading in settler imaginaries that absorb indigeneity into whiteness and also rely on the erasure of Black-Indigenous/Afro-Indigenous heritage. See Klopotek et al., "Ordinary and Extraordinary Trauma," 61; and Bruyneel, *Settler Memory*.
101. "Chicago Tonight," November 22, 1985, Moving Image and Recorded Sound Division; Schomburg Center for Research in Black Culture.
102. Ové et al., *Baldwin's N——*.
103. Sharpe, *Monstrous Intimacies*, 4.
104. Sharpe, *Monstrous Intimacies*, 4, 33–34; Hartman, *Scenes of Subjection*, 89.
105. Stoler, *Haunted by Empire*, 14.
106. Richardson, "A Black Woman Speaks."
107. Spillers, "Mama's Baby, Papa's Maybe," 67.
108. Spillers, "Mama's Baby, Papa's Maybe," 67; Holland, *The Erotic Life of Racism*, 23.
109. Ashon Crawley, "Stayed / Freedom / Hallelujah," *Los Angeles Review of Books*, May 10, 2015.
110. Spillers, "Mama's Baby, Papa's Maybe," 69.
111. Ové et al., *Baldwin's N——*.
112. "Transcript: Barack Obama's Speech on Race," *NPR*, March 18, 2008; Crenshaw, "How Colorblindness Flourished in the Age of Obama," 137; and Lowndes, "Barack Obama's Body," 485–486.
113. Sharpe, *Monstrous Intimacies*, 2.
114. HoSang and Lowndes, *Producers, Parasites, Patriots*, 82–83.
115. HoSang, *Racial Propositions*, 268.
116. Roberts, *Fatal Invention*, 5; Haney-López, *White By Law*, 11.
117. Lowndes, "Looking Forward to the History of the Tea Party."

Chapter 3

1. Jones and Engel, *What Would Martin Say?*, 192.
2. Other participants included television producer Henry Morgenthau (who would record and air Clark's interview of Baldwin), Edward Fales (Baldwin's secretary), Thais Aubrey (a friend of David Baldwin), and Robert P. Mills (Baldwin's literary agent).

3. Clark, *The Negro Protest*, 3.

4. Anand Commissiong, comments, WPSA Conference, April 13, 2017.

5. To be clear, I mean *identification with* a political commitment to ending anti-Black violence, not a white slide into "identification as" Black. See Shana Redmond's warnings about identificatory politics that enact violent displacements in "As Though It Were Our Own," 19–20.

6. Farah Godrej, conversation, April 18, 2018.

7. Baldwin, "Lorraine Hansberry at the Summit," in *The Cross of Redemption*, 135.

8. Pavlić, *Who Can Afford to Improvise?*, 23.

9. See McGuire, *At the Dark End of the Street*.

10. Telegram reprinted in Eckman, *The Furious Passage of James Baldwin*, 180.

11. See Berger on the ways white liberal media reduced the complexities of the civil rights movement's direct action campaigns into formulaic narratives of white-on-Black violence while Black media constructed a different visual record, including photographic sequences depicting a fuller story of resistance to police violence; accounts of Black political action framed without white people as central referents; and interviews and biographies of protestors or bystanders whose profiles represented political ambiguities, detailed personal histories, and practices of resistance. *Seeing Through Race*, 6–7, 10–11, 37–38, 11. See also Raiford, "Come Let Us Build a New World Together," 1135.

12. See Berger, *Seeing Through Race*, 48–49.

13. Tiffany Willoughby-Herard, correspondence, June 29, 2018.

14. HoSang, *Racial Propositions*, 21.

15. Leeming, *James Baldwin*, 221; and Beard, "James Baldwin on Violence and Disavowal," 344.

16. Baldwin, "The White Problem," in *The Cross of Redemption*, 96–97. From the fire hoses and police dogs to the bombing of the 16th Street Baptist Church, the racialized violence in Birmingham, Alabama, figures repeatedly in Baldwin's political essays and speeches in the 1960s. See, e.g., "Nobody Knows My Name" (1961, 192), "White Man's Guilt," (1965, 412–413) and "Introduction" (xviii), all in *The Price of the Ticket*; and "We Can Change the Country" (1963, 51), "The White Problem" (1964, 96–97), "Black Power" (1968, 82), and "The N—— We Invent" (1969; 115) in *The Cross of Redemption*. In a 1979 essay, Baldwin wrote that what Birmingham signifies and contains reaches both backward and forward in time—that what happened in Birmingham goes back "countless generations," and it moves forward through the ways it politicized young people like Angela Davis, Julian Bond, and Jerome Smith. See "Lorraine Hansberry at the Summit," 136.

17. On the informal set of agreements or meta-agreements that constitute the Racial Contract and that are characterized by evasion, misrepresentation, and self-deception on matters of race, see Mills, *The Racial Contract*, 11, 19. On the violence and shame that structure the formation of white racial identity, see Thandeka, *Learning to Be White*, 12–13, 17–19.

18. Willoughby-Herard, "Mammy No More/Mammy Forever," 160, 162.

19. Baldwin and Peck, *I Am Not Your Negro*, 31.

20. Tiffany Willoughby-Herard, comments, Scandal in Real Time Conference, May 2016, youtu.be/esELsb4Fw5M; and Willoughby-Herard, *Waste of a White Skin,* 185 and 245fn12.

21. Baldwin and Mead, *A Rap on Race,* 221.

22. McKittrick, *Demonic Grounds,* 12.

23. Lipsitz, "The Racialization of Space and the Spatialization of Race," 12; Gilmore, *Golden Gulag,* 28; Mills, *The Racial Contract,* 41–44, 51–52; and Cheng and Shabazz, "Introduction: Race, Space, and Scale in the Twenty-First Century."

24. "Robert Kennedy and Noel Coward," *The Mike Wallace Profiles,* Sc Visual VRC-2880, James Baldwin: The Price of The Ticket Documentary Film Collection, Schomburg Center for Research in Black Culture.

25. King, *Why We Can't Wait,* 85–112.

26. Baldwin, *The Fire Next Time,* 106; Lowndes, "Barack Obama's Body," 471–472.

27. Steinberg, *Race Relations,* 17, 39, 43, 52.

28. As a genre of appeal, prophecy is often (but not always) entrenched in nation-building and in masculinized charismatic leadership that is tied to the nation. See chapter 1.

29. See Tiffany Willoughby-Herard on the ways in which nation states are built on Racial Contracts, in *Waste of a White Skin,* 145–6 and 2–5, 29.

30. LaShonda Carter, correspondence, June 30, 2017.

31. Baldwin and Buckley, "Debate: Baldwin vs Buckley."

32. Jones and Engel, *What Would Martin Say?,* 192.

33. Baldwin, "Lorraine Hansberry at the Summit," 136.

34. Baldwin, "Lorraine Hansberry at the Summit," 136; Boyd, *Baldwin's Harlem,* 72; and James Baldwin and Kenneth Clark Interviews, Jean Stein Papers, John F. Kennedy Presidential Library.

35. Baldwin and Clark Interviews, Stein Papers.

36. Iton, *In Search of the Black Fantastic,* 28, 68–69. Robert Kennedy, for example, rejected the delegate's political claims and analyses through tropes that "they didn't know anything about government." "Sixth Oral History Interview with Robert F. Kennedy and Burke Marshall, December 6, 1964," 588, Robert F. Kennedy Oral History Collection, John F. Kennedy Presidential Library.

37. Robert Nemiroff to Lena Horne, March 15, 1963, Folder 3, Box 65; "A Salute to Southern Students," Folder 3, Box 65; "Chronology: Lorraine Hansberry," Folder 7, Box 68; and "Defenders of Worthy to Picket Banquet for Kennedy in D.C.," Folder 2, Box 72, Lorraine Hansberry Papers, Schomburg Center for Research in Black Culture; and Leeming, *James Baldwin,* 219.

38. Leeming, *James Baldwin,* 218.

39. Jerome M. Smith and Weldon J. Rougeau to Lorraine Hansberry, March 27, 1963, Folder 3, Box 65, Hansberry Papers; and see Figure 3.1.

40. *Hansberry v. Lee* (1940); and Hansberry, *To Be Young, Gifted, and Black,* 51.

41. Hansberry et al., *Lorraine Hansberry: The Black Experience in the Creation of Drama.*

42. Lipsitz, *How Racism Takes Place,* 199.

43. "Memoir," Folder 8, Box 68; and "The Riot," Folder 4, Box 60, Hansberry Papers; Perry, *Looking for Lorraine,* 11, 24.

44. "Make New Sounds," Folder 1, Box 3, Hansberry Papers.
45. "The Negro Writer and His Roots," Folder 4, Box 58, Hansberry Papers. Hansberry presented this talk to the *American Society of African Culture* on March 1, 1959. See also Hansberry's poem, "Three Hundred Years Later," Folder 15, Box 60, Hansberry Papers. Hansberry self-consciously adopted W. E. B. Du Bois' "legacy which insists that American Negroes do not follow their oppressors. . . . That we look out at the world through our own eyes and have the fibre not to call enemy friend or friend enemy," and explained that this international identification, Pan-Africanism, and sense of herself as a part of a world majority in the context of growing anticolonial movements are what gave her a sense of freedom and power that her father did not have in his lifetime. See "Remarks by Lorraine Hansberry at Memorial Meeting for W.E.B. Du Bois," February 29, 1964, Folder 21, Box 56; "To Pick your Leaders," March 27, 1964, Folder 6, Box 72; and "Five Writers and Their African Ancestors," Folder 7, Box 3, Hansberry Papers.
46. On Hansberry's publications at *The Ladder* and *ONE* and on her lesbian identity, see Perry, *Looking for Lorraine*, chapter 5, and Colbert, *Radical Vision*, 59–65.
47. "Playwright at Work," Folder 3, Box 3, Hansberry Papers. Hansberry names this craft of embedding visions of the future in a story of the present (or past) in her 1964 speech to young Black writers, in her call to "write about the world as it is and as you think it *ought* to be and must be—if there is to be a world." "To Be Young, Gifted, and Black," May 1, 1964, Folder 3, Box 59, Hansberry Papers. See also Colbert, *Radical Vision*, 21, 29.
48. "Lorraine Hansberry Discusses Her Play 'A Raisin in the Sun,'" Studs Terkel Radio Archive; Colbert, *Radical Vision*, 6, 30–32, 34, 44; Perry, *Looking for Lorraine*, 149, 157, 161, 167, 182; and Lorraine Hansberry interviewed by Mike Wallace, Folder 2, Box 3, Hansberry Papers. See also Colbert on Hansberry's existentialist thought.
49. The essay was originally written for a retrospective issue of *Freedomways* on Hansberry.
50. See also Hansberry's FBI records (especially Box 72) and also Folder 1, Box 4, and Folder 5, Box 65, Hansberry Papers. Michael Eric Dyson's book on the summit, *What the Truth Sounds Like,* draws on a number of the same primary materials, and there are certain resonances between our interpretations of the event. Differently than Dyson, however, I maintain that Hansberry, with support from Horne, was the theoretical lead at the summit. See also Soyica Diggs Cobert's account of the summit in *Radical Vision,* 134–135; and Barbara Tomlinson and George Lipsitz's account in *Insubordinate Spaces,* 2–6.
51. See, e.g., Clarence B. Jones to the *New York Times,* June 10, 1963, Burke Marshall Papers, John F. Kennedy Presidential Library, 1–4; and Jones and Engel, *What Would Martin Say?*, 194.
52. Jones and Engel, *What Would Martin Say?*, 193. See also Schlesinger, *Robert Kennedy and His Times,* 332.
53. Smith, "The Jump-Off Point," 61–62.
54. Perry, *Looking for Lorraine*, 163.
55. Clark Interview, Stein Papers.

56. Clark Interview, Stein Papers.

57. Baldwin Interview, Stein Papers, 1; Jones and Engel, *What Would Martin Say?*, 193. In the retrospective interview, Baldwin explained that in the Deep South, FBI agents were called "blood counters," which "meant that you got beaten to death under the eyes of the FBI and the Justice Department. And the FBI stood there and watched this man bleed to death, and sent a report into Washington saying, 'This man bled thirty-nine thousand drops of blood and we find no violation of his civil rights.'" Baldwin in "Robert Kennedy and Noel Coward."

58. Baldwin, "Lorraine Hansberry at the Summit," 137. Jones also describes Kennedy "turn[ing] away" from Smith at this point in the conversation. See "Robert Kennedy and Noel Coward."

59. Baldwin, "Lorraine Hansberry at the Summit," 137.

60. Jones and Engel, *What Would Martin Say?*, 193.

61. Horne in Jones and Engel, *What Would Martin Say?*, 193; Baldwin, "Lorraine Hansberry at the Summit," 137.

62. Baldwin, "Lorraine Hansberry at the Summit," 138; Baldwin Interview, Stein Papers.

63. Horne and Shickel, *Lena*, 278.

64. Leeming, *James Baldwin*, 221.

65. Leeming, *James Baldwin*, 224.

66. Horne and Shickel, *Lena*, 281.

67. Horne and Shickel, *Lena*, 278.

68. Clark Interview, Stein Papers; and Jones and Engel, *What Would Martin Say?*, 193–194. Baldwin recounts that they recommended Kennedy escort to school a "black girl already scheduled to enter a Deep South school." "Lorraine Hansberry at the Summit," 137.

69. Baldwin, "Lorraine Hansberry at the Summit," 138.

70. Clarence B. Jones to the *New York Times*, June 7, 1963; Marshall Papers, 2–3.

71. Clark Interview, Stein Papers, 11. Jones reflected that his dominant recollection of the meeting was Robert Kennedy's naïveté—that the "chief law enforcement officer was *surprised* and *shocked* to hear what a cross section of Black Americans were saying about the conditions of Black Americans in the South and North." Jones in "Robert Kennedy and Noel Coward." See also Jones to the *New York Times*, 4.

72. Baldwin, "Lorraine Hansberry at the Summit," 137; and Leeming, *James Baldwin*, 224.

73. To reconstruct this particular moment, I draw on Hansberry's description of her departure as quoted in the *Village Voice*, and Baldwin's retelling of her departure in his essay "Lorraine Hansberry at the Summit." As quoted by the *Voice*, Hansberry explains that "I did not . . . as was reported in some quarters, walk out. When I got up to leave, the meeting had gone on for about three hours, and everyone got up, said goodbye, and left." I take this newspaper account to be more likely reliable than some other newspaper accounts of the summit (see note 51), as Hansberry already had a relationship with the *Voice*—she had published there in prior years and would do so again. Where Hansberry did not see her *embodied departure* as a politics of refusal—she saw the meeting had come to an obvious closing—Baldwin read refusal in her departure. Both these accounts can exist alongside each other, as Baldwin is speaking

to the meaning he made of her departure. Additionally, I take Baldwin's rendering of Hansberry's final *remarks*—which I recount and analyze in this chapter—to hold weight, particularly given Hansberry's invocation of the same photograph in her Croton rally speech three weeks later. Diane Fisher, "Birthweight Low, Jobs Few, Death Comes Early," *Village Voice,* Folder 9, Box 3, Hansberry Papers, 9; and Baldwin "Lorraine Hansberry at the Summit," 138–139; and Hansberry, "Croton Rally," June 16, 1963, Folder 1, Box 56, Hansberry Papers, 2.

74. Baldwin quoting Hansberry in "Lorraine Hansberry at the Summit," 138.

75. Baldwin, "Lorraine Hansberry at the Summit," 138; Baldwin Interview, Stein Papers, 5, 12; and Hansberry, "Croton Rally," June 16, 1963, Folder 1, Box 56, Hansberry Papers, 2.

76. Baldwin, "Lorraine Hansberry at the Summit," 139.

77. Baldwin, "Lorraine Hansberry at the Summit," 139.

78. Clark Interview, Stein Papers, 5; Schlesinger, *Robert Kennedy and His Times,* 335.

79. Balfour, *The Evidence of Things Not Said*, 105.

80. Baldwin, "Lorraine Hansberry at the Summit," 135.

81. Schlesinger, *Robert Kennedy and His Times*, 333.

82. Baldwin, "Lorraine Hansberry at the Summit," 137.

83. Toni Morrison, " 'I wanted to carve out a world both culture-specific and race-free," *The Guardian,* August 8, 2019.

84. Friedner and Helmreich, "Sound Studies Meets Deaf Studies," 80.

85. I thank my reviewers for their clarity on this point.

86. Hansberry et al., *Lorraine Hansberry: The Black Experience in the Creation of Drama.*

87. Lorraine Hansberry, "The New Paternalists," 15, Folder 8, Box 58, Hansberry Papers.

88. Lorraine Hansberry, "Me Tink Me Hear Sounds in De Night," 9, Folder 1, Box 58, Hansberry Papers.

89. Baldwin, "Lorraine Hansberry at the Summit," 137.

90. Tiffany Willoughby-Herard, correspondence, June 30, 2017. See also Natasha Behl's account of and interventions into narrow definitions of the political in *Gendered Citizenship,* 25–26.

91. Meier and Rudwick, *CORE,* 298; and Horne and Shickel, *Lena,* 280.

92. Smith, "Jump-Off Point," 63.

93. Perry, *Looking for Lorraine,* 166.

94. "Rally to Support the Southern Freedom Movement June 16, 1963," Folder 1, Box 56, Hansberry Papers. Part of the funds for CORE went to purchase the station wagon that James Chaney, Andrew Goodman, and Michael Schwerner used for voter registration organizing the day they were murdered.

95. Hansberry, "Croton Rally," Hansberry Papers.

96. "Lorraine Hansberry: Make New Sounds," Folder 1, Box 3, Hansberry Papers.

97. Lorraine Hansberry, "Croton Rally," Hansberry Papers; "The Little Man Who Wasn't There: Negro Intellectuals Just Can't Reach Robert Kennedy," *National Guardian,* Folder 1, Box 4, Hansberry Papers.

98. Khanum Shaikh, correspondence, January 24, 2020.

99. Clark Interview, Stein Papers; Schlesinger, *Robert Kennedy and His Times,* 332.

100. On "assuming the persona of [an] office," see Accapadi, "When White Women Cry," 211.

101. Khanum Shaikh, correspondence, January 24, 2020.

102. Multiple reports indicated that Witherspoon resisted police authority/violence. This story did not fit the liberal white media's frames presenting white Southerners as active agents and Black people as passive victims. Berger, 115–116, 122.

103. Hansberry quoted in Baldwin, "Lorraine Hansberry at the Summit," 138. On SNCC's extensive media structure and the role of photography in SNCC's cultural and political work, see Leigh Raiford, "Come Let Us Build a New World Together."

104. "Student Nonviolent Coordinating Committee, Ivan Black, Press Representative," Folder 5, Box 65; and "Birthweight Low, Jobs Few, Death Comes Early," Folder 1, Box 4, Hansberry Papers. Confronting white epistemologies of ignorance and disavowal would animate Hansberry's incisive interventions at the 1964 Town Hall Debate "The Black Revolution and White Backlash"; her 1961 exchange with Norman Mailer in the *Village Voice*; and some of the characterization in *The Sign in Sidney Brustein's Window* and *Les Blancs*.

105. Clark Interview, Stein Papers.

106. The day after the summit, Belafonte relayed details to King over the phone—describing the meeting as a "disaster" and recounting Smith's comments. King reflected that "maybe that's exactly what Bobby needed to hear." See Belafonte, *My Song*, 270.

107. Don Paul, "Jerome Smith and his Freedom Fighting Peers' Enduring Light," *The New Orleans Tribune*, 2017; John F. Kennedy, "Televised Address to the Nation on Civil Rights," June 11, 1963; and "The Little Man Who Wasn't There," Folder 1, Box 4, Hansberry Papers.

108. One biographer argued that Robert Kennedy's contempt shifted a day or two after the meeting toward some understanding of Smith's absolute refusal to fight in the U.S. Army (Guthman, *We Band of Brothers*, 221), but Kennedy's December 1964 oral history interview on the matter still reveals contempt. When asked by Mike Wallace about Robert Kennedy's shift in later years, as well as about his having gained a reputation of having some understanding about Black politics, Clark explained that Kennedy "went through quite a bit to get to that understanding," and Baldwin explained that "he was different, yes, and something had happened to him, yes. He suffered. And I think for the first time he understood that suffering was real." Neither Baldwin nor Clark explains the summit as being a singular catalyst. See "Robert Kennedy and Noel Coward."

109. Baldwin in "Robert Kennedy and Noel Coward."

110. In a 1970 interview, Baldwin reflected on how surprising the delegates' relative unity must have been to Bobby Kennedy, asking rhetorically, "what really connects Lena Horne and Jimmy Baldwin? . . . What connects all of us to that student? No one had ever heard of him; he didn't sing or dance or act or anything. Why did he become the focal point? On what principle were we all united in defending him? Trying to explain what he was trying to say. That boy, after all, in some sense, represented to everybody in that room our hope. Our honor. Our dignity. But, above all, our hope. We

can't afford our black boys being beaten half to death. We can't afford it." See Baldwin Interview, Stein Papers, 21.

111. Baldwin Interview, Stein Papers.

112. King, *Why We Can't Wait*, 97. Baldwin later reflected on the historical significance of such an in-person meeting, explaining that even as the Kennedys were "exasperat[ing]," it was a moment in which "at least [there was] contact, . . . connection . . . [there was] something happening which makes other things possible. And that's gone! That's gone! Ain't anybody going to try to rap with Richard Nixon. Good Lord!" See Baldwin Interview, Stein Papers.

113. Clark Interview, Stein Papers, 14.

114. The summit took place a month after some of the first major signs (a fainting episode, followed by hospitalization and abdominal surgery) of Hanberry's illness. Hansberry passed away of pancreatic cancer in January 1965.

115. Clark Interview, Stein Papers.

116. Horne and Schickel, *Lena*, 280.

117. Horne and Schickel, *Lena*, 280.

118. Horne, then forty-six, had been acutely aware that "a new generation was taking over. And they were not interested in being symbols. They knew the symbol was obsolete—before I did. . . . They knew my generation had been sold a bill of goods—and I was just learning it." Horne had for years been reflecting upon her experiences of tokenism and objectification. She had resolved to "re-identify" herself with Black people after years of navigating white worlds, and she was determined to find her way in the civil rights movement. In her account, participation in the summit symbolized this turn. See Horne and Schickel, *Lena*, 271, 274.

119. Horne and Shickel, *Lena*, 289–290; and Raymond, *Stars for Freedom*, 136.

120. "Sixth Oral History Interview with Robert F. Kennedy and Burke Marshall," 586–588.

121. Tia Oso, "Say It: I Interrupted a Presidential Town Hall Because Black Women Matter," *The Atlantic*, July 23, 2015; Marissa Johnson, "1 Year Later: BLM Protestor Who Interrupted Bernie Sanders' Rally Discusses the Moment and the Movement," *The Root*, August 9, 2016; and Alex Lubben, "We Spoke to Ashley Williams, the Black Queer Organizers Who Interrupted Hillary Clinton," *The Nation*, February 26, 2016.

122. Jasmine Syedullah, conversation, August 2017.

123. S. I. Rosenbaum, "The Education of Daunasia Yancey," *Boston Magazine*, January 29, 2015.

124. The $30 billion bill was the largest crime control bill in U.S. history, implementing the "three strikes" mandatory life sentences policy; allocating money to hire 100,000 new police officers and $9.7 billion in funding prisons; and expanding death penalty–eligible offenses. See "H.R. 3355—Violent Crimes and Law Enforcement Act of 1994." For footage of the meeting, see *Democracy Now*, August 19, 2015.

125. Elizabeth Hinton, Julilly Hohler-Hausmann, and Vesla M. Weaver, "Did Blacks Really Endorse the 1994 Crime Bill?," *New York Times*, April 13, 2016; and Tiffany Willoughby-Herard, correspondence, June 29, 2018.

126. See "When Black Lives Matter Met Clinton," *Democracy Now*, August 19, 2015.

127. Melvin Rogers, conversation, December 1, 2016. See also Hooker, "Black Lives Matter and the Paradoxes of U.S. Black Politics," 456.

128. The two meetings illuminate different dimensions of boundness. In the first, Hansberry and Horne are asking Kennedy to be present to a testimony for something from which he cannot, as a white Northerner, be separated. In the second meeting, Yancey and Jones are asking Clinton to be accountable to violent effects of the Clinton administration's decisions in the 1990s. Georgia Warnke and John Medearis, discussion, April 18, 2018.

129. Beard, "James Baldwin on Violence and Disavowal," 355.

130. Shulman, *American Prophecy*, xiv.

131. Shulman, *American Prophecy*, 19.

132. As Shulman traces, critics of white supremacy have reworked rather than ceded prophetic language, employing this "extraordinarily resonant form of political speech" to upend the sacred iconography of American exceptionalism, to pose questions unvoiced in the liberal ordinary, to provoke acknowledgment, and redefine collective purpose. See *American Prophecy*, xii–xiii.

133. Shulman, *American Prophecy*, 136.

134. Shulman, *American Prophecy*, 19.

135. Accapadi, "When White Women Cry," 210.

136. This problem in the two meetings of what is unheard is emblematic of broader politics in both moments. At a distance, all that is heard is a narrow kind of dissent, rather than an appeal to boundness. Jasmine Syedullah, conversation, May 19, 2017.

137. Cory Gooding, Discussant comments, NCOBPS Conference, March 17, 2017.

138. Balfour, *The Evidence of Things Not Said*, 103–104.

139. Krause, *Civil Passions*, 201.

140. As Dyson has put it, "Baldwin knew that tinkering with public policy was of little use if the value of black life had not been established." See Dyson, *What the Truth Sounds Like*, 59.

141. Iton, *In Search of the Black Fantastic*, 33–34, 58, 68. In the Cold War, civil rights, and post–civil rights eras, Iton explains, the absence of significant representation within electoral politics due to structures of white supremacist domination, disenfranchisement, and racial terror meant that civil rights movement leaders and cultural actors provided much of the public leadership in Black communities. This leadership was fiercely policed. McCarthyism, countersubversion and political demonology, state surveillance, the strictures of Cold War patriotism, and the attempted containment of Black transnationalism structured the increasing demarcation and confinement of the "appropriate" role of the artist as being outside of politics or only in service to patriotic performance. See *In Search of the Black Fantastic*, 33, 36–38.

142. Melvin Rogers, conversation, December 1, 2016.

143. See Krause, *Civil Passions*, 3.

144. Thompson, "An Exoneration of Black Rage," 461.

145. Thompson, "An Exoneration of Black Rage," 461; and Willoughby-Herard, "More Expendable than Slaves?," 507. Through the terms of civility discourse, appeals issued by raced and gendered others are deemed angry and emotional, and are

discarded, unheard, and shut out of democratic engagement. I thank Bronwyn Leebaw for engagement on this point.

146. Thompson, "An Exoneration of Black Rage," 459–460, 469–470; and Cooper, *Eloquent Rage*, 169.

Interlude

1. Willoughby-Herard, "More Expendable than Slaves?," 507.
2. Smith interview in Harris, "From the Kennedy Commission to the Combahee Collective," 300. For Smith's account of the disjuncture between the original meaning of "identity politics" in the CRC statement and the meanings that have become attached to the term in succeeding decades, see "Feminist Scholar Barbara Smith on Identity Politics," *Democracy Now*, February 12, 2020. See also Taylor, *How We Get Free*, 11–12.
3. Pharr, *In the Time of the Right*, 100. There is also a related set of critiques in academic spaces around questions of solidarity, knowledge, and identification. Ernesto Javier Martínez, conversation, 2015; and Smith in "Feminist Scholar Barbara Smith on Identity Politics."
4. Garza, *The Purpose of Power*, 186–189.
5. Gilmore, "Forgotten Places and the Seeds of Grassroots Planning," 39. See also Alcoff, *Visible Identities*, Introduction and chapters 1–2; Willoughby-Herard, "South Africa's Poor Whites and Whiteness Studies," 482 fn9; and Alcoff and Mohanty, "Reconsidering Identity Politics," 1–2. Gilmore argues that a more useful critique of identity "reveals the contradictory ways in which identities fracture and reform in the crucibles of state and society, public and private, home and work, violence and consent."
6. Alcoff, *Visible Identities*, 6; Ransby, "Quilting a Movement," *In These Times*, April 4, 2011.
7. Alcoff, *Visible Identities*, 15.
8. Gilmore, "Forgotten Places," 39.
9. See, e.g., Lilla, *The Once and Future Liberal*.
10. Garza, *The Purpose of Power*, 194; Alcoff, *Visible Identities*, 17–18 and chapters 2 and 3.
11. Dean, *Cultural Studies and Political Theory*, 6.
12. Lowndes, "From New Class Critique to White Nationalism," 9.
13. Marlene Cimons, "AIDS: 'It's Changed Us Forever,'" *Los Angeles Times*, May 31, 1992.
14. Hall, "Fantasy, Identity, Politics," 67.
15. Hall, "Fantasy, Identity, Politics," 68.
16. Hall, "Fantasy, Identity, Politics," 67–68.
17. Durham, *The Christian Right*, 154; Lowndes, "From Pat Buchanan to Donald Trump."
18. Lowndes, "New Class Critique," 1; Zeskind, *Blood and Politics*, 288–292; Durham, *The Christian Right*, 155–158.

19. Francis, "Winning the Culture War," *Chronicles*, December 1993, 13.

20. Francis, "Winning the Culture War," 12.

21. Francis, "Winning the Culture War," 15.

22. Francis, "Winning the Culture War," 12.

23. In her report, "Violence in Houston," SONG co-founder Suzanne Pharr explains that in July 1992, after six months of organizing against the Christian Right in Oregon and returning to the Women's Project in Arkansas, she was afraid that people had begun to think she had become "obsessed and exaggerated" in her accounts of the growth and influence of the Christian Right. However, after traveling to Houston to work with national strategists in the lesbian and gay Left and participate in multiple protests at the RNC, she realized that prior to the Convention she "had not been outspoken enough." See Pharr, "Violence in Houston," Women's Project [AR] folder, Box 19, International Gay Information Center collection, NYPL.

24. Young, "Dan Quayle," 451. On the Eagle Form, Shlafly, and the context of resurgent right-wing politics, see Jean Hardisty's *Mobilizing Resentment*.

25. Lindsay Brice, "1992 Republican National Convention Protests," *Getty Images*, August 20, 1992; and Julie Morris, "AIDS Protestors Burn Flag as Turbulent First Day Outside GOP Convention Ends," *UPI*, August 18, 1992.

26. Pharr, "Violence in Houston," 4.

27. "'92 Republican Convention: GOP Takes the Field," *Los Angeles Times*, August 17, 1992; Pharr, "Violence in Houston."

28. "Pat Buchanan 1992 Republican Convention Address," August 17, 1992, c-span.org/video/?31255–1/pat-buchanan-1992-republican-convention-address; and americanrhetoric.com/speeches/patrickbuchanan1992rnc.htm.

29. Lowndes, "The Populist Violence of Donald Trump," 9.

30. Lowndes, "Populist Violence," 9; and Lowndes, "From Pat Buchanan to Donald Trump," 272.

31. Miller, "Patrick Joseph Buchanan," 52.

32. Miller, "Patrick Joseph Buchanan," 56.

33. Rogin, *Ronald Reagan The Movie*, xvi.

34. Hill, *Men, Mobs, and Law*, 117–120.

35. Swinth, *Feminism's Forgotten Fight*, Introduction.

36. Ruth Wilson Gilmore explains that antistate state actors are people and parties who gain state power by denouncing state power, including by denouncing government spending and arguing for "shrinking government" even as they increase spending on the military, prisons, and border militarization. See Gilmore, "In the Shadow of the Shadow State," 45–46.

37. Yamin, *American Marriage*, 99–100.

38. Yamin, *American Marriage*, 101.

39. Yamin, *American Marriage*, 104.

40. Kauffman, *Bad Girls and Sick Boys*, 237.

41. Kauffman, *Bad Girls and Sick Boys*, 236.

42. Rogin, *Ronald Reagan the Movie*, xiii.

43. Anker, *Orgies of Feeling*, 2–3. As Anker explains, melodrama became an influential political discourse after World War II with the rise of the Cold War and televisual political communication.

44. Anker, *Orgies of Feeling*, 84.

45. Rogin, *Ronald Reagan the Movie*, xvi. Rogin is referring to Reagan's March 16, 1986 nationwide address about Nicaragua.

46. "Managing the Crisis: The FDIC and RTC Experience—Chronological Overview," Federal Deposit Insurance Corporation; and Stanley, *The Crusader*, 153.

47. Willoughby-Herard, *Waste of a White Skin*, 92, 95. On the political and ideological labor that goes into constructing notions of white kinship and on the gendered articulations of "fraternal agreements" between white elites to see poor white people as kin, see Willoughby-Herard, *Waste of a White Skin*, chap. 2, especially 57–58, 61, 67; and Sherene Razack, symposium comments, *From Colorblindness to White Nationalism?: Emerging Racial Formations in the Trump Era*, UCLA, March 3, 2017, youtu.be/HkOI90ckNmM. See Thandeka's *Learning to Be White* on the processes through which white people train each other to identify against people of color (or to identify with people of color in a patronizing ways) and to identify with (masculinized and sexualized) whiteness.

48. Willoughby-Herard, *Waste of a White Skin*, 49.

49. Lowndes, *From the New Deal to the New Right*, 3–5, 92, 161; and Olson, "Whiteness and the Polarization of American Politics," 710.

50. On the gender and racial politics of whose economic precarity gets registered as a "crisis," see Strolovitch, "Of Mancessions and Hecoveries," 167–168, 170.

51. Willoughby-Herard, *Waste of a White Skin*, 57.

52. HoSang and Lowndes, *Producers, Parasites, Patriots*, 24–25.

53. HoSang and Lowndes, *Producers, Parasites, Patriots*, 26–27. Here, Buchanan's "makers" are loggers, mill workers, and shopkeepers, and the "takers" include elite Democrats—a framing that requires that he downplay the economic standing of Republican elites.

54. *New Orleans City Park Improvement Association v. Detiege* (1958); *Watson et al. v. City of Memphis et al.* (1963); and "Civil Rights in America: Racial Desegregation of Public Accommodations," National Park Service (2009) 162, 168–169.

55. See Gordon Parks' photograph, "Outside, Looking In, Mobile, Alabama" (1956), in which six Black children stand outside a chain-link fence looking into one such segregated park, bearing witness to the park as a site of race-making, to its occupation and its emptiness, and to this iteration of white conceptions of play and pleasure that lie in performing myths of superiority.

56. On nostalgic and privatized fantasies of the "American way of life," see Berlant, *The Queen of America Goes to Washington City*, 5.

57. As Suzanne Pharr emphasizes, this era was a time of legalized segregation and racial violence, a time when abortion was illegal and, for many people, it was a time when rape, battering, incest, and alcoholism were kept as secrets within the family. See Pharr, *In the Time of the Right*, 83.

58. Scheper, *Moving Performances*, 170. See also Hardisty, *Mobilizing Resentment*, 18–19.

59. Boym, "Nostalgia," *Atlas of Transformation*.

60. Boym, *Common Places*, 284–285.

61. Anderson, *Imagined Communities*, 6.

62. Boym, *Common Places*, 285.

63. Tiffany Willoughby-Herard, correspondence, October 11, 2018.

64. Durham, *The Christian Right*, 150.

65. Olson, "Whiteness and the Polarization of American Politics," 710; and Lowndes, "White Populism and the Transformation of the Silent Majority," 30.

66. Lowndes, "White Populism," 26.

67. Lowndes, "Populist Violence," 9; and Lowndes, "White Populism," 30.

68. Lowndes, "White Populism," 28.

69. Lowndes, "Populist Violence," 9; Lowndes, "White Populism," 30.

70. Olson, "Whiteness and the Polarization of American Politics," 711.

71. Margolin, "'Make America Great Again'—Who Said It First?," *NBC News*, September 9, 2016.

72. Maskovsky, "Toward the Anthropology of White Nationalist Postracialism," 435.

73. Antiracist activists and cultural workers have flipped MAGA, including issuing red hats and posters calling to "Make Racists Afraid Again." See Smithsonian National Museum of American History, americanhistory.si.edu/collections/search/object/nmah_1851077.

74. Kim, *Bitter Fruit*, 6, 51; Smith, "Affect and Respectability Politics"; and Beard, "James Baldwin on Violence and Disavowal," 340.

75. A defining feature of the culture wars in the late twentieth century was a shift in discourse from "race" to "culture"—with early articulations of "race relations" emerging from the University of Chicago in the 1920s, the 1944 Myrdal Report, and through George Wallace's use of culture as a proxy for race in the late 1960s into the 1970s. Across many of his speeches, Spiro Agnew pathologized African Americans and lauded (white) "forgotten Americans" as personifying values of work, faith, and family. "Out of these articulations of values," Joel Olson explains, "came a set of debates (over welfare policy, crime, family, anticommunism, and abortion) that superficially appeared to have nothing to do with race but in fact revolved around the perceived pathologies of the black poor and the implicit virtues of the normalized white middle." See Olson, "Whiteness and the Polarization of American Politics," 714; and Steinberg, *Race Relations*, 20, 52.

76. HoSang and Lowndes, *Producers, Parasites, Patriots*, 20; and Alexander, *Pedagogies of Crossing*, 98–99.

77. Crenshaw and Peller, "Reel Time/Real Justice," 57.

78. Crenshaw and Peller, "Reel Time/Real Justice," 58.

79. Lowndes, "From Pat Buchanan to Donald Trump," 274.

80. As Claire Jean Kim explains, the 1992 Los Angeles rebellion played a crucial role in "etching Black–Korean conflict into American popular consciousness" through a racial scapegoating story that was "rip[ped] out" of the larger context of how racial power operates in contemporary America. Racial power, Kim demonstrates, not only "shapes the structural setting for Black–Korean conflict . . . [and] conditions the form

and rhetoric of Black collective action that arises against Korean merchants within this setting" but also "determines how major opinion makers interpret and respond to such action." See Kim, *Bitter Fruit*, 2–3.

81. Morrison, "On the Backs of Blacks."
82. Florian Martin, "10 Years Since Katrina: When the Astrodome Was a Mass Shelter," *Houston Public Media*, August 17, 2015.
83. "Barbara Bush Calls Evacuees Better Off," *New York Times*, September 7, 2005.
84. Sam Sacks, "Pat Buchanan: 'I Am on the Wrong Side of History,'" *RT America*, December 31, 2013.
85. "The 1992 Campaign: Buchanan Returns to Offensive Against Bush," *New York Times*, April 19, 1992.
86. Tim Alberta, "The Ideas Made It, but I Didn't," *Politico*, May/June 2017.
87. Miller, "Patrick Joseph Buchanan, Culture War Speech," 52.
88. At the start of his campaign, Buchanan acknowledged to reporters that his candidacy was "a very long-shot thing" and said his best hope would be a "replay" of 1968, when Eugene McCarthy garnered 42 percent of the vote in New Hampshire's Democratic primary, after which Lyndon B. Johnson withdrew from the race; or a replay of 1952, when Harry S. Truman withdrew from the primaries after Estes Kefauver won the New Hampshire primary. Robin Toner, "Buchanan, Urging New Nationalism, Joins '92 Race," *New York Times*, December 11, 1991.
89. Joshua Plencner, correspondence, August 13, 2018. See also Lowndes, "Barack Obama's Body," 471–473.
90. Samuel Francis, "From Household to Nation," *Chronicles*, March 1996. See also Lowndes, "From Pat Buchanan to Donald Trump," 271.

Chapter 4

1. Breedlove in *All of Us North Carolina*, directed by Sowjanya Kudva, vimeo.com/68133777.
2. Breedlove quoted by Serena Sebring in personal interview, August 12, 2014; and "One Million Conversations on Porches: A Report on SONG's Organizing During the Amendment One Ballot Measure in North Carolina," southernersonnewground.org. SONG leadership anticipated that the campaign would create opportunities for base building, intersectional issue framing, rural organizing, culture shift work, and grassroots leadership development.
3. SONG, Sowjanya Kudva, and Mikel Barton, *The Day after Amendment One . . . OUR WIN IS BIGGER!*, vimeo.com/41802835.
4. Deborah Lilton, email correspondence, August 25, 2021.
5. See SONG's article "Our People Are Worth the Risks" for SONG's account of the right wing's attempts to organize voters around their "family values" agenda, take over the governance of public institutions, use homosexuality as a wedge issue, and convince progressive organizations to abandon the South.

6. In an article on the activist group Mothers Reclaiming Our Children, Ruth Wilson Gilmore considers how the group, in "Antonio Gramsci's formulation of a philosophy of praxis, 'renovates and makes critical already existing activities' of both action and analysis to build a movement." See Gilmore, "You Have Dislodged a Boulder," 13; and Gilmore, "Fatal Couplings of Power and Difference," 17. See also Collins, "It's All in the Family," 78.

7. Talley, "Feminists We Love."

8. Puar, *Terrorist Assemblages*, 4, 39; Yasmin Nair, "Why I Won't Come Out on National Coming Out Day," blog, October 9, 2008; Yamin, *American Marriage*, chap. 5; and Ferguson, *One-Dimensional Queer*, 14.

9. Tiffany Willoughby-Herard, correspondence, March 4, 2019; Sycamore, "There's More to Life Than Platinum," in *That's Revolting!*, 6–7; Melamed, *Represent and Destroy*, 11.

10. Tiffany Willoughby-Herard, correspondence, March 4, 2019; Robinson, *An Anthropology of Marxism*, 33.

11. Kate Shapiro, personal interview, August 18, 2014.

12. Kate Shapiro, personal interview, August 18, 2014.

13. SONG's listening campaigns should be understood as part of a long-standing practice and political principle of participatory research in the organization—a practice of "collect[ing] stories and draw[ing] answers for our work from our constituency" and "synthesiz[ing] this work to give back" to their base ("Co-Director thoughts on SONG History," file shared by Caitlin Breedlove). Suzanne Pharr, Cara Page, Paulina Helm-Hernández, and Caitlin Breedlove developed the Organizing School curriculum starting in 2006. Between 2009 and 2013, SONG organizing schools trained more than 200 LGBTQ leaders across seven states. See "SONG History Timeline by SONG Board 2009"; "SONG Grant Proposal 2013," file shared by Caitlin Breedlove; and the "Igniting the Kindred" report on Organizing Schools.

14. Stefanía García, correspondence, April 27, 2019.

15. "SONGdoc brochure," file shared by Caitlin Breedlove. As of 2021, SONG is using a version of this phrase in their tagline: "SONG is a home for LGBTQ liberation across all lines of race, class, abilities, age, culture, gender, and sexuality in the South." See southernersonnewground.org.

16. On mobilizing identities, see Bedolla, *Fluid Borders*, 6–7.

17. Serena Sebring, personal interview, August 12, 2014.

18. Anker, *Orgies of Feeling*, 182, 192–193.

19. See Rodríguez, *Sexual Futures, Queer Gestures, and other Latina Longings*, chap. 1, especially pp. 37, 50; Spade, *Normal Life*, chap. 2; and Conrad, *Against Equality*.

20. These two forms of recognition are more than distinct—the latter can work to undo the former. See Gilmore's account of activists forming a "provisionally syncretic identity"—a provisional *we*—that required struggling with the structures and boundaries (e.g., funding streams, mission statements) that made their organizations recognizable by the state. See Gilmore, "Forgotten Places and the Seeds of Grassroots Planning," 42–43. See Leanne Betasamosake Simpson's and Glen Coulthard's theorizations of Indigenous politics of self-recognition that turn away from

settler-colonial recognition politics. Simpson, *As We Have Always Done*, chap. 10; and Coulthard, *Red Skins, White Masks*, chap. 4.

21. Gilmore, "Forgotten Places," 42–43; Reddy, *Freedom with Violence*, 193; Melamed, "The Spirit of Neoliberalism," 2; Duggan, *The Twilight of Equality?*, chap. 3.

22. Gilmore, "You Have Dislodged a Boulder," 12, 24.

23. Gilmore, "Forgotten Places," 55.

24. "Street Transvestite Action Revolutionaries," Box 19, International Gay Information Center Collection, Ephemera Files—Organizations, NYPL. When Rivera and Johnson called people into STAR, they called them into forms of relationality that the U.S. state could not provide and into visions of self-determination.

25. King, "Black 'Feminisms' and Pessimism," 72, 75. See Priscilla Yamin and Alison Gash on how family as an institution operates as an arm of the state in "State, Status and the American Family," 148. As Kennan Ferguson describes, rhetorics of family have been "metaphorically synchronous with state power"; *All in the Family*, 2, 7. My focus here is less on family as an institution but as a "contested concept implicated in . . . relations of power," as Kath Weston has put it, and as a "crucial symbol and organizing principle," as Richard Rodríguez has put it. See Weston, *Families We Choose*, 3; and Rodríguez, *Next of Kin*, 2.

26. Collins, "It's All in the Family," 63, 77–78; Harris, "Kathryn Stockett Is Not My Sister and I Am Not Her Help"; Gilroy, *Small Acts*, chap. 14; Reid-Pharr, "It's Raining Men," 259–260; and Rodríguez, *Next of Kin*, 11–12, and chap. 1.

27. Lorde, *Sister Outsider*, 70, 116, 119; Moraga, "La Jornada," xxxvii; and Collins, "It's All in the Family," 78.

28. Collins, "It's All in the Family," 67; Rodríguez, *Next of Kin*, 2, 7; and Lugones, *Pilgrimages/Peregrinajes*, 177.

29. Collins, "It's All in the Family," 77–78.

30. Rodríguez, *Next of Kin*, 7.

31. Gilmore, "Fatal Couplings of Power and Difference," 16.

32. Gilmore, "You Have Dislodged a Boulder," 25.

33. Muñoz, *Disidentifications*, 58; and Scheper, *Moving Performances*, 166.

34. Bassichis, Lee, and Spade, "Building an Abolitionist Trans and Queer Liberation Movement," 29.

35. See, e.g., SONG's blog posts, "A Revolutionary's Revolutionary: Sharing Our Moments with Murph"; "Honoring SONG Co-Founder Joan Garner"; "A Thank You to Leslie Feinberg"; "For Jurina: A Letter for a Light Lost"; and "Aloha Is Not a Task, Nor a Courtesy, It Is Kuleana: ¡Melenie Mahinamalamalama Eleneke PRESENTE! 1959–2013," all at southernersonnewground.org; and "Honoring Sylvia Rivera, 1952–2002," in "SONG Notes, Spring 2002," Mandy Carter Papers, Box 237, Duke University.

36. Ferguson, *One-Dimensional Queer*, 2, 12.

37. Pat Hussain, phone conversation, September 29, 2019.

38. From the beginning of their work as co-directors, Paulina Helm-Hernández and Caitlin Breedlove explicitly prioritized building deep relationships with SONG founders and leaders from throughout SONG's history. See "Co-Director Thoughts on SONG History." See Cathy Cohen's critical analysis of single-identity or

single-oppression frameworks in lesbian, gay, bisexual, transgender, and queer politics in the 1990s, in "Punks, Bulldaggers, and Welfare Queens," 440–441.

39. Kate Shapiro, personal interview, August 18, 2014. See also "Theory of Change: Queer Liberation," file shared by Caitlin Breedlove.

40. Aesha Rasheed, personal interview, June 14, 2014; Rodríguez, *Sexual Futures, Queer Gestures, and Other Latina Longings*, 51; and King, "Black 'Feminisms' and Pessimism," 74–75, 78.

41. Paulina Helm-Hernández in SONG StoryCorps Interview, youtu.be/ERiUlvZZnKs.

42. Sebring in Breedlove, "From Gay Marriage to Ferguson."

43. Sebring in Breedlove, "From Gay Marriage to Ferguson."

44. "Marry the Movement," SONG blog, June 27, 2013.

45. *Marry the Movement,* produced by SONG and directed by Sowjanya Kudva; King, "Southern LGBT Activists' Call: Marry the Movement," *Colorlines*, June 27, 2013; Laura Flanders, "Marry the Movement!," *The Nation*, June 27, 2013; and Caitlin Breedlove, "How Does It Feel to Be Southern and LGBTQ After the SCOTUS Decisions?," *HuffPost*, June 29, 2013.

46. Caitlin Breedlove, personal interview, August 11, 2014. For an account of the contestation and theorizing around the political meaning of identity in the gay rights movement, see also Woodly, *The Politics of Common Sense,* 74.

47. Segrest, *Memoir of a Race Traitor,* 229–246.

48. Pharr interviewed by Norman, *Sinister Wisdom,* March 28, 2013. *Sinister Wisdom* interviews of SONG co-founders available at sinisterwisdom.org/SW93Supplement.

49. Pat Hussain, phone conversation, September 29, 2019.

50. Pharr interviewed by Norman, *Sinister Wisdom.*

51. Gilmore, "In the Shadow of the Shadow State," 46; Woodly, *The Politics of Common Sense,* 67–73; Gash, *Below the Radar,* chap. 3.

52. On the concept of the antistate state, which foregrounds the ways communities abandoned by the state in terms of welfare provision are also intensely occupied by state power, see note 36 in the Interlude of this book, and Gilmore, "In the Shadow of the Shadow State," 46.

53. Pat Hussain had just led as director of outreach and interim co-chair for the 1993 Lesbian Gay and Bi March on Washington for Equal Rights and Liberation; had founded a chapter of GLAAD in Atlanta; and was in the early stages of organizing what would be a successful campaign to keep the Olympics out of Georgia's Cobb County in protest of the County's anti-gay legislation. In 1993, Pam McMichael was working at the Fairness Campaign in Kentucky (focused on housing and employment discrimination against LGBTQ people); the Kentucky Alliance Against Racism and Political Oppression; and a multiracial women's group called the Alliance Against Women's Oppression, whose analysis connected patterns of state violence, linking, for example, the divestment in women's and children's health in the U.S. with the use of U.S. tax money to harm women and children in Central America. Mandy Carter was the national director of the National Black Gay and Lesbian Leadership Forum's Fight the Right Project and had been an organizer with the War Resister's League, North Carolina Senate Vote 90, the Human Rights Campaign Fund, and the

Steering Committees of the 1987 and 1993 marches on Washington. Suzanne Pharr had a background in the women's antiviolence movement in the late 1970s and 1980s; was the founder in 1980 of the Women's Project—a multiracial organization with a strong structural commitment to the leadership of women of color—in Arkansas; and, at the time of SONG's founding, was working with the Center for Democratic Renewal, a long-standing anti-Klan network. Mab Segrest held a PhD in English; had co-produced the Southern feminist journal *Feminary*, had co-founded the multira-cial anti-Klan organization North Carolinians Against Racist and Religious Violence (NCARRV); and had recently begun working for the Urban-Rural Mission. Joan Garner was director of the Fund for Southern Communities (1993–1997); was the co-convener of the African American Lesbian Gay Alliance; and had been appointed by Atlanta Major Maynard Jackson as a liaison to gay and lesbian communities. See Mandy Carter, "Divide and Conquer," Folder 31, Box 3, SONG Records, Archives & Manuscripts, Duke University; Mandy Carter, personal interview, June 14, 2014; Pat Hussain, personal interview, August 15, 2014, and phone conversation, September 29, 2019; Suzanne Pharr, Skype interview, August 14, 2014; and *Sinister Wisdom* interviews of SONG founders. See also Johnson, *Honeypot*, 140–147. Two months be-fore the 1993 Creating Change conference, Pam McMichael participated in the Fight the Right Summit convened by NGLTF and led by Suzanne Pharr, Barbara Smith, and Scot Nakagawa, with discussions focused on pushing "the lesbigaytrans move-ment" toward a broader agenda "beyond single identity focus around queerness." See McMichael, *Sinister Wisdom* interview.

54. Pat Hussain and Pam McMichael, "SONG Notes: The Journal of Southerners On New Ground," Folder 7, Box 2, SONG Records, 2; Johnson, *Honeypot*, 140; and Pat Hussain, personal interview, August 15, 2014.

55. Pat Hussain, personal interview, August 15, 2014. In the beginning, the six co-founders developed SONG in a fairly small container. Joan Garner explains that for the first few years, the founders were adamant about not having men in the group, and that "we felt we had more work to do in establishing it as a [feminist] organiza-tion with a solid foundation. We were getting to know each other, building bonds of trust between ourselves, and making sure the organization wasn't dependent on just one person or one personality." See Garner interviewed by Norman, *Sinister Wisdom*, April 12, 2013. Cherry Hussain also played a significant role in SONG's early devel-opment, including around establishing practices of stopping work to share food. Pat Hussain, personal interview, August 15, 2014.

56. Hussain and McMichael, "SONG Notes: The Journal of Southerners On New Ground 1, no. 1 (1996), 2–3," Folder 7, Box 2, SONG Records.

Although building deep relationships within a multiracial staff and board has been a keystone for SONG, SONG has from the beginning strongly supported au-tonomous people of color-led organizations and spaces, and in 1999 launched their Bayard Rustin Project to extend this work. See "Hopscotch House Transcript," 5, and "SONGgirls RETREAT February 3–4, 1995," Box 237, Mandy Carter Papers; "Bayard Rustin Project Letter February 8, 2001," Box 6; SONG Records; and Suzanne Pharr, personal interview, August 14, 2014.

In their first decade, when SONG convened people of color-only spaces, they sometimes also convened parallel workshops for white people, as in their parallel workshops held at the Womonwrites retreat in 1994, "Sister Talk: Women of Color," and "Southern Cooking: White Women Talk About Race." SONG largely moved away from programming specifically for white kin until their 2018 inaugural Hog Mountain Retreat and their Race Traitor call series. See "Womonwrites 1995," Folder 59, Box 2, and "Undoing Racism," Folder 10, Box 1, SONG Records. See also SONG's 2015 teaching tool, "There Is Honor in the Work: SONG on the Role of White People in the Movement at This Time."

57. Hussain and McMichael, "SONG Notes, *The Journal of Southerners On New Ground* 1, no. 1 (1996)," 2–3, Folder 7, Box 2, SONG Records.

58. Pat Hussain, personal interview, August 15, 2014.

59. Carter, "Divide and Conquer," Folder 31, Box 3, SONG Records; and "A New Video from Traditional Values Coalition" and Galst, "Reel Hate: Right Wing Tape Pits Gays Against Blacks," Folder 13, Box 45, New York Boycott Colorado Collection, LGBT Community Center.

60. See also María Lugones' reference to the *GRSR* film in her framing of the "split" of Latina and lesbian political subjectivities in *Pilgrimages/Peregrinajes*, 168–169. For a chapter-length study of *GRSR*, see Mookas, "Faultlines."

61. Carter, "Divide and Conquer."

62. Duggan, *The Twilight of Equality*, xx.

63. Carter interviewed by Norman, *Sinister Wisdom*, March 26, 2013.

64. "SONG Economy Trainings," and "The Economy and Lesbigaytrans Liberation," Box 84, Mandy Carter Papers.

65. Suzanne Pharr, personal interview, August 14, 2014.

66. The organization grew over the 1990s, then struggled with significant funding and staffing challenges in the early 2000s. Mandy Carter served as the sole SONG staff member between 2003 and 2005. In 2005, a think tank was convened to consider whether to rebirth SONG. That year, Suzanne Pharr, Kara Keeling, and Annette Shead rebuilt the board, which in 2006 renewed SONG with Paulina Helm-Hernández and Caitlin Breedlove as co-directors. Helm-Hernández and Breedlove had been working at the Highlander Center prior. See "Report from Mandy Carter," Box 85, Mandy Carter Papers; and "SONG History Timeline by SONG Board 2009," file shared by Caitlin Breedlove.

67. "Co-Director Thoughts on SONG History"; "Theory of Change: Queer Liberation"; and "Post-Hurricane Sandy Solidarity Letter," files shared by Caitlin Breedlove. See also Zein Murib's archival work on debates at the National Policy Roundtables in the late 1990s that revealed tensions at a national level between single-issue/assimilationist and multi-issue conceptualizations of LGBTQ politics, in "Rethinking GLBT as a Political Category in U.S. Politics," 28–29.

68. Pharr, "Rural Organizing," Folder 28, Box 1, SONG Records.

69. Pharr, "Rural Organizing."

70. Some of the other actions in this time frame included working in coalition against Georgia HB87 in 2011. See "Puentes con Posibilidades/Bridges with Possibilities," SONG blog. On this language, see also SONG, "Our People Are Worth the Risks."

71. "Congressional Equality Caucus Letter 2014," southernersonnewground.org.

72. Serena Sebring, personal interview, August 12, 2014. See also "LGBT History: The Hensons and Camp Sister Spirit," *Unity Mississippi,* November 6, 2014.

73. Serena Sebring, personal interview, August 12, 2014.

74. "Coming Out of Exile: SONG + the Not1More Campaign," SONG blog, March 3, 2014.

75. Redmond, "As Though It Were Our Own," 25, 38.

76. Fernandez and Olson, "To Live, Love and Work Anywhere You Please," 412–413.

77. "Land4SONG!," SONG blog, October 7, 2016.

78. Gould, *Moving Politics,* 178, 207, 209.

79. Hussain and McMichael, "SONG Notes," SONG Records.

80. Westermeyer, "Local Tea Party Groups," 126; Holland, *Identity and Agency in Cultural Worlds,* 60; and Melucci, "The Process of Collective Identity," 47.

81. Westermeyer, "Local Tea Party Groups," 126.

82. Minkoff cited in Polletta and Jasper, "Collective Identity and Social Movements," 291.

83. The Gaycation convenings are an outgrowth of SONG's CampOuts of the mid 2000s, which were an outgrowth of SONG retreats held throughout the 1990s. I attended the 2014 Gaycation retreat.

84. Credit for introducing the concept of third space goes especially to Najma Nazy'at and Paulina Helm-Hernández. "Igniting the Kindred," southernersonnewground.org; Kate Shapiro, personal interview, August 14, 2014; and "SONG Virginia Organizing School: Facilitator's Agenda [May 18, 2012]," file shared by Caitlin Breedlove.

85. "Facilitator's Agenda May 2009" and "SONG VA Organizing School," files shared by Caitlin Breedlove; and "Igniting the Kindred."

86. "Co-Director Thoughts on SONG History."

87. Vanessa Faraj, personal interview, August 17, 2014.

88. "Facilitator's Agenda May 2009"; and Jade Brooks, personal interview, August 9, 2014. Kai Lumumba Barrow led the design/development of SONG's political education curriculum in the early 2010s.

89. Guinier and Torres, *The Miner's Canary,* 22–25; Bell, *Faces at the Bottom of the Well;* Anzaldúa, *Borderlands/La Frontera,* 103; Kelley, *Freedom Dreams,* ix; Muñoz, *Cruising Utopia,* 1; and brown, *Emergent Strategy,* 160–164. See also Imarisha and brown, *Octavia's Brood.*

90. Mary Hooks, Roundtable comments, "Sureños En Nueva Tierra—Desde TLC a Abolición / Southerners On New Ground—From NAFTA to Abolition," American Studies Association Annual Meeting, November 10, 2018; "Labor de Amor: La Acción de Fianzas Para Mamás Negras," SONG blog, May 16, 2017.

91. "A Labor of Love: Black Mamas Bail Out Action + Reflection," southernersonnewground.org. The Black Mamas Bail Out Action was launched in Spring 2017.

92. Ferguson, "On the Specificities of Racial Formation," 48–50; and Ferguson, *One Dimensional Queer,* 35.

93. Lugones, "On Complex Communication," 76; Chávez, *Queer Migration Politics*, 7.
94. Lugones, "On Complex Communication," 76.

Conclusion

1. Obama, "Remarks by the President in Address to the Nation on Immigration," November 20, 2014; and Franco, "A Movement That's Committed, Experienced, and Ready," #Not1More, November 22, 2014. On the ways in which normative definitions of family exclude many LGBTQ undocumented immigrants, especially undocumented trans women of color, from protections under this rubric, see Isa Noyola and Valeria de la Luz, "Op-Ed: Obama's Order Ices Out Some LGBTQ Immigrants," *The Advocate*, November 12, 2014. On the 2014 executive actions and the Obama administration's immigration policy in the years prior, see Sampaio, *Terrorizing Latina/o Immigrants*, 140–145.
2. Cacho, *Social Death*, 6.
3. As Cacho explains, social value in the U.S. racial state is defined against those who are "ineligible for personhood." See Cacho, *Social Death*, 6. Franco and others have explained how immigrant and Latinx distancing from the most criminalized immigrants, on the one hand, and from Black protestors, on the other, should be understood as linked in that the very narratives that parse out "good immigrants" and "bad immigrants" are rooted in anti-Black schemas. On the framework of "good" versus "bad" immigrants, see also CR10 Publication Collective, *Abolition Now!*, 341.
4. Rally remarks by Marisa Franco recounted by Jade Brooks, personal interview, August 9, 2014. March information archived at http://www.notonemoredeportation.com/2014/07/07/august2/.
5. Beard, "James Baldwin on Violence and Disavowal," 349.
6. Franco, "Statement on the Baltimore Uprising," notonemoredeportation.com, April 28, 2015. See also Franco's call issued during the Ferguson uprising three weeks later, "Latino Communities Must See Ferguson's Fight as Their Own," *MSNBC*, August 20, 2021.
7. Morrison, "On the Backs of Blacks," *Time*, December 2, 1993. See also Willoughby-Herard, "More Expendable than Slaves?," 507; and Noguera, "Anything but Black," 194.
8. See lettersforblacklives.com.
9. Lugones, *Pilgrimages/Peregrinajes*, 9–10.
10. Lugones, *Pilgrimages/Peregrinajes*, 13.
11. Lowndes, *From the New Deal to the New Right*, 3–4; HoSang, *Racial Propositions*, 17–18; and Beltrán, *The Trouble with Unity*, 163.
12. As one of the oldest forms of identification in the United States, race is rearticulated across place and time but always tied to and carrying the freight of the past. See Lowndes, *From the New Deal to the New Right*, 158; and Lowndes et al., *Race and American Political Development*, 1–10.

13. Baker in Ransby, "Quilting a Movement"; and Lugones, *Pilgrimages/Peregrinajes*, 143.

14. Lugones, *Pilgrimages/Peregrinajes*, 78–80; Baldwin, "On Being White . . . and Other Lies," in *The Cross of Redemption*, 137; and LaShonda Carter, conversation, June 29, 2018.

15. Hong and Ferguson, "Introduction," in *Strange Affinities*, 8.

16. While some scholars find promise in dispensing of identity in reaching for a solidarity politics, I suggest that there is not solidarity without some practice or negotiation of identification. Some practices of solidarity might leave forms of identity quite intact, and others might deeply change them. I suggest that calls to go beyond identity themselves can be read as a kind of identificatory appeal. See Marso, *Politics with Beauvoir*, 243–244; and Dean, *Solidarity of Strangers*.

17. Khan-Cullors, *When They Call You a Terrorist*, 53.

18. Khan-Cullors, *When They Call You a Terrorist*, 54.

19. Brown, "What Has Happened Here?," 300. See also Ahmed, "Intimate Touches," 32.

20. Brown, "What Has Happened Here?," 298.

21. Lorde, *Sister Outsider*, 139.

22. Douglass, "What to the Slave Is the Fourth of July? (1852)," in *Great Speeches by Frederick Douglass*, 33.

23. Melanie Yazzie, Roundtable comments, *From Colorblindness to White Nationalism?: Emerging Racial Formations in the Trump Era*, UCLA, March 3, 2017, youtu.be/ Gg5fUi_5Lg8. See also Molina et al., *Relational Formations of Race*.

24. Du Bois, *The World and Africa*, 47.

25. Du Bois, *The World and Africa*, 46–47.

26. Jordan, "Report from the Bahamas," 16.

27. Baldwin, "White Man's Guilt," in *The Price of the Ticket*, 410.

28. Jasmine Syedullah, conversation, May 25, 2017.

29. Kelley, *Freedom Dreams*, 2.

Bibliography

Archival Sources

John F. Kennedy Presidential Library, Boston, MA
    Robert F. Kennedy Oral History Collection
    Burke Marshall Personal Papers
    Jean Stein Personal Papers

Lesbian Herstory Archives, Brooklyn, NY
    Organizational Files

The Lesbian, Gay, Bisexual & Transgender Community Center National History Archive, New York, NY
    CSLD Committee Papers
    Rudy Grillo Collection
    John Kearns Papers
    Bob Kohler Papers
    Illardo Collection
    New York Boycott Colorado Papers, 1993

Manuscripts and Archives Division, the New York Public Library, New York, NY
    Christopher Street Liberation Day Committee Records
    Arthur Bell Papers
    Martin B. Duberman Papers
    International Gay Information Center Collection
    Lesbian, Gay, Bisexual, and Transgender Periodicals Collection
    Eric Marcus Papers
    Testing the Limits Records

Oregon Shakespeare Festival Archives, Ashland, OR
    Film and Video Collection

Sallie Bingham Center for Women's History and Culture, Duke University, Durham, NC
    Mandy Carter Papers, 1970–2013
    Southerners on New Ground Records, 1993–2004

Schomburg Center for Research in Black Culture, the New York Public Library, New York, NY
    James Baldwin Collection, 1943–1946
    James Baldwin Letters and Manuscripts, 1950–1986
    James Baldwin: The Price of the Ticket Collection
    Lorraine Hansberry Papers

Selected Publications

Abelson, Miriam J. "Already Feminists: Transfeminist Histories, Hurdles, and Futures." In Jo Reger, ed., *Nevertheless They Persisted: Feminisms and Continued Resistance in the U.S. Women's Movement*. New York: Routledge, 2019.

Accapadi, Mamta Motwani. "When White Women Cry: How White Women's Tears Oppress Women of Color." *The College Student Affairs Journal* 26, no. 2 (2007): 208–215.

Ahmed, Sara. "Intimate Touches: Proximity and Distance in International Feminist Dialogues." *Oxford Literary Review* 19, no. 1–2 (1997): 19–46.

Alcoff, Linda Martín. *The Future of Whiteness*. Malden, MA: Polity Press, 2015.

Alcoff, Linda Martín. *Visible Identities: Race, Gender, and the Self*. New York: Oxford University Press, 2006.

Alcoff, Linda Martín, Michael Hames-García, Satya P. Mohanty, and Paula M. L. Moya, eds., *Identity Politics Reconsidered*. New York: Palgrave, 2006.

Alexander, M. Jaqui. *Pedagogies of Crossing: Meditations of Feminism, Sexual Politics, Memory, and the Sacred*. Durham: Duke University Press, 2005.

Anderson, Benedict. *Imagined Communities: Reflections on the Origin and Spread of Nationalism*. New York: Verso, 2006.

Anker, Elizabeth R. *Orgies of Feeling: Melodrama and the Politics of Freedom*. Durham: Duke University Press, 2014.

Anzaldúa, Gloria. *Borderlands/La Frontera: The New Mestiza*. San Francisco: Aunt Lute Books, 2007.

Armstrong, Elizabeth A., and Suzanna M. Crage. "Movements and Memory: The Making of the Stonewall Myth." *American Sociological Review* 71, no. 5 (2006): 724–751.

Baldwin, James. *The Cross of Redemption: Uncollected Writings*. New York: Vintage International, 2010.

Baldwin, James. *The Fire Next Time*. New York: Vintage International, 1963.

Baldwin, James. *The Price of the Ticket: Collected Nonfiction, 1948–1985*. New York: St. Martin's Press, 1985.

Baldwin, James, and William F. Buckley. "Debate: Baldwin vs Buckley." Sponsored by the Cambridge Union Society, June 6, 1965. youtu.be/VOCZOHQ7fCE.

Baldwin, James, and Margaret Mead. *A Rap on Race*. Philadelphia: J.B. Lippincott, 1971.

Baldwin, James, and Raoul Peck. *I Am Not Your Negro: A Major Motion Picture Directed by Raoul Peck*. New York: Vintage Books, 2017.

Baldwin, James, Frank Shatz, and Russell Banks. "John Brown's Body." *Transition* 81/82 (2000): 250–266.

Balfour, Lawrie. *The Evidence of Things Not Said: James Baldwin and the Promise of American Democracy*. Ithaca: Cornell University Press, 2001.

Balfour, Lawrie. "Vexed Genealogy: Octavia Butler and Political Memories of Slavery." In Patrick J. Deneen and Joseph Romance, eds., *Democracy's Literature: Politics and Fiction in America*. New York: Rowman & Littlefield, 2005.

Bassichis, Morgan, Alexander Lee, and Dean Spade. "Building an Abolitionist Trans and Queer Liberation Movement with Everything We've Got." In Eric A. Stanley and Nat Smith, eds., *Captive Genders: Trans Embodiment and the Prison Industrial Complex*. Oakland: AK Press, 2011.

Beard, Lisa. "James Baldwin on Violence and Disavowal." In Susan McWilliams, ed., *A Political Companion to James Baldwin*. Lexington: University Press of Kentucky, 2017.

Behl, Natasha. *Gendered Citizenship: Understanding Gendered Violence in Democratic India*. New York: Oxford University Press, 2019.

Belafonte, Harry. *My Song: A Memoir*. New York: Knopf, 2011.

Bell, Derrick. *Faces at the Bottom of the Well: The Permanence of Racism*. New York: Basic Books, 1992.

Beltrán, Cristina. *The Trouble with Unity: Latino Politics and the Creation of Identity*. New York: Oxford University Press, 2010.

Berger, Dan. *Captive Nation: Black Prison Organizing in the Civil Rights Era*. Chapel Hill: University of North Carolina Press, 2014.

Berger, Martin A. *Seeing Through Race: A Reinterpretation of Civil Rights Photography*. Berkeley: University of California Press, 2011.

Berlant, Lauren. "Intimacy: A Special Issue." *Critical Inquiry* 24, no. 2 (1998): 281–288.

Berlant, Lauren. *The Queen of America Goes to Washington City: Essays on Sex and Citizenship*. Durham: Duke University Press, 1997.

Bettcher, Talia M. "A Conversation with Jeanne Córdova." *TSQ: Transgender Studies Quarterly* 3, no. 1–2 (2016): 285–293.

Boyd, Herb. *Baldwin's Harlem: A Biography of James Baldwin*. New York: Atria, 2008.

Boym, Svetlana. *Common Places: Mythologies of Everyday Life in Russia*. Cambridge, MA: Harvard University Press, 1994.

Boym, Svetlana. "Nostalgia." *Atlas of Transformation*. monumentoftransformation.org/atlas-of-transformation.

Brennan, Teresa. "Essence Against Identity." *Metaphilosophy* 27, no. 1/2 (1996): 92–103.

brown, adrienne maree. *Emergent Strategy: Shaping Change, Changing Worlds*. Oakland: AK Press, 2017.

Brown, Elsa Barkley. "'What Has Happened Here': The Politics of Difference in Women's History and Feminist Politics." *Feminist Studies* 18, no. 2 (1992): 295–312.

Bruyneel, Kevin. *Settler Memory: The Disavowal of Indigeneity and the Politics of Race in the United States*. Chapel Hill: University of North Carolina Press, 2021.

Burlein, Ann. *Lift High the Cross: Where White Supremacy and the Christian Right Converge*. Durham: Duke University Press, 2002.

Cacho, Lisa Marie. *Social Death: Racialized Rightlessness and the Criminalization of the Unprotected*. New York: New York University Press, 2012.

Carbado, Devon W. "Racial Naturalization." *American Quarterly* 57, no. 3 (2005): 633–658.

Chacón, Justin Akers, Mike Davis, and Julián Cardona. *No One Is Illegal: Fighting Violence and State Repression on the U.S.-Mexico Border*. Chicago: Haymarket Books, 2006.

Chávez, Karma R. *Queer Migration Politics: Activist Rhetoric and Coalitional Possibilities*. Chicago: University of Illinois Press, 2013.

Cheng, Wendy, and Rashad Shabazz. "Introduction: Race, Space, and Scale in the Twenty-First Century." *Occasion* 8 (August 2015).

Clark, Kenneth B. *The Negro Protest: James Baldwin, Malcolm X, and Martin Luther King Talk with Kenneth B. Clark*. Boston: Beacon Press, 1963.

Clendinen, Dudley, and Adam Nagourney. *Out for Good: The Struggle to Build a Gay Rights Movement in America*. New York: Simon & Schuster, 1999.

Clover, David. "Dispersed or Destroyed: Archives, The West Indian Students' Union, and Public Memory." *The Society for Caribbean Studies Annual Conference Papers*. London: Society for Caribbean Studies, 2005.

Cohen, Cathy J. *The Boundaries of Blackness: AIDS and the Breakdown of Black Politics*. Chicago: University of Chicago Press, 1999.

Cohen, Cathy J. "Punks, Bulldaggers, and Welfare Queens: The Radical Potential of Queer Politics?" *GLQ* 3, no. 4 (1997): 437–465.

Cohen, Stephan L. *The Gay Liberation Youth Movement: "An Army of Lovers Cannot Fail."* New York: Routledge, 2008.

Colbert, Soyica Diggs. *Radical Vision: A Biography of Lorraine Hansberry*. New Haven: Yale University Press, 2021.

Collins, Patricia Hill. *Black Feminist Thought: Knowledge, Consciousness, and the Politics of Empowerment*. New York: Routledge, 2009.

Collins, Patricia Hill. "It's All in the Family: Intersections of Gender, Race, and Nation." *Hypatia* 13, no. 3 (1998): 62–82.

Collins, Patricia Hill. "Like One of the Family: Race, Ethnicity, and the Paradox of U.S. National Identity." *Ethnic and Racial Studies* 24, no. 1 (2001): 3–28.

Combahee River Collective. "The Combahee River Collective Statement." In Barbara Smith, ed., *Home Girls: A Black Feminist Anthology*. New Brunswick: Rutgers University Press, 2000.

Conrad, Ryan, ed. *Against Equality: Queer Revolution, Not Mere Inclusion*. Oakland: AK Press, 2014.

Cooper, Brittney C. *Eloquent Rage: A Black Feminist Discovers Her Superpower*. New York: Picador, 2019.

Coulthard, Glen. *Red Skin, White Masks: Rejecting the Colonial Politics of Recognition*. Minneapolis: University of Minnesota Press, 2014.

Crenshaw, Kimberlé Williams. "How Colorblindness Flourished in the Age of Obama." In Kimberlé Williams Crenshaw, Luke Charles Harris, Daniel Martinez HoSang, and George Lipsitz, eds., *Seeing Race Again: Countering Colorblindness across the Disciplines*. Oakland: University of California Press, 2019.

Crenshaw, Kimberlé, and Gary Peller. "Reel Time/Real Justice." In Robert Gooding-Williams, ed., *Reading Rodney King/Reading Urban Uprising*. New York: Routledge, 1993.

Crenshaw, Kimberlé Williams, and Andrea J. Ritchie. *Say Her Name: Resisting Police Brutality Against Black Women*. African American Policy Forum. 2015.

CR10 Publications Collective. *Abolition Now! Ten Years of Strategy and Struggle Against the Prison Industrial Complex*. Oakland: AK Press, 2008.

Davis, Angela, and Gina Dent. "Prison as a Border: A Conversation on Gender, Globalization, and Punishment." *Signs: Journal of Women in Culture and Society* 26, no. 4 (2001): 1235–1241.

Dean, Jodi, ed., *Cultural Studies and Political Theory*. Ithaca: Cornell University Press, 2000.

Dean, Jodi. *Solidarity of Strangers: Feminism After Identity Politics*. Berkeley: University of California Press, 1996.

Díaz-Cotto, Juanita. *Gender, Ethnicity, and the State: Latina and Latino Prison Politics*. Albany: State University of New York Press, 1996.

DiPietro, Pedro J., Jennifer McWeeny, and Shireen Roshanravan, eds., *Speaking Face to Face: The Visionary Philosophy of María Lugones*. Albany: State University of New York Press, 2019.

Douglass, Frederick. *Great Speeches by Frederick Douglass*, edited by James Daley. New York: Dover, 2013.

Douglass, Frederick. *Narrative of the Life of Frederick Douglass*. Chapel Hill: University of North Carolina Academic Affairs Library, 1999.

Du Bois, W. E. B. *The World and Africa and Color and Democracy*. New York: Oxford University Press, 2007.

Dudziak, Mary L. *Cold War Civil Rights: Race and the Image of American Democracy*. Princeton: Princeton University Press, 2000.

Duggan, Lisa. *The Twilight of Equality?: Neoliberalism, Cultural Politics, and the Attack on Democracy*. Boston: Beacon Press, 2003.

Dunham, Cyrus. "Out of Obscurity: Trans Resistance, 1969–2016." In Eric A. Stanley, Tourmaline, and Johanna Burton, eds., *Trap Door: Trans Cultural Production and the Politics of Visibility*. Cambridge, MA: MIT Press, 2017.

Durham, Martin. *The Christian Right, the Far Right, and the Boundaries of American Conservatism*. New York: Manchester University Press, 2000.

Dyson, Michael Eric. *What the Truth Sounds Like: Robert F. Kennedy, James Baldwin, and Our Unfinished Conversation About Race in America*. New York: St. Martin's, 2018.

Eckman, Fern Marja. *The Furious Passage of James Baldwin*. New York: M. Evans, 1966.

Edwards, Erica R. *Charisma and the Fictions of Black Leadership*. Minneapolis: University of Minnesota Press, 2012.

Enck-Wanzer, Darrel, ed. *The Young Lords: A Reader*. New York: New York University Press, 2010.

Ferguson, Kennan. *All in the Family: On Community and Incommensurability*. Durham: Duke University Press, 2012.

Ferguson, Roderick A. "On the Specificities of Racial Formation: Gender and Sexuality in Historiographies of Race." In Daniel Martinez HoSang, Oneka LaBennett, and Laura Pulido, eds., *Racial Formation in the Twenty-First Century*. Berkeley: University of California Press, 2012.

Ferguson, Roderick A. *One-Dimensional Queer*. Medford, MA: Polity Press, 2019.

Fernandez, Luis, and Joel Olson. "To Live, Love and Work Anywhere You Please." *Contemporary Political Theory* 10, no. 3 (2011): 412–419.

Field, Douglas. "Looking for Jimmy Baldwin: Sex, Privacy, and Black Nationalist Fervor." *Callaloo* 27, no. 2 (2004): 457–480.

Friedner, Michele, and Stefan Helmreich, "Sound Studies Meets Deaf Studies." *The Senses & Society* 7, no. 1 (2012): 72–86.

García Bedolla, Lisa. *Fluid Borders: Latino Power, Identity, and Politics in Los Angeles*. Berkeley: University of California Press, 2005.

Gash, Alison. *Below the Radar: How Silence Can Save Civil Rights*. New York: Oxford University Press, 2015.

Gash, Alison, and Priscilla Yamin. "State, Status and the American Family." *Polity* 48, no. 2 (2016): 146–164.

Garza, Alicia. "A Herstory of the #BlackLivesMatter Movement." *The Feminist Wire*, October 7, 2014.

Garza, Alicia. *The Purpose of Power*. New York: One World Press, 2020.

Gilmore, Ruth Wilson. "Fatal Couplings of Power and Difference: Notes on Racism and Geography." *Professional Geographer* 54, no. 1 (2002): 15–24.

Gilmore, Ruth Wilson. "Forgotten Places and the Seeds of Grassroots Planning." In Charles R. Hale, ed., *Engaging Contradictions: Theory, Politics, and Methods of Activist Scholarship*. Berkeley: University of California Press, 2008.

Gilmore, Ruth Wilson. *Golden Gulag: Prisons, Surplus, Crisis, and Opposition in Globalizing California*. Berkeley: University of California Press, 2007.

Gilmore, Ruth Wilson. "In the Shadow of the Shadow State." In INCITE!, ed., *The Revolution Will Not Be Funded: Beyond the Non-Profit Industrial Complex*. Cambridge, MA: South End Press, 2007.

Gilmore, Ruth Wilson. "You Have Dislodged a Boulder: Mothers and Prisoners in the Post Keynesian California Landscape." *Transforming Anthropology* 8, no. 1/2 (1999): 12–38.

Gilroy, Paul. *Small Acts: Thoughts on the Politics of Black Cultures*. New York: Serpent's Tail, 1993.

Glaude, Eddie S., Jr. *In a Shade of Blue: Pragmatism and the Politics of Black America*. Chicago: University of Chicago Press, 2007.

Glaude, Eddie S., Jr. *Begin Again: James Baldwin's America and Its Urgent Lessons for Our Own*. New York: Crown, 2020.

Gómez, Alan Eladio. "Resisting Living Death at Marion Federal Penitentiary, 1972." *Radical History Review* 96 (2006): 58–86.

Gould, Deborah. *Moving Politics: Emotion and ACT UP's Fight Against AIDS*. Chicago: University of Chicago Press, 2009.

Guinier, Lani, and Gerald Torres. *The Miner's Canary: Enlisting Race, Resisting Power, Transforming Democracy*. Cambridge, MA: Harvard University Press, 2002.

Guthman, Edwin O. *We Band of Brothers*. New York: Harper & Row, 1971.

Hall, Stuart. "Cultural Identity and Diaspora." In Jonathan Rutherford, ed., *Identity: Community, Culture, Difference*. London: Lawrence & Wishart, 1994.

Hall, Stuart. "Fantasy, Identity, Politics." In Erica Carter, James Donald, and Judith Squires, eds., *Cultural Remix: Theories of Politics and the Popular*. London: Lawrence & Wishart, 1995.

Hall, Stuart. *The Hard Road to Renewal: Thatcherism and the Crisis of the Left*. New York: Verso, 1988.

Hall, Stuart. "New Ethnicities." In Stuart Hall, David Morley, and Kuan-Hsing Chen, eds., *Stuart Hall: Critical Dialogues in Cultural Studies*. New York: Routledge, 1996.

Hall, Stuart. "Who Needs 'Identity'?" In Paul du Gay, Jessica Evans, and Peter Redman, eds., *Identity: A Reader*. Thousand Oaks: SAGE Publications in association with the Open University, 2000.

Hames-García, Michael. *Identity Complex: Making the Case for Multiplicity*. Minneapolis: University of Minnesota Press, 2011.

Haney-López, Ian. *White by Law: The Legal Construction of Race*. New York: New York University Press, 1996.

Hansberry, Lorraine. *Les Blancs: The Collected Last Plays*. New York: Vintage, 1994.

Hansberry, Lorraine. *A Raisin in the Sun and The Sign in Sidney Brustein's Window*. New York: Vintage, 1995.

Hansberry, Lorraine. *To Be Young, Gifted, and Black: Lorraine Hansberry in Her Own Words*. New York: Signet, 1969.

Hansberry, Lorraine, Claudia McNeil, and Ralph J. Tangney. *Lorraine Hansberry: The Black Experience in the Creation of Drama*. Princeton: Films for the Humanities, 1975.

Hardisty, Jean. *Mobilizing Resentment: Conservative Resurgence from the John Birch Society to the Promise Keepers*. Boston: Beacon Press, 2000.

Harris, Duchess. "From the Kennedy Commission to the Combahee Collective: Black Feminist Organizing 1960–80." In Bettye Collier-Thomas and V. P. Franklin, eds., *Sisters in the Struggle: African American Women in the Civil Rights-Black Power Movement*. New York: New York University Press, 2001.

Harris, Duchess. "Kathryn Stockett Is Not My Sister and I Am Not Her Help." *The Feminist Wire*, August 12, 2011.

Hartman, Saidiya V. *Scenes of Subjection: Terror, Slavery, and Self-Making in Nineteenth-Century America*. New York: Oxford University Press, 1997.

Hattam, Victoria. *In the Shadow of Race: Jews, Latinos, and Immigrant Politics in the United States*. Chicago: University of Chicago Press, 2007.

Hattam, Victoria, and Joseph Lowndes. "The Ground Beneath Our Feet: Language, Culture, and Political Change." In Stephen Skowronek and Matthew Glassman, eds., *Formative Acts: American Politics in the Making*. Philadelphia: University of Pennsylvania Press, 2007.

Hill, Rebecca N. *Men, Mobs, and Law: Anti-lynching and Labor Defense in U.S. Radical History*. Durham: Duke University Press, 2008.

Holland, Dorothy C. *Identity and Agency in Cultural Worlds*. Cambridge, MA: Harvard University Press, 1998.

Holland, Sharon Patricia. *The Erotic Life of Racism*. Durham: Duke University Press, 2012.

Hong, Grace Kyungwon. *Death Beyond Disavowal: The Impossible Politics of Difference*. Minneapolis: University of Minnesota Press, 2015.

Hong, Grace Kyungwon, and Roderick A. Ferguson, eds. *Strange Affinities: The Gender and Sexual Politics of Comparative Racialization*. Durham: Duke University Press, 2011.

Hooker, Juliet. "Black Lives Matter and the Paradoxes of U.S. Black Politics: From Democratic Sacrifice to Democratic Repair." *Political Theory* 44, no. 4 (2016): 448–469.

Hooker, Juliet. *Race and the Politics of Solidarity*. New York: Oxford University Press, 2009.

Horne, Lena, and Richard Schickel. *Lena*. Garden City, NY: Doubleday, 1965.

HoSang, Daniel Martinez. *Racial Propositions: Ballot Initiatives and the Making of Postwar California*. Berkeley: University of California Press, 2010.

HoSang, Daniel Martinez, and Joseph E. Lowndes. *Producers, Parasites, Patriots: Race and the New Right-Wing Politics of Precarity*. Minneapolis: University of Minnesota Press, 2019.

Imarisha, Walidah, and adrienne maree brown. *Octavia's Brood: Science Fiction Stories from Social Justice Movements*. Oakland: AK Press, 2015.

Iton, Richard. *In Search of the Black Fantastic: Politics and Popular Culture in the Post-Civil Rights Era*. New York: Oxford University Press, 2008.

James, Joy, ed. *Imprisoned Intellectuals: America's Political Prisoners Write on Life, Liberation, and Rebellion*. Lanham, MD: Rowman & Littlefield, 2003.

James, Joy, ed. *The New Abolitionists: (Neo)Slave Narratives and Contemporary Prison Writings*. Albany: State University of New York Press, 2005.

Johnson, E. Patrick. *Honeypot: Black Southern Women Who Love Women*. Durham, Duke University Press, 2019.

Jones, Clarence, and Joel Engel. *What Would Martin Say?* New York: Harper, 2008.

Jordan, June. "Report from the Bahamas, 1982." *Meridians* 3, no. 2 (2003): 6–16.

Joseph, Peniel E. *Dark Days, Bright Nights: From Black Power to Barack Obama*. New York: Basic Civitas Books, 2010.

Kauffman, Linda S. *Bad Girls and Sick Boys: Fantasies in Contemporary Art and Culture*. Berkeley: University of California Press, 1998.

Keating, Cricket. "Building Coalitional Consciousness." *NWSA Journal* 17, no. 2 (2005): 86–103.

Kelley, Robin D. G. *Freedom Dreams: The Black Radical Imagination*. Boston: Beacon Press, 2002.

Khan-Cullors, Patrisse, and asha bandele. *When They Call You a Terrorist: A Black Lives Matter Memoir*. New York: St. Martin's Press, 2017.

Kim, Claire Jean. *Bitter Fruit: The Politics of Black-Korean Conflict in New York City*. New Haven: Yale University Press, 2000.

King, Martin Luther, Jr. *Why We Can't Wait*. New York: Signet, 2000.

King, Tiffany Lethabo. "Black 'Feminisms' and Pessimism: Abolishing Moynihan's Negro Family." *Theory & Event* 21, no. 1 (January 2018): 68–87.

Klinkner, Philip A., and Rogers M. Smith. *The Unsteady March: The Rise and Decline of Racial Equality in America*. Chicago: University of Chicago Press, 1999.

Klopotek, Brian, Brenda Lintinger, and John Barbry. "Ordinary and Extraordinary Trauma: Race, Indigeneity, and Hurricane Katrina in Tunica-Biloxi History." *American Indian Culture and Research Journal* 32, no. 2 (2008): 55–77.

Koné, Mzilikazi. "Transnational Sex Worker Organizing in Latin America: RedTraSex, Labour and Human Rights." *Social and Economic Studies* 65, no. 4 (2016): 87–108.

Krause, Sharon. *Civil Passions: Moral Sentiment and Democratic Deliberation*. Princeton: Princeton University Press, 2008.

Kunzel, Regina. "Lessons in Being Gay: Queer Encounters in Gay and Lesbian Prison Activism." *Radical History Review* no. 100 (2008): 11–37.

Law, Victoria. *Resistance Behind Bars: The Struggles of Incarcerated Women*. Oakland: PM Press, 2009.

Lebron, Christopher J. *The Color of Our Shame: Race and Justice in Our Time*. New York: Oxford University Press, 2013.

Leeming, David A. *James Baldwin: A Biography*. New York: Knopf, 1994.

Lewis, Abram J. "Trans History in a Moment of Danger: Organizing Within and Beyond 'Visibility' in the 1970s." In Eric A. Stanley, Tourmaline, and Johanna Burton, eds., *Trap Door: Trans Cultural Production and the Politics of Visibility*. Cambridge, MA: MIT Press, 2017.

Lilla, Mark. *The Once and Future Liberal: After Identity Politics*. New York: Harper, 2017.

Lipsitz, George. *How Racism Takes Place*. Philadelphia: Temple University Press, 2011.

Lipsitz, George. "The Racialization of Space and the Spatialization of Race: Theorizing the Hidden Architecture of Landscape." *Landscape Journal* 26, no. 1 (2007): 10–23.

Lopez Bunyasi, Tehama, and Candis Watts Smith. "Do All Black Lives Matter Equally to Black People? Respectability Politics and the Limitations of Linked Fate." *Journal of Race, Ethnicity and Politics* 4, no. 1 (2019): 180–215.

Lorde, Audre. *Sister Outsider: Essays and Speeches*. Trumansburg, NY: Crossing Press, 1984.

Lowe, Lisa. *The Intimacies of Four Continents*. Durham: Duke University Press, 2015.

Lowndes, Joseph E. "Barack Obama's Body: The Presidency, the Body Politic, and the Contest over American National Identity." *Polity* 45, no. 4 (2013): 469–498.

Lowndes, Joseph E. "From New Class Critique to White Nationalism: Telos, the Alt Right, and the Origins of Trumpism." *Konturen* 9 (2017): 8–14.

Lowndes, Joseph E. *From the New Deal to the New Right: Race and the Southern Origins of Modern Conservatism*. New Haven: Yale University Press, 2008.

Lowndes, Joseph E. "From Pat Buchanan to Donald Trump: The Nativist Turn in Right-Wing Populism." In Kathleen Belew and Ramón A. Gutiérrez, eds., *A Field Guide to White Supremacy*. Oakland: University of California Press, 2021.

Lowndes, Joseph E. "Looking Forward to the History of the Tea Party." *Logos: A Journal of Modern Society and Culture* 10, no. 3 (2011).

Lowndes, Joseph E. "The Populist Violence of Donald Trump." *Counterpunch Magazine* 22, no. 7 (2015).

Lowndes, Joseph E. "Response to Shane Hamilton's Review of *From the New Deal to the New Right: Race and the Southern Origins of Modern Conservatism*." *Perspectives on Politics* 7, no. 2 (2009): 380.

Lowndes, Joseph E. "White Populism and the Transformation of the Silent Majority." *The Forum* 14, no. 1 (2016): 25–37.

Lowndes, Joseph, Julie Novkov, and Dorian T. Warren, eds. *Race and American Political Development*. New York: Routledge, 2008.

Lugones, María. "On Complex Communication." *Hypatia* 21, no. 3 (Summer 2006): 75–85.

Lugones, María. *Pilgrimages/Peregrinajes: Theorizing Coalition Against Multiple Oppressions*. Lanham, MD: Rowman & Littlefield, 2003.

Lushetich, Natasha. *Interdisciplinary Performance: Reformatting Reality*. New York: Palgrave, 2016.

Marshall, Stephen H. *The City on the Hill from Below: The Crisis of Prophetic Black Politics*. Philadelphia: Temple University Press, 2011.

Marso, Lori Jo. *Politics with Beauvoir: Freedom in the Encounter*. Durham: Duke University Press, 2017.

Martel, James R. *The Misinterpellated Subject*. Durham: Duke University Press, 2017.

Martínez, Ernesto Javier. "Dying to Know: Identity and Self-Knowledge in Baldwin's *Another Country*." *PMLA* 124, no. 3 (May 2009): 782–797.

Maskovsky, Jeff. "Toward the Anthropology of White Nationalist Postracialism." *HAU Journal of Ethnographic Theory* 7, no. 1 (Spring 2017): 433–440.

Mathiowetz, Dean. *Appeals to Interest: Language, Contestation, and the Shaping of Political Agency*. University Park: Pennsylvania State University Press, 2011.

Maxwell, Lida. "Queer/Love/Bird Extinction: Rachel Carson's *Silent Spring* as a Work of Love." *Political Theory* 45, no. 5 (2017): 682–704.

McBride, Dwight A., ed. *James Baldwin Now*. New York: New York University Press, 1999.

McClintock, Anne. *Imperial Leather: Race, Gender, and Sexuality in the Colonial Contest*. New York: Routledge, 1995.

McGuire, Danielle L. *At the Dark End of the Street: Black Women, Rape, and Resistance—A New History of the Civil Rights Movement from Rosa Parks to the Rise of Black Power*. New York: Knopf, 2010.

McKittrick, Katherine. *Demonic Grounds: Black Women and the Cartographies of Struggle*. Minneapolis: University of Minnesota Press, 2006.

McWilliams, Susan, ed. *A Political Companion to James Baldwin*. Lexington: University Press of Kentucky, 2017.

Meier, August, and Elliott M. Rudwick. *CORE: A Study in the Civil Rights Movement, 1942–1968*. New York: Oxford University Press, 1973.

Melamed, Jodi. *Represent and Destroy: Rationalizing Violence in the New Racial Capitalism*. Minneapolis: University of Minnesota, 2011.

Melamed, Jodi. "The Spirit of Neoliberalism: From Racial Liberalism to Neoliberal Multiculturalism." *Social Text* 24, no. 4 (2006): 1–24.

Melucci, Alberto. "The Process of Collective Identity." In Hank Johnston and Bert Klandermans, eds., *Social Movements and Culture*. Minneapolis: University of Minnesota Press, 1995.

Menzel, Annie. "Generations of White Women's Violence Stop Here: On Watching the Amy Cooper Video with My 5-Year-Old White Daughter." *The Feminist Wire*. June 22, 2020.

Miller, Eric. "Patrick Joseph Buchanan, Culture War Speech: Address to the Republican National Convention." *Voices of Democracy: The U.S. Oratory Project* 7 (2013): 47–59.

Mills, Charles W. *The Racial Contract*. Ithaca: Cornell University Press, 1997.

Molina, Natalia, Daniel Martinez HoSang, and Ramón A. Gutiérrez, eds. *Relational Formations of Race: Theory, Method, and Practice*. Oakland: University of California Press, 2019.

Mookas, Ioannis. "Faultlines: Homophobic Innovation in Gay Rights/Special Rights." In Linda Kintz and Julia Lesage, eds., *Media, Culture, and the Religious Right*. Minneapolis: University of Minnesota Press, 1993.

Moraga, Cherríe. "La Jornada." In Cherríe Moraga and Gloria Anzaldúa, eds., *This Bridge Called My Back: Writings by Radical Women of Color*. Albany: State University of New York Press, 2015.

Morgan, Jennifer. "*Partus sequiter ventrem*: Law, Race, and Reproduction in Colonial Slavery." *Small Axe* 55 (March 2018): 1–17.

Morrison, Toni. *Playing in the Dark: Whiteness and the Literary Imagination*. Cambridge, MA: Harvard University Press, 1992.

Muñoz, José Esteban. *Cruising Utopia: The Then and There of Queer Futurity*. New York: New York University Press, 2009.

Muñoz, José Esteban. *Disidentifications: Queers of Color and the Performance of Politics*. Minneapolis: University of Minnesota Press, 1999.

Murib, Zein. "Rethinking GLBT as a Political Category in U.S. Politics." In Marla Brettschneider, Susan Burgess, and Christine Keating, eds., *LGBTQ Politics: A Critical Reader*. New York: New York University Press, 2017.

Namaste, Viviane K. *Invisible Lives: The Erasure of Transsexual and Transgendered People*. Chicago: University of Chicago Press, 2000.

Nero, Charles I. "Why Are the Gay Ghettos White?" In E. Patrick Johnson and Mae G. Henderson, eds., *Black Queer Studies: A Critical Anthology*. Durham: Duke University Press, 2005.

Noguera, Pedro A. "Anything but Black: Bringing Politics Back to the Study of Race." In Percy C. Hintzen and Jean Muteba Rahier, eds., *Problematizing Blackness: Self-Ethnographies by Black Immigrants to the United States*. New York: Routledge, 2003.

Olson, Joel. "Whiteness and the Polarization of American Politics." *Political Research Quarterly* 61, no. 4 (2008): 704–718.

Oparah, Julia Chinyere. "Maroon Abolitionists: Black Gender-Oppressed Activists in the Anti-Prison Movement in the US and Canada." In Eric A. Stanley and Nat Smith, eds. *Captive Genders: Trans Embodiment and the Prison Industrial Complex*. 2nd ed. Oakland: AK Press, 2015.

Osorio, Ruth. "Embodying Truth: Sylvia Rivera's Delivery of *Parrhesia* at the 1973 Christopher Street Liberation Day Rally." *Rhetoric Review* 36, no. 2 (2017): 151–163.

Painter, Nell Irvin. *The History of White People*. New York: W.W. Norton, 2010.

Pascoe, Peggy. *What Comes Naturally: Miscegenation Law and the Making of Race in America*. New York: Oxford University Press, 2009.

Pavlić, Edward M. *Who Can Afford to Improvise? James Baldwin and Black Music, the Lyric and the Listeners*. New York: Fordham University Press, 2015.

Perry, Imani. *Looking for Lorraine: The Radiant and Radical Life of Lorraine Hansberry*. Boston: Beacon Press, 2018.

Pharr, Suzanne. *In the Time of the Right: Reflections on Liberation*. Berkeley: Chardon Press, 1996.

Phillips, Layli, and Shomari Olugbala. "Sylvia Rivera: Fighting in Her Heels: Stonewall, Civil Rights, and Liberation." In Susan M. Glisson, ed., *The Human Tradition in the Civil Rights Movement*. Lanham, MD: Rowman & Littlefield, 2006.

Polletta, Francesca, and James M. Jasper. "Collective Identity and Social Movements." *Annual Review of Sociology* 27, no. 1 (2001): 283–305.

Puar, Jasbir K. *Terrorist Assemblages: Homonationalism in Queer Times*. Durham: Duke University Press, 2007.

Pulido, Laura. *Black, Brown, Yellow, and Left: Radical Activism in Los Angeles*. Berkeley: University of California Press, 2006.

Raiford, Leigh. "'Come Let Us Build a New World Together': SNCC and Photography of the Civil Rights Movement." *American Quarterly* 59, no. 4 (2007): 1129–1157.

Ransby, Barbara. *Ella Baker and the Black Freedom Movement: A Radical Democratic Vision*. Chapel Hill: University of North Carolina Press, 2003.

Raymond, Emilie. *Stars for Freedom: Hollywood, Black Celebrities, and the Civil Rights Movement*. Seattle: University of Washington Press, 2015.

Reddy, Chandan. *Freedom with Violence: Race, Sexuality, and the US State*. Durham: Duke University Press, 2011.

Redmond, Shana. "'As Though It Were Our Own': Against a Politics of Identification." In Nada Elia, David M. Hernández, Jodi Kim, Shana L. Redmond, Dylan Rodríguez, Sarita Echavez See, eds., *Critical Ethnic Studies: A Reader*. Durham: Duke University Press, 2016.

Reed, Adolph L. *Stirrings in the Jug: Black Politics in the Post-Segregation Era*. Minneapolis: University of Minnesota Press, 1999.

Reid-Pharr, Robert F. "It's Raining Men: Notes on the Million Man March." In Rudolph P. Byrd and Beverly Guy-Sheftall, eds., *Traps: African American Men on Gender and Sexuality*. Bloomington: Indiana University Press, 2001.

Reyes-Santos, Alaí. *Our Caribbean Kin: Race and Nation in the Neoliberal Antilles*. New Brunswick: Rutgers University Press, 2015.

Richardson, Beulah. "A Black Woman Speaks . . . of White Womanhood, of White Supremacy, of Peace." New York: American Women for Peace, 1951.

Rivera, Sylvia. "Queens in Exile: The Forgotten Ones." In Riki Wilchins, Clare Howell, and Joan Nestle, eds., *GenderQueer: Voices from Beyond the Sexual Binary*. Los Angeles: Alyson Books, 2002.

Rivera, Sylvia. "Sylvia Rivera's Talk at LGMNY, June 2001 Lesbian and Gay Community Services Center, New York City." *Centro Journal* 19, no. 1 (2007): 116–123.

Rivera, Sylvia. "Transvestites: Your Half Brothers and Half Sisters of the Revolution." In Steven F. Dansky, Perry Brass, and John Knoebel, eds., *The Come Out! Reader*. Christopher Street Press, 2012.

Roberts, Dorothy. *Fatal Invention: How Science, Politics, and Big Business Re-Create Race in the Twenty-first Century*. New York: New Press, 2011.

Roberts, Dorothy. *Killing the Black Body: Race, Reproduction, and the Meaning of Liberty*. New York: Pantheon Books, 1997.

Robinson, Cedric J. *An Anthropology of Marxism*. Chapel Hill: University of North Carolina Press, 2019.

Rodríguez, Juana María. *Sexual Futures, Queer Gestures, and Other Latina Longings*. New York: New York University Press, 2014.

Rodríguez, Richard T. *Next of Kin: The Family in Chicano/a Cultural Politics*. Durham: Duke University Press, 2009.

Roediger, David. "Making Solidarity Uneasy: Cautions on a Keyword from Black Lives Matter to the Past." *American Quarterly* 68, no. 2 (2016): 223–248.

Rogers, Melvin L. "David Walker and the Political Power of the Appeal." *Political Theory* 43, no. 2 (2015): 208–233.

Rogin, Michael. *Ronald Reagan, the Movie: And Other Episodes in Political Demonology*. Berkeley: University of California Press, 1988.

Sampaio, Anna. *Terrorizing Latina/o Immigrants: Race, Gender, and Immigration Politics in the Age of Security*. Philadelphia: Temple University Press, 2015.

Sánchez, Rosaura, and Beatrice Pita. "Theses on the Latino Bloc: A Critical Perspective." *Aztlán: A Journal of Chicano Studies* 31, no. 2 (2006): 25–53.

Scarpinato, Bebe, and Rusty Moore. "Sylvia Rivera—A Remembrance." *Transgender Tapestry* 98, (Spring 2002).

Segrest, Mab. *Memoir of a Race Traitor*. Boston: South End Press, 1994.

Shah, Nayan. *Stranger Intimacy: Contesting Race, Sexuality, and the Law in the North American West*. Berkeley: University of California Press, 2011.

Sharpe, Christina. *Monstrous Intimacies: Making Post-Slavery Subjects*. Durham: Duke University Press, 2010.

Shepard, Benjamin. "From Community Organization to Direct Services: The Street Trans Action Revolutionaries to Sylvia Rivera Law Project." *Journal of Social Science Research* 39, no. 1 (2013): 95–114.

Shepard, Benjamin. "Sylvia and Sylvia's Children: A Battle for A Queer Public Space." In Mattilda Bernstein Sycamore, ed., *That's Revolting!: Queer Strategies for Resisting Assimilation*. Brooklyn: Soft Skull Press, 2004.

Scheper, Jeanne. *Moving Performances: Divas, Iconicity, and Remembering the Modern Stage*. New Brunswick: Rutgers University Press, 2016.

Schlesinger, Arthur M. *Robert Kennedy and His Times*. Boston: Houghton Mifflin, 1978.

Sedgwick, Eve Kosofsky. *Epistemology of the Closet*. Berkeley: University of California, 1990.

Sexton, Jared. *Amalgamation Schemes: Antiblackness and the Critique of Multiracialism*. Minneapolis: University of Minnesota Press, 2008.

Shaikh, Khanum. "Intimate Critique: Toward a Feminism from Within." *Feminist Studies* 48, no. 2 (2022): 369–394.

Shulman, George. *American Prophecy: Race and Redemption in American Political Culture*. Minneapolis: University of Minnesota Press, 2008.

Simien, Evelyn M. "Race, Gender, and Linked Fate." *Journal of Black Studies* 35, no. 5 (2005): 529–550.

Simpson, Leanne Betasamosake. *As We Have Always Done: Indigenous Freedom Through Radical Resistance*. Minneapolis: University of Minnesota Press, 2017.

Singh, Nikhil Pal. *Black Is a Country: Race and the Unfinished Struggle for Democracy*. Cambridge, MA: Harvard University Press, 2004.

Slack, Jennifer Daryl. "The Theory and Method of Articulation in Cultural Studies." In Stuart Hall, David Morley, and Kuan-Hsing Chen, eds., *Stuart Hall: Critical Dialogues in Cultural Studies*. New York: Routledge, 1996.

Smith, Jerome. "The Jump-Off Point." In Juan Williams, ed., *My Soul Looks Back in Wonder: Voices of the Civil Rights Experience*. New York: AARP/Sterling, 2005.

Southerners On New Ground. "Our People Are Worth the Risks: A Southern Queer Agenda from the Margins and the Red States." *S&F Online* 10.1–10.2 (Spring 2012).

Spade, Dean. "Fighting to Win." In Mattilda Bernstein Sycamore, ed., *That's Revolting!: Queer Strategies for Resisting Assimilation*. Brooklyn: Soft Skull Press, 2004.

Spade, Dean. *Normal Life: Administrative Violence, Critical Trans Politics, and the Limits of Law*. Durham: Duke University Press, 2015.

Spillers, Hortense J. "Mama's Baby, Papa's Maybe: An American Grammar Book." *Diacritics* 17, no. 2 (1987): 65–81.

Stanley, Eric A. *Atmospheres of Violence: Structuring Antagonism and the Trans/Queer Ungovernable*. Durham: Duke University Press, 2021.

Stanley, Eric A., Dean Spade, and Queer (In)Justice. "Queering Prison Abolition, Now?" *American Quarterly* 64, no. 1 (2012): 115–127.

Stanley, Eric A., Tourmaline, and Johanna Burton, eds. *Trap Door: Trans Cultural Production and the Politics of Visibility*. Cambridge, MA: MIT Press, 2017.

Stanley, Timothy. *The Crusader: The Life and Tumultuous Times of Pat Buchanan*. New York: Thomas Dunne Books, 2012.

Steinberg, Stephen. *Race Relations: A Critique*. Stanford, CA: Stanford University Press, 2007.

Stewart, Maria W., and Marilyn Richardson. *Maria W. Stewart, America's First Black Woman Political Writer: Essays and Speeches*. Bloomington: Indiana University Press, 1987.

Stoler, Ann Laura. *Haunted by Empire: Geographies of Intimacy in North American History*. Durham: Duke University Press, 2006.

Strolovitch, Dara Z. "Of Mancessions and Hecoveries: Race, Gender, and the Political Construction of Economic Crises and Recoveries." *Perspectives on Politics* 11, no. 1 (2013): 167–176.

Stryker, Susan. *Transgender History*. Berkeley: Seal Press, 2008.

Stryker, Susan, and Talia M. Bettcher. "Introduction: Trans/Feminisms." *Transgender Studies Quarterly* 3, no. 1/2 (2006): 5–14.

Swinth, Kirsten. *Feminism's Forgotten Fight: The Unfinished Struggle for Work and Family*. Cambridge, MA: Harvard University Press, 2018.

Sycamore, Mattilda Bernstein. *That's Revolting!: Queer Strategies for Resisting Assimilation*. Brooklyn: Soft Skull Press, 2004.

Syedullah, Jasmine, and Rae Leiner. "'Take a Moment to Ask Yourself, If This Is How We Fall Apart?' Practices for Mutually Reinforced Resilience in the Time of Reckoning More Lessons from The Manual for Liberating Survival." *Journal of Women, Politics & Policy* 42, no. 1 (2021): 23–37.

Talley, Heather Laine. "Feminists We Love: Caitlin Breedlove & SONG." *The Feminist Wire*, November 8, 2013.

Tang, Jeannine. "Contemporary Art and Critical Transgender Infrastructures." In Eric A. Stanley, Tourmaline, and Johanna Burton, eds., *Trap Door: Trans Cultural Production and the Politics of Visibility*. Cambridge, MA: MIT Press, 2017.

Taylor, Keeanga-Yamahtta, ed. *How We Get Free: Black Feminism and the Combahee River Collective*. Chicago: Haymarket Books, 2017.

Teal, Donn. *The Gay Militants*. New York: St. Martin's Press, 1995.

Thandeka. *Learning to Be White: Money, Race, and God in America*. New York: Continuum, 1999.

Thompson, Debra. "An Exoneration of Black Rage." *The South Atlantic Quarterly* 116, no. 3 (2017): 457–481.

Thorsen, Karen, director and producer. *James Baldwin: The Price of the Ticket*. San Francisco: California Newsreel, 1990.

Threadcraft, Shatema. *Intimate Justice: The Black Female Body and the Body Politic*. New York: Oxford University Press, 2016.

Thuma, Emily L. *All Our Trials: Prisons, Policing, and the Feminist Fight to End Violence*. Chicago: University of Illinois Press, 2019.

Tomlinson, Barbara, and George Lipsitz. *Insubordinate Spaces: Improvisation and Accompaniment for Social Justice*. Philadelphia: Temple University Press, 2019.

Turner, Jack. *Awakening to Race: Individualism and Social Consciousness in America*. Chicago: University of Chicago Press, 2012.

Wells-Barnett, Ida B., and Jaqueline Jones Royster. *Southern Horrors and Other Writings: The Anti-Lynching Campaign of Ida B. Wells, 1892–1900*. Boston: Bedford Books, 1997.

Westermeyer, William H. "Local Tea Party Groups and the Vibrancy of the Movement." *Political and Legal Anthropology Review* 39, no. S1 (2016): 121–138.

Weston, Kath. *Families We Choose: Lesbians, Gays, Kinship*. New York: Columbia University Press, 1997.

Willoughby-Herard, Tiffany. "Let Me Introduce You to My Family . . . That Is, My Property." PowerPoint slides, 2011. Received June 20, 2015.

Willoughby-Herard, Tiffany. "Mammy No More/Mammy Forever: The Stakes and Costs of Teaching Our Colleagues." In Stephanie A. Fryberg and Ernesto Javier Martínez, eds., *The Truly Diverse Faculty: New Dialogues in American Higher Education*. New York: Palgrave, 2014.

Willoughby-Herard, Tiffany. "More Expendable Than Slaves? Racial Justice and the After-life of Slavery." *Politics, Groups, and Identities* 2, no. 3 (2014): 506–521.

Willoughby-Herard, Tiffany. "South Africa's Poor Whites and Whiteness Studies: Afrikaner Ethnicity, Scientific Racism, and White Misery." *New Political Science* 29, no. 4 (2007): 479–500.

Willoughby-Herard, Tiffany. *Waste of a White Skin: The Carnegie Corporation and the Racial Logic of White Vulnerability*. Berkeley: University of California Press, 2015.

Woodly, Deva R. *The Politics of Common Sense: How Social Movements Use Public Discourse to Change Politics and Win Acceptance*. New York: Oxford University Press, 2015.

Yamin, Priscilla. *American Marriage: A Political Institution*. Philadelphia: University of Pennsylvania Press, 2012.

Young, Iris Marion. *On Female Body Experience: "Throwing Like a Girl" and Other Essays*. New York: Oxford University Press, 2005.

Young, E. Michael. "Dan Quayle." In Roger Chapman, ed., *Culture Wars: An Encyclopedia of Issues, Viewpoints, and Voices*. Armonk, NY: M.E. Sharpe, 2010.

Zeskind, Leonard. *Blood and Politics: The History of the White Nationalist Movement from the Margins to the Mainstream*. New York: Farrar Straus Giroux, 2009.

Index

For the benefit of digital users, indexed terms that span two pages (e.g., 52–53) may, on occasion, appear on only one of those pages.

Figures are indicated by *f* following the page number